Bounded Rationality and Economic Diplomacy

The Politics of Investment Treaties in Developing Countries

Lauge N. Skovgaard Poulsen
University College London

CAMBRIDGE
UNIVERSITY PRESS

University Printing House, Cambridge CB2 8BS, United Kingdom

Cambridge University Press is part of the University of Cambridge.

It furthers the University's mission by disseminating knowledge in the pursuit of education, learning and research at the highest international levels of excellence.

www.cambridge.org
Information on this title: www.cambridge.org/9781107119536

© Lauge N. Skovgaard Poulsen 2015

This publication is in copyright. Subject to statutory exception and to the provisions of relevant collective licensing agreements, no reproduction of any part may take place without the written permission of Cambridge University Press.

First published 2015

A catalogue record for this publication is available from the British Library

Library of Congress Cataloging-in-Publication Data
Poulsen, Lauge N. Skovgaard, author.
Bounded rationality and economic diplomacy : the politics of investment treaties in developing countries / Lauge N. Skovgaard Poulsen, University College London.
    pages   cm
Includes bibliographical references and index.
ISBN 978-1-107-11953-6 (Hardback : alk. paper)
1. Investments, Foreign–Developing countries.   2. International economic relations.   3. Investments, Foreign (International law)   4. International commercial arbitration.   I. Title.
HG5993.P68 2015
332.67'3091724–dc23   2015010885

ISBN 978-1-107-11953-6 Hardback

Cambridge University Press has no responsibility for the persistence or accuracy of URLs for external or third-party internet websites referred to in this publication, and does not guarantee that any content on such websites is, or will remain, accurate or appropriate.

To Misha

Contents

List of figures	*page* viii
List of tables	ix
Selected abbreviations	x
Acknowledgements	xi
Preface	xiii

1	Unanticipated consequences	1
2	Bounded rationality and the spread of investment treaties	25
3	A difficult beginning	47
4	Promoting investment treaties	71
5	A less than rational competition	110
6	Narcissistic learning	135
7	Letting down the guard: a case study	162
8	Expanding the bounds of rationality in the investment regime	192

Appendix	204
References	206
Archives	235
Agreements, arbitration awards, and constitutions	236
Index	237

Figures

1.1 The spread of bilateral investment treaties	*page* 1
1.2 Investment treaty arbitration and direct expropriation	2
1.3 Take-off in BIT adoption coincided with domestic FDI liberalization	11
1.4 Poor publicity stunts	15
2.1 Rational learning about risks	37
2.2 Rational learning and the zone of agreement	38
2.3 Bounded rational learning about risks	40
2.4 Bounded rational learning and the zone of agreement	42
4.1 Reference to ICSID in bilateral investment treaties	73
4.2 Investment projects with MIGA guarantees, 1990–1999	75
4.3 FIAS advisory projects, 1986–1998	78
4.4 The rush to BITs in Central and Eastern Europe, median total number of BITs by region	88
6.1 The rise of investment treaty arbitration and the slowdown in BIT adoption	143
6.2 Slowdown in BIT adoption after first claim	144
7.1 Bounded rationality in South Africa's investment treaty programme	190

Tables

2.1	Investment treaty adoption: competition and learning	*page* 31
3.1	The first decade of the BIT movement, German and Swiss treaties	54
3.2	The early BIT programme of the United Kingdom, 1971–1979	61
4.1	World Bank programmes and BIT adoption	80
4.2	CEELI operations by 1994	84
4.3	UNCTAD's negotiation matrix for G-15 countries	93
4.4	UNCTAD's BIT facilitation rounds and signing ceremonies	95
4.5	Private lawyers as government advisers	97
5.1	Adoption patterns show no evidence of rational competition	113
5.2	Adoption patterns show no evidence of rational learning about economic benefits	115
5.3	Subsequent treaties among US BIT partners	117
5.4	Anchoring of Thai BITs to UK treaty	128
6.1	When the claim hits	145
7.1	South Africa's BITs	164
A.1	Sources for country FDI liberalization years	205

Selected abbreviations

BIT	bilateral investment treaty
FCN treaty	friendship, commerce, and navigation treaty
FCO	Foreign and Commonwealth Office, London
FDI	foreign direct investment
FIAS	Foreign Investment Advisory Services
FTA	free trade agreement
ICSID	International Centre for the Settlement of Investment Disputes
MAI	Multilateral Agreement on Investment
MFN	most favoured nation
MIGA	Multilateral Investment Guarantee Agency
NAFTA	North American Free Trade Agreement
OPIC	Overseas Private Investment Corporation
PRI	political risk insurance
PTA	preferential trade agreement
UNCTAD	United Nations Conference on Trade and Development
UNCTC	United Nations Centre on Transnational Corporations

Acknowledgements

The volume has benefitted from support, input, and inspiration from a great number of colleagues and friends. Most of the book was written at Nuffield College, Oxford, where the manuscript benefitted greatly from book workshops organized by Kalypso Nicolaidis and Ngaire Woods. From my time at Nuffield, I owe particular debts to Duncan Snidal, who was always available to discuss ideas, as well as to Nick Turner, Lisa Brahms, and Niels van Wanrooij for excellent research assistance.

The original research for the book was conducted as I worked on my PhD dissertation at the London School of Economics (LSE). The idea stemmed from a conversation with the former Attorney General of Pakistan – Makhdoom Ali Khan – and I am grateful to my in-laws for facilitating access to the Pakistani bureaucracy in order to verify Makhdoom's incredible story. From LSE, I am indebted to my two supervisors, Stephen Woolcock and Andrew Walter, as well as to the dissertation examiners Federico Ortino and Kurt Weyland. My time at LSE was funded by a grant from the Danish Council for Independent Research, which was administered by the Copenhagen Business School. At CBS, I received useful feedback from staff at the Department of Business and Politics and generous support from Leonard Seabrooke, Ove Kaj Pedersen, Lars Bo Kaspersen, and Bo Bøgeskov.

Several organizations provided vital support. FIAS declassified a number of reports, UNCTAD assisted in tracking BIT negotiators and allowed me access to their archives, and the Danish Ministry of Foreign Affairs kindly opened up their recent archives as well. While I was a visiting scholar at the Brookings Institution, USTR officials provided helpful insights on the nature of the American BIT program as well as current and past negotiations.

In addition, I gratefully acknowledge the comments and support received over the years by Anne van Aaken, Faisal Ahmed, Todd Allee, Chris Arnold, Axel Berger, Nathalie Bernasconi, Shelagh Brooks, Tomer Broude, Quentin Bruneau, Tony Cole, Eileen Denza, Yoram Haftel, Tom Hale, Todd Hall, Gus Van Harten, Christian Ibsen, Srividya xii Acknowledgements

Jandhyala, Noel Johnston, Anna Joubin-Bret, Mark Kantor, Jan Kleinheisterkamp, Toby Landau, Mark Manger, Noel Maurer, Covadunga Meseguer, Santiago Montt, Eric Neumayer, Martins Paparinskis, Antonio Parra, Clint Peinhardt, Luke Peterson, Mona Pinchis, Prabash Ranjan, Anthea Roberts, Patrick Robinson, Jeswald Salacuse, Philippe Sands, Karl Sauvant, David Schneiderman, Elisabeth Tuerk, Kenneth Vandevelde, Jörg Weber, and Jason Yackee. The final manuscript benefitted especially from discussions with Jonathan Bonnitcha, Michael Waibel, and Lou Wells, as well as detailed comments by Wolfgang Alschner, N. Jansen Calamita, Geoff Gertz, Taylor St John, and two anonymous reviewers. John Haslam, Carrie Parkinson, Ezhilmaran Sugumaran, and Alyson Platt provided excellent editorial assistance at Cambridge University Press.

Some of the findings have been published in 'When the claim hits: bilateral investment treaties and bounded rational learning,' *World Politics,* 65(2): 273–313 (2013); and 'Bounded rationality and the diffusion of modern investment treaties,' *International Studies Quarterly* 58(1): 1–14 (2014) – both reproduced with permission. I am indebted to Emma Aisbett for agreeing to co-author the article for *World Politics.* Aisbett's econometric work has been updated for Chapter 6 and our discussions helped me sharpen several of the claims that ended up in the book.

Finally, the book would not have been possible without feedback from policy-makers in all corners of the world. Although you have to remain anonymous I am sincerely grateful for your time. I should also make clear from the outset that even though the book is about information processing biases, it is not a critique of your efforts to build the international investment regime from the ground up. Not only did you work under considerable pressure and administrative constraints, we also know from cognitive psychology that inferential biases are simply a fact of life. Had I been in your shoes during the 1990s my own cognition constraints could very well have resulted in far less rational behaviour.

The book is dedicated with love to my wife, Misha, who generously listened to my monologues on the intricacies of bounded rationality and economic diplomacy for much too long.

Preface

The curious case of Pakistan

In October 2001 Pakistan's Secretary of Law received a letter. It related to a dispute between the Pakistani government and a Swiss company, Société Générale de Surveillance (SGS). The dispute had begun in 1996 after the Sharif government terminated a contract with SGS due to suspicions that it had been obtained through bribes. SGS objected and began a series of legal proceedings in both Switzerland and Pakistan. All failed. The letter received five years after the dispute had begun was not from Switzerland or the Pakistani courts. This time it was from Washington DC. It came from a World Bank institution called the International Centre for the Settlement of Investment Disputes. ICSID said SGS was claiming more than US $110 million in compensation based on a so-called bilateral investment treaty (BIT). This puzzled the Secretary, as neither ICSID nor the BIT had been mentioned by SGS while the contractual dispute had lasted.[1] He therefore called up his Attorney General to ask what he knew about ICSID, and how SGS could possibly use a BIT to file such a claim. Although one of the most notable experts on international public and commercial law in Pakistan, the attorney general couldn't give him an answer. 'To be perfectly honest,' he later said to me, 'I did not have a clue.'[2] After hanging up, the attorney general therefore went on to Google. Here he typed in two questions: 'What is ICSID?' and 'What is a BIT?' And that is how he learned of these instruments for the first time.

It didn't take long before the attorney general realized that the letter from ICSID was serious indeed. Unlike the contract with SGS, which involved specific commercial rights, the six-page BIT provided SGS a right to compensation for a wide range of regulatory conduct based on

---

[1] ICSID Case No. ARB/01/13, Decision on Jurisdiction, 6 August 2003, par. 63.
[2] Interview, Karachi, January 2009.

xiii

xiv   Preface

very vague treaty language. Pakistan was obliged to fully compensate Swiss investors for expropriation, indirect expropriation, or any other measures having the same nature or effect. What that meant remained unspecified. Swiss investors could also claim damages owing to war, revolts, states of emergency or other armed conflicts, none of which were strangers in a Pakistani context. They were promised free repatriation of their profits and other capital out of Pakistan, which again was a very significant obligation for a country facing serious foreign exchange shortages at the time. The treaty also obliged Pakistan to treat Swiss investors in the same way as Pakistani investors (national treatment) or investors from other third countries (most-favoured-nation treatment), whichever was more favourable. Finally, it included a vague – but potentially far-reaching – clause providing for fair and equitable treatment, which again remained unspecified. In essence, the BIT provided SGS something akin to an 'economic constitution' while operating in Pakistan that was independent of Pakistan's own laws and regulations.

As important, it gave Swiss investors the right to settle disputes with the Pakistani government outside Pakistan's own legal system, for instance by using ICSID as the arbitration forum. This was in contrast to the usual procedure of international arbitrations, where foreign investors traditionally needed to go through domestic courts before international proceedings could be initiated. The tribunal had the authority to admit SGS's claim, rule on its own jurisdiction, as well as award damages binding upon Pakistan and with no real options for appeal.

Some corners of the Pakistani bureaucracy proposed to stay away from the proceedings and not comply with any potential arbitral awards, but the attorney general realized this was a bad idea. Like the vast majority of investment arbitration claims, SGS had asked for monetary compensation as a remedy. In case of non-compliance, the award would be enforceable against Pakistan's commercial assets around the world. Courts in enforcing states would have only limited options to refuse execution. Even more important, Pakistan was crucially dependent on financial assistance from the International Financial Institutions, so reneging on international legal obligations within a World Bank forum like ICSID would be imprudent.

Clearly, this was not a claim to be taken lightly, so the attorney general wanted more information on the BIT and why it had been signed in 1995. But when inquiring with the relevant ministries, he was unable to trace any records of negotiations ever taking place with Switzerland. There were no files or documentation and no indication that the treaty had ever been discussed in Parliament. In fact, no one could find the treaty itself, so Pakistan had to ask Switzerland for a copy through formal channels. For a treaty with such a considerable scope, this was somewhat

Preface xv

of a mystery. Yet, the attorney general later learned that this was no exception, as hardly any records existed of Pakistan's past BIT negotiations.

This was peculiar. For although Pakistan was no stranger to allowing *individual* investors a right to international arbitration based on specific contracts, its BITs had provided a 'standing offer' to international arbitration to foreign investors *as a group*. When signing BITs Pakistan had given all existing *and* future investors covered by the treaties the option of taking their disputes to international arbitration. Combined with their vague and broad treaty language, this not only gave investors a second chance at adjudicating contract disputes, as in the SGS case, but also implied a potentially infinite number of claims involving Pakistan's regulatory conduct. But even though Pakistan had actually been the first country to ever sign a BIT in 1959 with West Germany, and had concluded a total of 40 similar treaties since then, no one could seem to find any documentation that they had been carefully negotiated.

This was not because the negotiations were considered too sensitive to document in written form. On the contrary, when foreign delegations had come to the country, or the Pakistani leadership went abroad, BITs had merely been considered a diplomatic token of goodwill. There was an expectation that the treaties would lead to increased inflows of foreign investment, something Pakistan desperately needed, but they were not thought to have any potential liabilities or regulatory constraints. The claim by SGS made it obvious to the attorney general that this view was mistaken.

For many, however, this probably sounds a little too convenient: now that Pakistan had to adhere to her international legal obligations, it appears opportunistic of a bureaucrat to claim ignorance on behalf of his former colleagues. So to corroborate the story, I contacted a considerable number of officials involved in Pakistan's BIT program in the past. All confirmed more or less the same narrative, and today even government files admit to this view: 'BITs were initially instruments that were signed during visits of high level delegations to provide for photo opportunities'.[3] It was thereby not until Pakistan was hit by a multimillion-dollar arbitration claim that officials realized the implications of treaties signed by shifting governments since 1959.

This book will show that Pakistan's experiences have not been unique. During the 1990s and early 2000s, only few developing country governments realized that by consenting to investment treaty arbitration, they

---

[3] Communication between Pakistan's Board of Investment and Ministry of Law concerning re-negotiation of German-Pakistan BIT, 23 November 2009. On file with author.

agreed to offer international investors enforceable protections with the potential for costly and far-reaching implications. The majority of developing countries thereby signed up to one of the most potent international legal regimes underwriting economic globalization without even realizing it at the time.

This not only means that the history of the international investment regime has to be rewritten; it also provides more general lessons for our understanding of economic diplomacy. For even if policy-makers try to pursue their own preferences when designing the rules that shape global economic governance, they are not always as careful and sophisticated as much international relations literature would have us believe. Instead, economic diplomats are no different from the rest of us by often struggling to make sense of their surroundings due to limited problem-solving capabilities. It is only through studying the nature and role of these cognitive constraints that we will understand the often irrational, yet predictable, nature of international economic relations.

1 Unanticipated consequences

The bilateral investment treaty (BIT) between Pakistan and Switzerland is one of more than 3,000 investment treaties signed by practically all countries in the world, particularly during the 1990s and early 2000s (Figure 1.1). The vast majority are bilateral and closely follow decade-old provisions going back to the 1959 agreement between West Germany and Pakistan – with one key exception. For whereas early investment treaties referred disputes to inter-state adjudication, BITs adopted in recent decades have included a broad and binding consent to investor–state arbitration. As realized by the attorney general of Pakistan, this made the treaties some of the most potent legal instruments in the global economy.

Today, foreign investors increasingly resort to treaty-based arbitration when disputes arise. Not all claims have to be made public, but by 2015 we knew of more than 600 filed against nearly 100 states. Most have been brought in recent years and the majority of respondents are developing countries. The claims have dealt with a very wide range of government activities. For although investment treaties emerged in response to the wave of expropriations during the post-colonial era, outright expropriation of foreign investments came out of fashion in the late 1970s. Instead, the vague terms of investment treaties have been

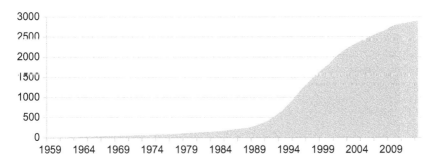

Figure 1.1 The spread of bilateral investment treaties

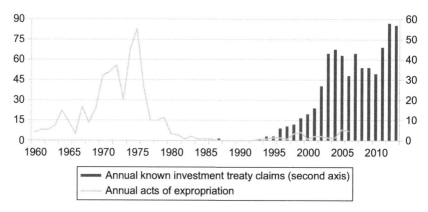

Figure 1.2 Investment treaty arbitration and direct expropriation
Note: Expropriation data, from Hajzler (2012), ends in 2006.

used to raise broader complaints about lacking transparency, stability, and predictability in government decisions affecting a large number of actors apart from claimants themselves. Investors have targeted measures at all levels of government, including legislative and judicial acts, and disputes have often been in vital areas of public regulation, such as environmental protection or the provision of key utilities.

Foreign investors have not always won. In the SGS case, for instance, Pakistan was fortunate to have the tribunal ultimately deny the claim. But almost three out of five concluded cases have been decided against the host state or settled on, typically, unknown terms.[1] This has resulted in considerable controversy in recent years, particularly because some arbitrators have granted compensation for measures that may have been permissible in domestic legal systems of most developed countries.[2]

Such expansive interpretations have raised eyebrows among critics, who argue that vague treaties have been used to give foreign investors too far-reaching protections. Moreover, the identity of arbitrators themselves has come under scrutiny. For unlike domestic judges, arbitrators have often been private commercial lawyers.[3] And should private lawyers really be granted such extensive powers over public regulation made by

---

[1] UNCTAD 2014a.
[2] Douglas 2006, pp. 27–8; Johnson and Volkov 2013; Montt 2009; Van Harten 2013.
[3] Waibel and Wu 2014; Van Harten 2013.

Unanticipated consequences

sovereign states? Can they be trusted not to inflate the judicial scope of the regime in order to boost the number of claims brought by investors?

Also, whereas governments have routinely been told by arbitrators that they are not sufficiently stable and predictable in their dealings with foreign investors, arbitrators themselves have taken inconsistent, and occasionally contradictory, positions. In the SGS case, for instance, one of the clauses appeared to the tribunal 'susceptible of almost indefinite expansion' and it ultimately ruled in favour of Pakistan by taking a narrow interpretation.[4] Five months later, however, a contradictory interpretation of a largely similar clause went in SGS's favour in a separate claim against the Philippines. This is but one example of how the vague nature of investment treaties combined with an ad hoc dispute settlement process has made investment treaty arbitration often unpredictable, which makes it difficult to foresee exactly which measures violate the treaties, and why.

Another set of concerns relate to the size of the monetary awards.[5] In 2003, for instance, one dispute led to more than $350 million in damages against the Czech government including interest, which was equal to the entire health budget of the Czech government and effectively doubled the public-sector deficit for that year.[6] This was a glimpse of what was yet to come. Nine years later a split tribunal awarded an American company $2.37 billion in compensation from Ecuador including interest, despite acknowledging that the investor had broken Ecuador's own laws as well as the contract with the Ecuadorian government.[7] The award amounted to almost 7 per cent of the Ecuadorian government's total government budget[8] and, adjusted for GDP, an equivalent award against the United Kingdom would be almost $70 billion and for the United States $458 billion.

Then finally, in 2014, Russia was asked to pay $50 billion to shareholders of the defunct oil company Yukos, amounting to 12 per cent of the government's total revenue.[9] Just the legal fees involved were staggering: the shareholders paid Shearman and Sterling, an American law firm, $74 million to represent them and the tribunal took almost $9 million for themselves – $7.4 million to the three arbitrators and $1.4 million to their assistant.[10] These cases were extreme, of course, and the

---

[4] *S.A.* v. *Islamic Republic of Pakistan, Decision on Jurisdiction*, Société Générale de Surveillance, 6 August 2003, para. 167–8.

[5] For statistics, see Franck 2007; Gallagher and Shrestha 2011; Hodgson 2014; Rosert 2014.

[6] *CME Czech Rep. B.V.* v. *Czech Republic*, UNCITRAL, Final Award, 14 March 2003; Kellner 2003; Peterson 2004, pp. 25–6.

[7] ICSID Case No. ARB/06/11, Award, 5 October 2012.   [8] Rosert 2014.   [9] Ibid.

[10] "The Cost of Yukos," *Global Arbitration Review*, 29 July 2014. About 4 per cent of the arbitrators' costs were to cover personal expenses. On top of that a further $1.3 million

4   Unanticipated consequences

Yukos claim did in fact involve outright expropriation. Yet, they highlight the potential liabilities that investment arbitration can impose on states.

So given the scope and interpretive practice of investment treaty arbitration, it should come as no surprise that the regime has become one of the most controversial areas of global economic governance. As one arbitrator has lamented: 'the more [people] find out what we do and what we say, and how we say it, the more appalled they are'.[11] This includes policy-makers in a growing number of developing countries. By 2015, several countries had decided to withdraw from the regime after coming on the receiving end of controversial investment treaty claims.[12] South Africa had begun terminating its BITs, and Bolivia, Ecuador, and Venezuela had left the International Centre for the Settlement of Investment Disputes (ICSID) and cancelled some of their investment treaties. Also Indonesia was considering following suit, and India had put a hold to negotiations in order to rethink its investment treaty programme.[13] Most other developing countries have stayed in the regime for now and instead pursued more incremental reforms, but there is no doubt that the legitimacy of investment treaty arbitration has been put to the test in recent years.

Yet, the vast majority of respondent governments have nevertheless complied with awards promptly and voluntarily. The main calculus has been that in the absence of overriding political concerns it would be imprudent to sign up to investment treaties and the ICSID Convention to attract investment and then proceed to scare away the same investors by refusing to comply with awards. Also, the very few states that have postponed payment of awards have faced significant political and legal challenges. For instance, when Argentina initially refused to pay a number of outstanding ICSID awards owed to American companies, Washington suspended trade benefits to the country and sought to block international credit from the World Bank and the IMF. President Kirchner finally relented and decided to settle the outstanding ICSID awards, paying out half a billion dollars to five American companies.

Some investors have also taken the matter in their own hands and used the ICSID and New York Conventions to confiscate assets of the

---

went towards 'tribunal costs' and a $1.2 million fee to the Permanent Court of Arbitration for administering the proceedings.

[11] Comments by Johnny Veeder QC at Wilmer Hale seminar on international arbitration, 23 April 2014.

[12] On investment treaties and investment treaty arbitration as a 'regime', see Salacuse 2010. *A contrario*, Wells 2010.

[13] See 'Indonesia to terminate more than 60 bilateral investment treaties', *Financial Times*, 26 March 2014; Ranjan 2014.

respondent government.[14] This is neither easy nor cheap due to sovereign immunity laws, but it is possible, and at the time this book went to press, President Putin could expect Yukos shareholders to try to enforce their award around the globe for years to come. Yet, in the vast majority of cases this hasn't been necessary as international investment law is no different from other international regimes, where 'almost all nations observe almost all principles of international law and almost all of their obligations almost all of the time'.[15]

This raises a significant puzzle. For why did practically all developing countries suddenly rush to sign largely identical treaties, which significantly constrained their sovereignty? Why did they expose themselves to expensive investment claims and give such a remarkable degree of flexibility to private lawyers to determine the scope of their regulatory autonomy? This is the core question of this book.

Traditional accounts

Crucial credible commitments

The standard answer from political scientists and a large number of legal practitioners is straightforward: if developing countries wanted to attract investment they *had* to sign the treaties. Because without offering recourse to investment treaty arbitration, developing countries couldn't give risk-averse foreign investors a credible commitment that their investments would be safe. The theory is simple. As a starting point, developing country governments are expected to not fully internalize the costs of regulating foreign investors. They favour local firms at the expense of foreigners, even when the latter are more efficient.[16] This is typically explained in terms of a dynamic inconsistency problem, where governments have an incentive to renege on promises made to foreign investors after their investments have been sunk in the host state.[17] This could be through outright expropriation or more indirectly through changes in tax codes, requirements for local content requirements, repatriation restrictions, introducing new operation fees, and so forth. Although rational ex post this has negative ex ante implications, as foreign investors are aware of these risks and therefore refrain from otherwise efficient investment

---

[14] See e.g. Peterson and Balcerzak 2014.
[15] Henkin 1979, p. 47. See generally; von Stein 2013.
[16] See discussion in Bonnitcha and Aisbett 2013.
[17] Guzman 1998. On obsolescent bargains and foreign investment, see generally, Vernon 1971; Woodhouse 2006.

6   Unanticipated consequences

decisions.[18] According to the standard narrative, investment treaties credibly commit against such behaviour by raising the costs of existing and future governments to extract value from foreign investors, which in turn should make them more attractive investment decisions. By signing investment treaties, developing countries thereby traded their sovereignty for credibility as this was the 'cost of seeking additional FDI inflows'.[19]

Although this assumption underlies a large share of political science literature on the international investment regime, it is unconvincing. First of all, during the time investment treaties spread rapidly, the long-term reputational costs of mistreating foreign investors prevented (most) developing countries from taking the types of measures foreseen by obsolescent bargaining models. Although there were, of course, examples of egregious conduct against foreign investors during the 1990s, most developing countries were strongly committed to attracting foreign capital, which meant regulatory risk premiums were often quite limited even in 'high-risk' sectors with major sunk investments.[20]

In cases where uncompensated expropriation or other regulatory abuses of foreign investors were a genuine concern, political risk management could often be effectively handled through market-based strategies. Investors could enter into joint ventures with local companies, obtain financing from local creditors, structure investments over long time periods, or bring in powerful partners such as major foreign banks or public aid agencies.[21] Such options ensure that the host country has a long-term interest in protecting foreign capital. And even if these business strategies were deemed insufficient, investors could still obtain investment insurance. Political risk insurance covers many of the same risks as investment treaties and is often a more direct, quick, and straightforward option of investment protection than the prospect of going through lengthy and expensive arbitration proceedings.[22] Particularly when insurance providers are state sponsored, the host government has a strong incentive to protect the assets of foreign investors, as they may otherwise risk future aid and loans. As a result, 'once the full cost of prospective action against an insured investor is realized, these

---

[18] Markusen 2001.

[19] Montt 2009, p. 128. Although not deal with here, it is important to note that investment treaty protections could also, in theory, encourage inefficient investment decisions by preventing efficiency-improving government measures; Aisbett, Karp, and McAusland 2010.

[20] See Yackee 2008, pp. 125–7.

[21] Ramamurti 2003; Wells and Ahmed 2006; West 1999; Woodhouse 2006.

[22] See e.g. Bekker and Ogawa 2013; Jensen 2005.

Traditional accounts 7

disputes often become "misunderstandings" which are quietly and successfully resolved'.[23]

Finally, the notion that investment treaties were the only instruments that could 'tie governments to the mast' of international law is inaccurate. Although they are not necessarily perfect substitutes for investment treaties, carefully drafted investment contracts can secure many investments with the same – or greater – standards, including recourse to international arbitration backed by the New York or ICSID Conventions.[24] Throughout the post-war era, international tribunals have recognized their jurisdiction over contractual disputes and relied on international law principles to provide meaningful compensation for both expropriation and other contractual breaches.[25] Contracts do not *guarantee* that host countries will uphold their commitments, of course, but neither do investment treaties.[26] Also, it is true that some investment treaty claims have been pursued by medium-size investors, who may not be in a position to negotiate advantageous contracts, but the majority of claims have involved investors in a contractual relationship with the host state, where the contracts have often included their own dispute settlement clause.[27] In those cases, the effect of investment treaties is mainly to provide investors yet another avenue to adjudicate the same dispute. Just like the claim by SGS against Pakistan.

In short, there is a wide range of options available to foreign investors concerned with political risks, including market-based mechanisms, political risk insurance offered by governments and private providers, as well as contracts with recourse to international arbitration. None of these instruments can eliminate political risks entirely, but they do make investment treaties less crucial commitment devices than typically assumed by political scientists.

It is therefore not surprising that only a few investors seem to have found the treaties critical when considering whether to invest in developing countries. Sophisticated firms occasionally set up holding companies in third countries to obtain protection,[28] but the treaties have hardly ever influenced where the investments are going in the first place. It can

---

[23] West 1999.   [24] See generally: Yackee 2008b; 2009b.   [25] Yackee 2009b, pp. 61–2.
[26] On why, and when, governments breach investor–state contracts, see e.g. Wellhausen 2014; Wellhausen and Johns 2014.
[27] Bonnitcha 2014, pp. 76–7; OECD 2012a, p. 17; Van Harten 2013, pp. 122–4.
[28] In the absence of ratified Brazilian BITs, for instance, Petrobas is reported to have invested abroad via third countries to obtain investment treaty protection; see wikileaks.org/cable/2007/05/07BRASILIA833.html. Accessed on 10 June 2013. See also ICSID Case No. ARB/02/18, Decision on Jurisdiction, 29 April 2004; ICSID Case No. ARB/06/5, Award on Jurisdiction, 15 April 2009; ICSID Case No. ARB/07/27, Decision on Jurisdiction, 10 June 2010.

8   Unanticipated consequences

happen,[29] but it is exceedingly rare. For instance, the World Bank published a survey of foreign investors in 1991 and concluded that BITs had a negligible, if any, role for investment decisions. Only '[p]rofessional advisors, such as accountants or merchant bankers, would be people to concern themselves with such minutia, only after detailed project planning was already underway'.[30] The report noted that UK investors 'rarely if ever take into account the existence of [a BIT] when deciding whether or not to invest'.[31] Similarly, although German public institutions considered BITs to be effective investment promotion tools, the World Bank noted that 'empirical evidence does not necessarily support this',[32] and evidence to sustain that the treaties promoted investment was 'limited'.[33] Interviews with Swedish investors similarly revealed that BITs were 'relatively unknown and therefore have little to no impact on FDI flows'.[34] American investors didn't find BITs that important either. This was in contrast with double taxation treaties, which were considered crucial for FDI decisions.[35]

Later surveys have largely confirmed this view.[36] Nor have investment treaties been crucial for the financing of the vast majority of foreign investment projects, as even political risk insurers have rarely found them relevant when determining the availability and pricing of insurance for expropriation and other political risks. Germany's tying of state-backed insurance to investment treaties has been important for German investors

---

[29] When Venezuela ratified the Dutch BIT in 1993, for instance, the Dutch ambassador reported to his Danish counterpart that recourse to investor–state arbitration in the treaty was instrumental for Royal Dutch Shell's participation in a large natural gas project, Cristóbal Colon; UM.400.E.13.Venezuela.12. It is unclear from the report whether a binding arbitration clause in a contract could have been sufficient for Shell.

[30] MIGA PAS 1991, p. 92.   [31] Ibid., p. 89.   [32] Ibid., p. 135.   [33] Ibid., p. 140.

[34] Ibid., p. 199.   [35] Ibid., p. 41.

[36] For a review, see Poulsen 2010. See also Yackee 2010 (in-house legal counsel in American multinationals report that BITs are ineffective in protecting against political risks and the treaties are unlikely to be important for the vast majority of establishment decisions as senior executives are rarely aware of their existence); Economist Intelligence Unit 2011 (only a small minority of 316 executives find BITs very important for expropriation risk, though with somewhat higher figures for large investors and investors from industries with large sunk costs); Copenhagen Economics 2012 (European investors in China are rarely familiar with their relevant BITs and only a few find the treaties relevant for investment decisions); Economist Intelligence Unit 2015 (even the relatively small number of investors who said they found the treaties crucial had nevertheless invested in risky jurisdictions without treaty protections. BITs were found to be very important for investing in China, in stark contrast with 2012 Copenhagen Economics survey, but the authors suggest that much feedback was likely aspirational rather than reflecting real investment decisions, as the questionnaire was sent out during highly politicized discussions over the future of European investment treaties.)

Traditional accounts 9

on occasion, as we shall see, but most public and private providers of insurance rarely find the treaties crucial. As noted by this underwriter:

> While they should perhaps have a role to play, I would say [BITs] are likely to be considered completely irrelevant by underwriters today and thus irrelevant for the pricing of risk insurance. . . Rather than having a role in the investment decision, they are just an extra arrow in the lawyer's quiver on the occasions where disputes arise.[37]

All in all, investment treaties have undoubtedly been significant for some establishment decisions of some investors – particularly when it comes to the legal structure of their investments – but the impact of the treaties on investment flows to the developing world has been small.[38]

At least to date. Because even if surveys indicated that BITs were less than crucial for establishment decisions in the past, a growing number of investors and underwriters could find the treaties to be increasingly important as they realize the potential of investment treaty arbitration. The spike in claims in recent years indicates that this is not unlikely. Yet, even if investment treaties are becoming slightly more important for investment flows, it still leaves the question of why governments in developing countries signed the treaties in such great numbers from the late 1980s to early 2000s. There were many ways in which developing countries could attract investment, so why did these agreements become so widespread? If only few investors cared about BITs, and that too only 'after detailed project planning was already underway', why were the treaties so popular?

Coercion

One answer could be that developing countries were somehow coerced into the regime. Critics of BITs occasionally argue that Western states relied on power-asymmetries to get developing countries to sign the treaties and that explains why there is no multilateral investment agreement.[39] This is misleading. During the 1960s and 1970s the sceptical attitude towards foreign investment in large parts of the developing world meant Western states had difficulties getting the vast majority of developing country governments to sign on to BITs. When invited to negotiate,

---

[37] Quoted in Poulsen 2010.
[38] There is a large amount of econometric literature on these questions, but findings are often conflicting because of the limited data available. For a review of studies until 2010, see Poulsen 2010. See also Berger, Busse, Nunnemkamp, and Roy 2011 (finding a positive effect from 'strong' BITs); Peinhardt and Allee 2012 (finding no effect of American treaties); Jandhyala and Weiner 2012 (finding a positive effect on pricing of oil reserves); Kerner and Lawrence 2014 (finding a positive, but very limited, effect).
[39] See e.g. Kaushal 2009.

10 Unanticipated consequences

most governments responded that protections enshrined in domestic laws were sufficient to protect foreign investors, and the book will present archival records showing that even small and weak capital importing states were able to resist Western pressure.

Rather than external imposition, it was internal reforms that led the way for the investment treaty movement. With the Latin American debt crisis and the drying up of official aid flows during the 1980s, a consensus emerged that attracting foreign direct investment (FDI) was key to economic development. In John Williamson's 10-point list summarizing the 'Washington Consensus' towards development policies, a restrictive attitude towards FDI was considered outright 'foolish'.[40] Many developing countries agreed, and governments in practically all corners of the world began to liberalize their investment regimes. Fair and equitable treatment of foreign investors, compensation for expropriation at fair market value, and non-discrimination – all are principles that were not just enshrined in Western BIT templates, but also in many national investment codes and practices during this period.[41]

Investment treaties seemed like the perfect instrument to complement domestic investment reforms. A judge from Sri Lanka's Court of Appeal accurately summarized the attitude like this:

Although substantial aid is given by the developed countries and their agencies to the Third World countries, the latter are unhappy about the conditions attached to such aid programs. Thus, they prefer foreign direct investments, in which they are equal partners with the investors ... The concept upon which [BITs] are based, namely reciprocity, accords well with that thinking; the principle of reciprocity is in conformity with the concept of sovereignty.[42]

So after they had begun liberalizing their investment regimes at home, practically every developing country began signing treaties enshrining the very protections they had resisted just decades before (Figure 1.3). This included Latin American countries as well as governments in the former Socialist block. Immediately before the end of the Cold War even the Kremlin had begun to negotiate investment treaties after Gorbachev embraced the virtues of international law[43] and the Soviet leadership no longer saw foreign investors as 'the last poisonous flowers on the dung-heap of capitalism'.[44]

---

[40] Williamson 1990, ch. 2.   [41] Alvarez 2009, pp. 52–6; Montt 2009, p. 129.
[42] Gunawardana 1992, p. 546.
[43] See e.g. comments made by Gorbachev in the UN in Koh 1997, ftn. 156.
[44] Sahlgren quoted in Sagafi-Nejad 2008, p. 92. Foreign investors were invited to enter into joint ventures governed by Soviet laws and regulations, but 'with exceptions provided for by inter-state and intergovernmental agreements, which the USSR is part to'; Decree No. 49 of the USSR Council of Ministers 13 January 1987.

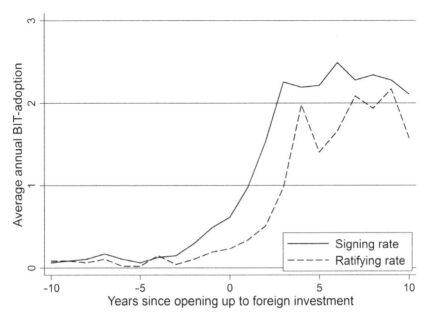

Figure 1.3 Take-off in BIT adoption coincided with domestic FDI liberalization
Note: Figure is based on 46 developing countries; see Appendix 1.

Also regional agreements with investment protection chapters emerged during this period. This included the 1991 Energy Charter Treaty (ECT), signed by a large number of OECD countries as well as countries in Eastern European and the Commonwealth of Independent States. The 1994 North American Free Trade Agreement (NAFTA) was signed as well between the United States, Canada, and Mexico. Yet, the vast majority of treaties remained bilateral. Between 1994 and 1996 an average of four BITs was signed every week[45] and unlike the early years of the investment treaty movement, it was now typically developing countries that initiated negotiations. European governments could largely pick and choose with whom they wished to sign BITs and the United States also managed to sign a growing number of agreements. Whereas the Reagan administration had significant difficulties getting the American BIT program off the ground, the United States succeeded in signing 28 between 1990 and 1995 alone. Washington even had to

[45] UNCTAD 2013a, p. xx.

12   Unanticipated consequences

decline some invitations to negotiate during the 1990s,[46] as was the case for several European countries as well.

During the same period it proved impossible to agree to a multilateral investment agreement, but this was not because developing countries resisted BIT-like protections. In the 1980s and 1990s investment was covered during the Uruguay Round of GATT negotiations, but efforts were focused primarily on investment liberalization – not protection (like BITs).[47] And although OECD countries tried to negotiate a Multilateral Agreement on Investment (MAI) during the mid 1990s, it was disagreements amongst developed countries themselves that made the project crumple rather than developing country opposition.[48] When developing countries expressed concerns with the project, it was the forum – not the substance – that was the main lightening rod: for why should rules intended primarily to protect investment in developing countries be negotiated solely by OECD members?

Finally, developing countries did manage to exclude investment from WTO's Doha-Round, but the blocking coalition was small and only few developing countries were active in the discussions.[49] Supported primarily by Indonesia and Malaysia, India was the main stumbling block – not exactly the most likely candidate to be pushed around in bilateral negotiations – and one of the primary arguments was that BITs were the preferred instruments to deal with investment protection. Delhi's WTO representative said that bilateral treaties were 'favoured by countries like India' and Malaysia agreed that its interests were 'best served by bilateral investment treaties'.[50]

In short, investment treaties were adopted willingly by capital-importing states seeing the treaties as useful supplements to parallel reforms of domestic investment regimes. BITs were 'often a codification, not a source, of pro-foreign-investment policies'.[51] Power was naturally important for the investment treaty movement, as we shall see, and there were instances where unbalanced power relations were important for bilateral negotiations. But the treaties were nothing akin to 'contracts of adhesion'.

---

[46] This was the case with Pakistan, for instance, where talks over a BIT began already in the 1980s. But when in 1995, Pakistan asked the United States to take the talks further, the Clinton administration refused until Islamabad signed a treaty on intellectual property right protection. See "United States no to talks to investment treaty before IPR record," *Business Recorder*, 19 March 1995; USAID 1990, p. 17.

[47] Stewart 1993.

[48] NGO pressure and failing business support meant there was little political buy-in in Western capitals, so when France walked away from negotiations due to concerns about its cultural industries the project was shelved; Graham 2000; Walter 2001.

[49] Sauvé 2006.   [50] WT/WGTI/M/14.   [51] Salacuse and Sullivan 2005, p. 96.

Again, however, this still leaves the question largely unanswered: although investment treaties may have complemented domestic reforms in broad terms, their arbitration clauses invited all existing and future foreign investors to file compensation claims based on exceptionally vague provisions. Chief Justice Roberts of the US Supreme Court wrote in 2014 that by consenting to investment arbitration 'a state permits private adjudicators to review its public policies and effectively annul the authoritative acts of its legislature, executive, and judiciary'.[52] Why would so many governments voluntarily agree to such a thing?

Emulation

Perhaps developing countries merely signed BITs based on what political scientists call a logic of appropriateness. Just as 'civilized' nations had to adhere to certain standards during the Imperial era, for instance, countries with widely different backgrounds also use a number of policy programmes today to signal their commitment to the norms of political and economic liberalism without necessarily having the capacity, or even inclination, to implement them in practice.[53] Along the same lines, some scholars argue that investment treaties were signed by developing countries not because they expected any material benefits or were coerced into adopting them, but rather because state leaders and their bureaucracies thought it was one of those things (self-perceived) modern, liberal, and law-abiding states were *supposed* to do after the end of the Cold War and the rise of neoliberalism.[54]

The claim is backed up by the spread of 'strange' BITs among developing countries themselves. Although the process started in 1964 with the Kuwait-Iraq BIT, the share of South-South BITs out of the global BIT landscape remained rather small until the mid 1990s. Today, however, almost 40 per cent of all BITs are between developing countries – an astonishing share given that BITs were initially tailored to protect Western investors in the developing world. With only a few exceptions,[55] these treaties are very much similar to 'normal' North-South BITs. And because many are among countries with few, if any, commercial links, they could indicate that investment treaties were intended as nothing but political symbolism.

---

[52] *BG Group plc* v. *Republic of Argentina*, Supreme Court of the United States, No. 12–138, Dissenting Opinion by Chief Justice Roberts, 5 March 2014.
[53] See, e.g. Ramirez, Meyer, Wotipka, and Drori 2002.
[54] Jandhyala, Henisz, and Mansfield 2011.   [55] Poulsen 2010.

14   Unanticipated consequences

This account is also unconvincing. As will become clear throughout this book, investment treaties were repeatedly justified by their capacity to attract investment by both promoters of the treaties as well as developing country governments themselves. Normative considerations were not irrelevant, but they were rarely at the forefront. Both the discourse trail and interviews with officials themselves show that developing country governments around the world genuinely thought the treaties were important to attract foreign investment and that was the main driver behind their investment treaty programmes.[56]

Also, if BITs were signed primarily as acts of political symbolism, it is peculiar that unlike human rights treaties, for instance, they were typically signed entirely under the radars of public discourse and received little attention by parliaments, the press, or the public at large. Because both the signing and ratification of the treaties were usually very low-profile events, only few paid much attention to BITs before the early 2000s, with the possible exception of treaties entered into with the United States. Figure 1.4 shows that whereas hundreds of BITs were signed annually up through the 1990s, it is not until the claims began that the treaties attracted much attention in the press. By comparison, preferential trade agreements (PTAs) were mentioned almost 70 times more frequently during the 1990s. The spread of BITs was one of those 'supranational governance activities that go virtually unnoticed',[57] and the treaties were therefore rather poor marketing instruments if used to signal adherence to global norms.

Also, despite the 'poor publicity' of BITs, developing countries themselves have done very little to advertise the fact that they have signed the treaties, even in recent years.[58] This, too, is surprising if they were merely signed as 'ceremonial acts'.[59] For even if developing countries didn't care whether the treaties were actually effective,[60] some amount of publicity was necessary in order for the symbolic content of investment treaties to be recognized and endorsed by international organizations, foreign investors, or other spectators.[61]

Finally, most investment treaties very closely follow Western BIT templates, occasionally word for word, but it is notable that during the height of the BIT movement, developing countries primarily followed the templates of European countries. The United States had

---

[56] On the relevance of the discourse trail for testing norm-emulation models, see Finnemore and Sikkink 1998, p. 892; Gurowitz 2006.
[57] Esty 2006, p. 1509; quoted in Montt 2009, p. 143.   [58] Yackee 2014.
[59] On 'ceremonial' acts in World Polity theory, see Meyer 2000; Strang and Meyer 2009.
[60] On de-coupling and institutional choice, see again the works of Meyer.
[61] See generally, Lamertz and Heugens 2009.

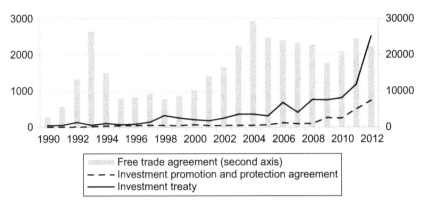

Figure 1.4 Poor publicity stunts
Note: Figure shows number of times the phrases 'free trade agreement', 'investment promotion and protection agreement' (the British term for a BIT), and 'investment treaty' was mentioned in English-speaking newspapers from 1990 to 2012. The latter also covers the number of times 'bilateral investment treaty' was mentioned.
Source: FACTIVA

a different model. It was longer and more clearly specified but also significantly more ambitious by including liberalization provisions and prohibitions on performance requirements (such as local contents requirements). These two omissions make a former American negotiator go so far as to argue that European models are in fact somewhat 'antithetical to economic liberalism'.[62] Yet, not only was the United States relatively unsuccessful in developing a wide network of investment treaties compared to European countries, it was also not until recently that the American model gained in popularity. This, too, is puzzling if BITs were merely the result of normative emulation during the 1990s; for what better option to show a government's adherence to the Washington consensus than mimicking the most investor-friendly treaties possible?

So although we shall see that some treaties were indeed signed for ceremonial reasons, it is not a satisfactory explanation overall. For most developing countries, the BIT movement has not been about lofty aspirations of international justice or symbolic attempts to adhere to neoliberal ideals. Rather it was about something as mundane as

---

[62] Vandevelde 1998, p. 634.

16   Unanticipated consequences

attracting foreign investment. A former American negotiator is correct to note that during the 1990s, 'many developing countries [now saw] the BIT [as] a tangible way of signalling their captivity to foreign investment, and thus may seem to assist in attracting capital from the United States and other developed countries'.[63] This is what Salacuse has described as the 'grand bargain' of BITs: developing countries promised foreign investors extensive protections in return for the prospect of more capital.[64]

But, although foreign investors got their end of the bargain – extensive protections – the treaties have rarely been important to attract investment. So why did so many developing countries radically overestimate the economic benefits of BITs? Also, if it was not because of emulation, why did practically all developing countries almost completely sign off on European BIT templates? Although negotiating around model agreements can be entirely rational, it is puzzling that so many BITs have been practically identical despite diverse institutional, political, economic, and cultural contexts. Why haven't we seen more tailoring to local circumstances? If not functionalism, coercion, or emulation, what then explains the adoption and design of the treaties?

The argument

Suffice it to say that with more than 3,000 investment treaties signed over more than half a century, any single – or monocausal – explanation is impossible, and it would fall outside the scope of any book to explain why every single developing country has signed and ratified every single investment treaty. The aim with this volume, therefore, is to explain the main factors driving developing countries to sign up to the modern investment treaty regime.[65] And the core argument is that the way developing countries assessed and negotiated investment treaties fits

---

[63] Vandevelde 1993, p. 638.   [64] Salacuse 2013.

[65] Different organizations use different definitions of developing countries, and any classification is bound to be crude, particularly in studies over time. For the purpose of this book, developing countries are those the World Bank has not classified as 'high-income' countries for the majority of the period listed in its World Development Indicators, starting in 1987 and ending in 2013. The 'developed country' category therefore includes Andorra, Aruba, Australia, Austria, Bahamas, Bahrain, Belgium, Bermuda, Brunei, Canada, Cyprus, Denmark, Finland, France, Germany, Greece, Hong Kong, Iceland, Ireland, Israel, Italy, Japan, Korea, Kuwait, Luxembourg, Malta, Netherlands, New Zealand, Norway, Portugal, Qatar, Singapore, Slovenia, Spain, Sweden, Switzerland, Taiwan, United Arab Emirates, the United Kingdom, and the United States. All other countries are grouped under the umbrella term of *developing countries* in this study.

The argument 17

hand-in-glove with expectations on bounded rationality from behavioural psychology and economics. From this perspective, policy-makers are not expected to blindly follow a logic of appropriateness – as in emulation models – but are instead seen as 'intended rational', who *try* to strategically pursue their own preferences.[66] But in contrast with the unrealistic expectations of judgment common to approaches based on 'comprehensive rationality', a bounded rationality framework is based on what we actually know about the capacities, and limits, of human decision-making.[67] It acknowledges that policy-makers are subject to cognitive constraints and often prone to make mistakes. For rather than engaging in sophisticated cost–benefit calculations when assessing the implications of different policies, their inferences are often skewed by systematic information processing biases.

Once we account for these cognition constraints, it is suddenly possible to explain much of the behaviour of developing countries in the international investment regime. BITs were rarely the result of developing countries pursuing 'optimizing' behaviour to achieve their national interests, as assumed in models based on unbounded rationality.[68] Instead, policy-makers often entirely misjudged their environment by failing to factor in and accurately assess relevant information about the agreements. This manifested itself in numerous ways, three of which are worth highlighting now.

First of all, developing countries' strong commitment to attracting foreign investment during the height of the Washington Consensus made policy-makers *want* investment treaties to work. Rather than conducting an unbiased search and assessment of information, they often based their expectations about the economic benefits of the treaties on wishful thinking. This is an example of what experimental psychology calls 'motivated reasoning': people tend to be inherently sceptical about evidence that goes against their preferences, whereas evidence they want to believe is accepted with little scrutiny.[69] We see what we want to see. For instance, we know from experiments that strong political beliefs lead people to seek confirming evidence to sustain their pre-existing conceptions and at the same time strongly resist unwanted information.[70] Along

---

[66] Simon 1957.

[67] Comprehensive rationality is understood as decision-makers' having a set of fixed, transitive preferences for alternatives, and the ability to calculate the trade-offs of their choices, both future and present; Jones 2001, p. 35.

[68] On the care with which rational governments should negotiate binding treaties as opposed to informal agreements, see Abbott and Snidal 2000; Lipson 1991.

[69] Dawson, Gilovich, and Regan 2002; Gilovich 2000.   [70] Taber and Lodge 2006.

18 Unanticipated consequences

the same lines, motivated optimism was a core reason for the highly inflated expectations about the economic benefits of BITs.

Similar 'mistakes' took place when learning about the risks of the treaties. For although states would normally be expected to exercise careful scrutiny and bureaucratic review when negotiating potentially costly international obligations, this rarely took place when it came to investment treaties. Even while claims began ticking in at ICSID, officials failed to seek and consider relevant information about the liabilities and regulatory constraints that could arise from investment treaty arbitration. When a country hadn't been subject to a claim itself, officials typically assumed such claims were entirely unlikely – just as in the case of Pakistan.

This may seem peculiar, but it is what we would expect if policymakers were bounded rational. Because rather than efficiently seeking and processing information to make unbiased judgments, as assumed in fully rational models, countless studies have shown that decisions are often based mostly on information that is particularly salient.[71] Even though this can be useful to form inferences, it can also lead people to ignore highly relevant information if it is not sufficiently 'vivid'. In the investment regime, the result was that most developing country governments failed to learn from claims against other countries, as only claims against themselves were salient enough to warrant attention.

Salience biases were aggregated by the fact that officials in charge of considering and negotiating investment treaties often lacked both experience and expertise in the field. Time and again the negotiators of developed countries had to explain to their developing country counterparts the meaning of even simple treaty terms, and stakeholders often mistook the vague and short European templates for soft law. Terms such as *fair and equitable treatment* or *indirect expropriation* were rarely given any attention, as the 'devils in the details' were not sufficiently salient for generalist bureaucrats. This meant that agencies and officials with an individual interest in promoting BITs had free reign to adopt them right, left, and centre with little, if any, discussion. Western BIT models were signed off in a rush and the treaties spread like wildfire. Many of the 'strange' BITs among developing countries, for instance, were not the result of transnational mimicry but rather bureaucrats and politicians promoting the treaties for their own selfish reasons.

Investment treaties with the United States and Canada were somewhat different. Not only were North American templates much longer and

---

[71] The starting point was Tversky and Kahneman 1973.

The argument 19

complex, the implications of their market access provisions were also clearer to negotiators and stakeholders. The short and simple European models only covered established investors, however, and were therefore more popular as the potential for costly investment arbitration wasn't realized.

Finally, and related, most developing countries were satisfied with signing off on European BIT templates without considering whether alternative, or revised, provisions might have been more optimal. This, too, is what we would expect from a bounded rationality perspective, as it conforms with what is called the status quo bias.[72] Although relying on 'focal points' is not necessarily irrational,[73] we know from numerous experimental and observational studies that bounded rationality gives decision-makers an excessive preference for whatever solution is the 'default'. Experimental studies on negotiations, for instance, have shown that entirely random offers made in the initial stages of a negotiation can have a considerable impact on both counteroffers and final outcomes.[74] And again, this deviation from rational decision-making strategies is particularly prevalent in the absence of experience and expertise, as generalists are especially disinclined from opting out of default solutions.[75] This can be critical for negotiations, and the book will show that an excessive reliance on default rules goes a long way towards explaining the remarkable similarity of investment treaties over time and across countries. Typically, developing countries only tinkered with Western BIT models rather than carefully considering alternatives. After having been asked to pay compensation based on vague treaty provisions, many government today regret that (non-)decision.

Unanticipated consequences are, of course, not unique to the investment area. Just as few were able to predict the current authority that investment arbitral tribunals have over governments' regulatory discretion, few foresaw the wide-ranging role of the European Court of Justice, for instance.[76] States have also found their sovereignty constrained in ways they didn't anticipate both in the WTO and the International Court of Justice.[77] Even in the context of human rights treaties, developing countries have occasionally been shocked to realize that what they thought were merely pieces of paper later permitted transnational actors to use them for effective political pressure.[78] But by contrast with human

---

[72] See e.g. Kahneman, Knetsch, and Thaler 1991.   [73] Abbott and Snidal 2002.
[74] E.g. Galinsky and Mussweiler 2001; Neale and Bazerman 1991.   [75] Sunstein 2013.
[76] Alter 1998; Burley and Mattli 1993; Mattli and Slaughter 1995.   [77] Alter 2008.
[78] Sikkink 1993.

20   Unanticipated consequences

rights treaties, BITs have not merely been useful points of reference for companies and other actors advocating investor-friendly policies; in the vast majority of cases they are actually enforceable in practice. In the spectrum between diplomacy and legalism, the two types of treaties are at separate ends.[79] Also, the unanticipated consequences of investment treaty arbitration are not (only) a case of tribunals strategically trying to expand their own jurisdiction through creative lawyering. More important is the almost complete lack of attention by developing country negotiators in the 1990s due to bounded rationality. Although incomplete contracting is seen in many other areas of international law, the fact that private tribunals were given such considerable flexibility in 'filling out the blanks' of vague and broadly drafted treaties was rarely even considered at the time they proliferated.

Suffice it to say that these conclusions will sound paternalistic to some. One arbitrator, Jan Paulsson, calls this line of reasoning outright insulting to negotiators;[80] and his colleague Francisco Vicuña concurs:

> The guns are pointing ... to the vast network of bilateral investment treaties. ... The argument is based on the false assumption that developing countries have been ignorant of what they were actually signing ... Thank you for that paternalistic thought, but with respect I must say that lawyers from developing countries are not dummies.[81]

The claim made in this book is not that negotiators were 'dummies'. However, when arbitrators and political scientists suggest that a great number of developing countries invested considerable expertise to engage in BIT negotiations during the 1980s and 1990s, they are out of touch with realities on the ground. Whereas officials in some countries did manage to appreciate the implications of the treaties, they were the exception – not the rule. Even some colleagues of Paulsson and Vicuña accede that BITs were often entirely misunderstood by adopting governments until hit by a claim. In his expert testimony to one case, for instance, Christoph Schreuer was asked whether 'he really believed that two sovereign States will negotiate, sign and ratify a Bilateral Investment Treaty without caring to consider what was put in it'. Although far from a critic of the treaties, Schreuer replied:

> [M]any times, in fact in the majority of times, BITs are among clauses of treaties that are not properly negotiated... and I have heard several representatives who

---

[79] See generally Smith 2000.   [80] Paulsson 2010, p. 344.   [81] Vicuña 2002, p. 31.

The argument 21

have actually been active in this Treaty-making process ... say that, 'We had no idea that this would have real consequences in the real world.'[82]

This book will show that whereas Schreuer's impression is in stark contrast to commonly held beliefs about the international investment regime, it is nevertheless accurate. For whatever one may think of BITs as instruments of global economic governance,[83] the *process* with which the treaties were adopted was typically bounded rational.

Apart from providing a better understanding of the international investment regime, the findings of the book also have broader theoretical implications. For although experimental studies on bounded rationality have spurred a large and rapidly growing body of work throughout the social sciences, the findings have thus far been largely ignored in international relations and particularly in studies on international political economy (IPE).[84] When bounded rationality is factored into international relations scholarship on occasion, it has typically been rooted in organizational studies instead of the rigorous micro-foundation from behavioural psychology and economics.[85] This is unfortunate. For although questions of external validity should be carefully considered when using insights from experimental studies,[86] experiments on bounded rationality were not started in a vacuum but due to the existence of biased judgments in the real world.[87] Similar to the assertions of any other theoretical framework, studies may prove them wrong in various contexts, but at least they are derived through empirically grounded observations rather than hypothetical speculation. And their growing application to understand political and social processes outside experimental settings imply that studies in IPE are missing out on considerable insights about the role of bounded rationality in international economic relations.

This study is one of the few works that is beginning to fill this gap.[88] Through its analysis of the international investment regime it will

---

[82] ICSID Case No ARB/04/14, Award, 8 December 2008, par 85.
[83] For normative discussions of investment treaty arbitration, see e.g. Bonnitcha 2014; Schwebel 2008.
[84] For behavioural legal scholarship, see e.g. Sunstein 2000; and for recent calls to draw on behavioural economics in international law, see Broude 2013; Galbraith 2013; Van Aaken 2014. For seminal studies in political science, see Jones 2001; Jones and Baumgartner 2005.
[85] See Jupille, Mattli, and Snidal 2013; Keohane 1984, ch. 7. For the security realm, see Allison 1971; Jervis 1976; Reiter 1996; Vertzberger 1998. Even prospect theory – now a standard reference in international security studies – has been largely ignored by IPE scholars: Elms 2013, p. 104.
[86] Levy 1992, pp. 98–100; McDermott 2004, p. 27; Shafir 1992, pp. 320–1.
[87] Gilovich and Griffin 2002, p. 11.
[88] Bamert, Gilardi, and Wasserfallen 2014; Hafner-Burton, Leveck, Victor, and Fowler 2012; Mintz 2007; Odell 2000, ch. 5; Walter and Willett 2012; Weyland 2006; 2009; 2010.

22   Unanticipated consequences

hopefully remind scholars of IPE that deviations from fully rational behaviour should not always be treated as 'noise' that cancels out in the aggregate. Instead, our theoretical models need to address, rather than ignore, the fact that economic diplomats are 'predictably irrational' – just like the rest of us.[89]

Strategy

Ascertaining why developing countries entered into investment treaties is no easy task. One approach typically taken by legal scholars is to rely primarily on comparing treaty texts. Yet, this has obvious limitations, as it does little to identify policy processes or actor motivations. Also, the negotiating history of investment treaties is rarely documented: with the exception of the ICSID Convention itself and BITs signed with the United States, even tribunals wanting to resort to investment treaties' negotiating records often go away empty-handed. In developing countries there are rarely *any* files available, as in the case of Pakistan, and in developed countries, archives still remain classified for the period in which investment treaties spread like wildfire. Even if they had been more readily available, official negotiating histories would certainly not have been sufficient to understand why governments pursued BITs. But the absence of considerable written documentation after the 1970s does present a considerable challenge.

As an alternative, political scientists have tended to rely on statistical techniques. This follows the dominant trend in mainstream IPE studies, which increasingly rely on econometric models as their methodological foundation. But whereas such an empirical strategy is often helpful, a challenge is the often considerable gap between underlying concepts, such as 'competition', and the quantitative indicators actually available. Past literature on BITs is no exception. Here, the increasing complexity of the statistical models used stands in stark contrast to the dearth of quantitative data needed. Also, even if they had the necessary data, studies purely based on statistics tend to have difficulties identifying plausible underlying causal mechanisms. This book will therefore complement econometrics with a wide range of other evidence.

This is particularly important when studying information processing biases. Because to take insights on bounded rationality seriously, one needs to discuss not only substantive issues of opportunities and constraints – including constraints on information – but also procedural

---

[89] Term is from Ariely 2008.

Strategy 23

questions essentially relating to human cognition.[90] Rationalist studies of IPE tend to include information solely on actors' goals (e.g. attracting investment) and the objective characteristics of their situation, namely the costs and benefits of the policy (e.g. to sign a BIT) compared to alternative causes of action.[91] This is a useful starting point, but to understand if, and under what circumstances, cognitive constraints intervene between preferences and contexts, one would often have to apply qualitative methodologies. Throughout the book, illustrations will thus be included from developing countries around the world, where I have been able to trace relevant officials involved in investment treaty negotiations.

This, of course, is not a strategy without risks. Just as there are perils with quantitative research, qualitative methods involve their own pitfalls. Practically all interviewees spoke on the condition of anonymity, so rather than detailed information on interviewees the book will merely refer to them in footnotes as 'official from Ghana' or 'official from Germany'. Suffice it to say, this reduces the transparency of the information gathering. More importantly, individuals may have forgotten key events or slant them in ways that serve their own preferences. This is a particular challenge as investment treaty negotiations were typically done by just a single or a couple of individuals in developing countries. Whenever possible, attempts were therefore made to corroborate the narratives with alternative sources – such as archival records – as well as testimony of interviewees from developed countries. And the main conclusions in the book were indeed confirmed by a very large number of officials around the world independently of each other. It is very unlikely all were disingenuous, not least because narratives from developing country officials rarely did them any favours in terms of portraying their decisions as sophisticated and informed (which is the typical bias associated with interview work).

So for all the potential biases associated with using personal testimonies, this book will show that they are crucial if we want a better understanding of the political history of the international investment regime. More broadly, by combining elite interviews from all corners of the world with quantitative analyses and archival sources, the study will provide a much-needed reminder to international relations scholars that instead of relying exclusively on either qualitative or quantitative evidence, their work would often benefit from engaging rigorously with both.

---

[90] Simon 1997, pp.18–19. [91] See generally Simon 1985, p. 294; Simon 1982, ch. 8.

24   Unanticipated consequences

The book will proceed as follows. The next chapter will develop the theoretical framework briefly summarized above by drawing on insights from both rationalist literature on policy diffusion, negotiation studies, as well as behavioural economics and psychology. Chapter 3 will provide the necessary historical context and show that early investment treaty negotiations had some puzzling characteristics if developing country policy-makers were fully rational. As negotiation records are more than scarce, however, I will refrain from making strong inferences about the role of bounded rationality in the early years of the investment treaty movement. This will be left for the remaining chapters, which will focus on the 1980s until September 2014, when the book was sent to press. Chapter 4 will show that although Western 'BIT entrepreneurs' promoted the treaties as easy and simple instruments to attract foreign investment, developing countries didn't seem to adopt them in ways expected from standard rationalist models. Taking this perspective further, Chapters 5 and 6 will use a range of qualitative and quantitative evidence to show that the competition for capital in the international investment regime corresponds with the predictions of a bounded rationality approach. Chapter 7 will complement these aggregate findings with a detailed case study of South Africa, and the concluding chapter will outline the implications for the arbitration community and policy-makers themselves.

2 Bounded rationality and the spread of investment treaties

This chapter offers a simple theory of why, and how, developing countries signed up to investment treaties. It will be rooted in standard rationalist models of economic diplomacy and international political economy. But unlike traditional 'armchair' frameworks of rational choice, it will base its predictions on how real people make actual decisions. The underlying premise is simple. We know from behavioural psychology and economics that cognitive constraints often result in behaviour that is difficult to explain by frameworks based on the all-capable optimizing actor. Instead, they base their decisions on systematic, and therefore predictable, cognitive shortcuts, which often result in biased judgments. And if the rest of us are subject to these constraints there is no reason to expect that policy-makers should be any different. In turn, this could be important for our understanding of how international economic policies are made in practice.

Simplifying assumptions

Just as rational choice theory can lead to innumerable predictions, there is no *one* bounded rational theory of government decision-making – in the investment regime or elsewhere. And although incorporating cognition constraints is a novelty in rationalist studies on international political economy, it does open up a Pandora's box of complex hypotheses and ideas. So to avoid sacrificing too much parsimony compared to theoretical alternatives, the framework developed here will be kept deliberately simple. This involves a series of restrictive assumptions.

The first has already been mentioned. Although experimental insights on bounded rationality have considerable promise in constructivist work, this is not the approach taken here.[1] Instead, I follow standard applications in political science by using bounded rationality as a variant of

---

[1] See e.g. Herrera 2007.

26   Bounded rationality and the spread of investment treaties

rational choice theory studying preference-based and goal-oriented behaviour while catering for cognitive constraints. From this perspective, actors try to pursue their own preferences but are constrained not just by the complexity of their environment but also by the limitations to their own problem-solving capabilities. The implication in this context is that BITs are not seen merely as solutions looking for a problem – as expected by emulation frameworks – but rather as instruments adopted by developing country policy-makers seeking to pursue their own preferences. For instance, governments may not necessarily have been right to think BITs would promote significant amount of investment, but they should at least have *tried* to engage rationally with the treaties. But unlike in fully rational frameworks, policy-makers were constrained by information processing biases when assessing the costs and benefits of different policy options.

Second, I keep the framework simple by focusing squarely on how bounded rationality results in 'biases', or errors. Although bounded rational decision-making can be useful in some contexts by providing 'fast and frugal' ways of solving problems, this is not the perspective in the framework developed here. Choosing to see bounded rationality as constraining rather than enabling is just that, a choice, but it follows the bulk of experimental literature.[2]

Third, countless biases have been identified in experimental studies thus far, so I focus only on three to avoid excessive complexity. They were already introduced in the previous chapter: motivated reasoning, salience bias, and status-quo bias. Recall that motivated reasoning refers to the fact that decision-makers judge evidence systematically different depending on whether or not they *want* it to be true. As stated by Kunda, 'people do not realize that the [inferential] process is biased by their goals, that they are only accessing a subset of their relevant knowledge, that they would probably access different beliefs and [inferential] rules in the presence of different goals'.[3] Salience bias is the tendency to rely excessively on information that is particularly salient. Whereas the rational decision-maker will process information efficiently, the bounded rational decision-maker will often forget about information that is not immediately available and 'vivid'. Finally, status-quo bias refers to the preference for 'default' solutions, even when others are more

---

[2] For a pragmatic discussion on when, and under what conditions, bounded rationality leads to mistakes as well as when it improves decision-making quality, see Kelman 2011. For an argument about the efficiency-enhancing aspects of bounded rationality in international relations, see Keohane 1984, ch. 7.

[3] Kunda 1990, p. 485.

optimal. This provides the micro-foundation for Herbert Simon's original notion of 'satisficing': because bounded rational decision-makers seek solutions that are merely 'good enough', rather than optimal, it often leads to path-dependency over and beyond what would be predicted in rationalist models. These three biases are some of the most widely acknowledged and are therefore useful as core elements of the model.

A fourth simplifying assumption relates to the treatment of preferences of policy-makers. These can include both normative goals as well as material interests, but I keep them exogenous at any given point in time. For instance, the preference for neoliberal policies in the 1980s and 1990s is crucial to understanding the sudden rapid spread of investment treaties, but this book does not seek to answer where this change in priorities came from in the first place. Similarly, we can think of a number of government actors with strong private motives to pursue BITs.[4] These could be embassies using the treaties to show the 'results' of their diplomatic efforts, or investment promotion officials using them to facilitate foreign travels or augment their budgets and discretionary power.[5] By contrast, the costs of investment treaties should be particularly important for finance ministers, who would have to 'pay the bill' in case of disputes, law ministries, who could be blamed for poorly drafted provisions, or regulatory agencies whose discretion could be curtailed by the treaties. As we shall see, these 'public choice' considerations are important for understanding the investment treaty movement, but I do not seek to explain why officials may want to promote their careers or other private objectives in the first place. On this point I follow standard rationalist models by taking preferences as given.[6] But recall that whereas preferences themselves may be exogenous, I expect they will skew cost–benefit assessments of different policies in ways often unrealized by policy-makers themselves (motivated reasoning).

The bounds of bounded rationality: institutional conditions

The final restriction on the framework requires some more clarification. For just as aggregating individual rationality to the level of collectives requires significant assumptions, it is unclear when bounded rationality

---

[4] On incorporating 'public choice' considerations into international relations, see generally Abbott 2007; Colombatto and Macey 1996.

[5] Note that unlike investor–state contracts, where private investors are parties themselves, corruption is unlikely to have been a considerable motive for inter-governmental treaty negotiations.

[6] See generally, Stigler and Becker 1977.

28   Bounded rationality and the spread of investment treaties

for individual policy-makers translates into bounded rationality at the level of their government.[7] When is it reasonable to assume that inferential biases balance out in policy-making processes, and when may they be reinforced? This is fortunately less of a thorny issue for our purposes, as the vast majority of developing countries only had few officials involved in BIT-adoption until recently, which makes the role of individual biases easier to study than in more politicized contexts. That said, this book does make the following simplifying assumption about the interaction between institutions and individual biases: developed country governments, international organizations, and non-state actors (such as foreign investors and epistemic communities) are treated *as if* they are perfectly rational, whereas developing country governments are not. This significantly reduces the complexity of the framework. And although it may sound parochial, it is not unreasonable to expect that bureaucratic structures in many developing countries augment information processing biases.[8]

First of all, developing countries often lack expertise within their bureaucracies. This is important for their economic diplomacy, as negotiators and stakeholders may routinely make 'mistakes' by failing to grasp all the devils in the details when dealing with complex international economic rules and regulations. A bounded rationality framework is perfectly suited for such situations: an absence of expertise is ultimately a cognition constraint and is therefore difficult to account for in rationalist models without reference to individual limitations on information processing.[9] Experts are naturally also disposed to biased judgments and inferences,[10] but their prior knowledge makes them less prone to make mistakes within their areas of expertise.[11] For instance, generalists tend to have a much broader and more multidimensional perspective on risks than do experts.[12] For many purposes this can be healthy to avoid too narrow conceptions of risk within a given area,[13] but it is common sense that an incomplete understanding of key causal mechanisms at play is problematic for any policy-maker. And whereas experts may not

---

[7] Van Aaken 2014; Levy 1997, pp. 102–4; McDermott 2004, p. 3. See also Alvarez 2005, p. 969 (warning of the dangers of 'pop psychology' when projecting individual biases to the level of the state).

[8] Weyland 2006, p. 225.

[9] Conlisk 1996, p. 691. For recent public choice literature on bureaucratic expertise and delegation, see e.g. Huber and McCarty 2004. On 'policy expertise', see Callander 2008.

[10] See e.g. Rowe and Wright 2001; Tversky and Kahneman 1971; Wright, Bolger, and Rowe 2002.

[11] Nisbett and Ross 1980; Reyna and Lloyd 2006; Reyna, Lloyd, and Brainerd 2003; Ste-Marie 1999.

[12] Slovic 1987.   [13] Kahan, Slovic, Braman, and Gastil 2006.

Bounded rationality and the spread of investment treaties 29

necessarily agree on the magnitude of risks associated with certain policies, they are better able than generalists to understand their plausible implications.[14]

In the absence of expertise gained from higher education officials can nevertheless develop a level of experience through learning and feedback.[15] Yet, bureaucratic realities in many developing countries make this difficult. To quote from Weyland's study of policy reforms in Latin America:

> Since many bureaucracies in the region diverge starkly from Weberian principles, political appointees and even technical experts often face uncertain tenure. In many social agencies, turnover in the upper, decision-making echelons is exceedingly high … They therefore design reform projects under tremendous time pressure and cannot afford a comprehensive, proactive search for relevant information.[16]

Such conditions are not unique to Latin America but are a general problem in much of the developing world.[17] They obstruct learning and specialization as those officials who actually gain some level of experience are transferred to other departments before being able to take advantage of it. So although experience – just as expertise – is no guarantee against biased judgments and inferences, we would nevertheless expect that bureaucratic conditions preventing officials from gaining domain-specific experience would limit the rationality in decision-making.

In short, the empirical conclusions reached in this book may in practice be applied to some developed countries as well, but I leave this for others to address. For as a simplifying assumption, the introduction of bounded rationality to the study of economic diplomacy is particularly well suited to the developing world.

Bounded rationality and the spread of investment treaties

To illustrate the role of bounded rationality for the spread of BITs, it is useful to contrast with expectations from models based on comprehensive rationality. Especially when rational choice theories incorporate the costs of seeking information, there could be converging expectations with frameworks based on information processing biases.[18] What may appear

---

[14] See generally Einhorn 1974; Mieg 2001, pp. 143–6.
[15] Neale and Bazerman 1991, pp. 86–7, 90.   [16] Weyland 2006, pp. 46–7.
[17] In the context of trade negotiations, see e.g. Busch, Reinhardt, Shaffer 2009.
[18] Meseguer 2006.

30   Bounded rationality and the spread of investment treaties

to be biasing information processing constraints could in practice be a function of imperfect information, and vice versa.[19] So to adequately assess the predictive qualities of a bounded rationality framework, we need some rational baselines.

Here, I'll use two models from literature on international policy diffusion that are intuitively useful to explain how rational governments would have considered the costs and benefits of BITs. The first is 'rational competition', which is the standard analytical framework in political economy literature on BITs.[20] From this perspective, developing countries signed up to investment treaties in a strategic and rational competition for foreign capital and that's why we see such similarity across otherwise dissimilar contexts. The second baseline is 'rational learning'. From this perspective, developing countries are expected to have learned about the risks of BITs based on careful observation and interpretation of experiences with the treaties.[21] Suffice it to say that these are merely analytical ideal types and in empirical work both mechanisms are found in different combinations, as they will be in this book.[22] For instance, just as competitive pressures will have different effects depending on how governments perceive the costs of investment treaties, learning is not only relevant when it comes to the risks of BITs but also to the benefits. But to keep the baselines simple I'll use the competition model to focus primarily on the benefits of the treaties, and the learning model to focus on the costs. This allows greater clarity to identify predictions from a bounded rational framework, which are not observationally equivalent with those in standard rationalist literature.

Table 2.1 outlines the key expectations. Note that they relate solely to the *process* with which the treaties were adopted. Whether signing some BITs turned out to be the 'right' choice for some developing countries is not the question addressed in this book, as the analysis will only address how policy-makers reached their decisions in the first place.

---

[19] In his own discussion of transaction costs, for instance, Williamson embeds it in bounded rationality; yet formal treatments of his insights often chose to model them purely as information costs; Conlisk 1996.

[20] See e.g. Bubb and Rose-Ackerman 2007; Elkins, Guzman, and Simmons 2006; Guzman 1998; Neumayer, Nunnemkamp, and Roy 2014.

[21] Seminal in the context of policy diffusion is Meseguer 2009. See generally, Levy 1994.

[22] Literature on international policy diffusion also incorporates coercion and emulation as causal drivers. But the previous chapter already showed that although not irrelevant for the investment treaty movement, they are not overly helpful analytical ideal types to explain the popularity of the treaties. See generally, Dobbin, Simmons, and Garrett 2007; Gilardi 2014.

Bounded rationality and the spread of investment treaties 31

Table 2.1 *Investment treaty adoption: competition and learning*

	Rational	Bounded rational
Competition	Optimizing strategy based on careful assessment of competitive pressures	Satisficing strategy and systematic overestimation of economic benefits
Learning	Optimizing strategy based on careful assessment of risks	Satisficing strategy and low-probability risks ignored until salient

Competition

In a competition framework, the core prediction is that developing countries adopted BITs to compete for foreign investment. As we shall see, this account is largely accurate. Proponents of investment treaty arbitration often argue that it 'de-politicizes' investment disputes by replacing diplomatic protection with international adjudication and helps build an international rule of law. Both claims are disputed.[23] But for the vast majority of developing countries these were rarely important considerations when signing up the treaties. Instead, the main expected benefit of BITs was their perceived ability to promote foreign capital.

In itself, however, this tells us little about *how* governments adopted the treaties. Here, models based on comprehensive rationality expect policy-makers to have carefully 'optimized' their investment treaty policies to attract as much foreign investment as possible. More specifically, because rationalist models assume that all governments were aware of the sovereignty costs of BITs when they signed up to them, or at least learned about the costs relatively quickly (see below), developing countries should only have signed the treaties if the expected economic benefits were significant. As noted by Elkins, Guzman, and Simmons: 'The decision to sign a BIT always involves an assessment by the host of whether the expected benefit of attracting an additional increment of foreign capital outweighs these costs.'[24] This has several observable implications.

First of all, rational policy-makers would try to assess whether the treaties were in fact useful to attract investment based on a rigorous

---

[23] For discussions on de-politicization, see Maurer 2013; Paparinskis 2010; Jandhyala, Gertz, and Poulsen 2015. On investment arbitration and the rule of law, see Bonnitcha 2014, ch. 3, and Brower and Schill 2009.

[24] Elkins, Guzman, and Simmons 2006, p. 825. Italics added.

32   Bounded rationality and the spread of investment treaties

and balanced search of available information.[25] This would have involved a comparison of BITs with alternative ways of attracting foreign investment, such as market-based mechanisms (e.g. insurance and joint ventures) over individual arrangements (e.g. concession contracts and subsidies) to other forms of inter-state arrangements (e.g. visa agreements and double taxation agreements). This was not easy during the 1980s and 1990s as there were only a few studies available about the economic implications of the treaties.[26] As a result, policy-makers had a strong incentive to conduct simple investor surveys, for instance, or ask international organizations or other external actors to come up with concrete evidence that the economic benefits of the treaties outweighed their costs. At a minimum, we should expect that rational policy-makers tried to learn from other countries' experiences. One study found a positive association between developing countries' decisions to enter into the treaties and whether countries experienced FDI inflows after having signed up to BITs.[27] If true, this is exactly what we would expect if governments sought whatever limited information was available about whether the treaties did in fact 'work'.

Another expectation in traditional competition frameworks is that developing countries responded strategically to BIT-adoption of their 'competitors'. The basic logic is simple. Assume three countries: e, a stereotypical capital-exporting developed country seeking a high level of protection for its investors abroad; i, a capital-importing developing country; and c, another capital-importing developing country competing with i for investment. Even if i was initially hesitant to sign on to investment treaties, fears of investment diversion would make it inclined to sign them once c signed a BIT with e. If i regarded investment treaties as a specific commitment device it would be particularly concerned with signing a BIT with e.[28] If the treaties were seen as a general signal to all foreign investors, i would mainly be interested in the number of BITs signed by the competitor, c, rather than treaties signed with specific sources of investment.[29] Shared by both accounts, however, is the expectation that developing country governments carefully considered the interests and strategies of the countries with which they competed for capital.

---

[25] Bubb and Rose-Ackerman 2007; Elkins, Guzman, and Simmons 2006, p. 825; Neumayer, Nunnenkamp, and Roy 2014, p. 9.
[26] See comments in MIGA PAS 1991, p. 170. The first publicly available study on the economic impact of BITs came in 1998; see UNCTAD 1998b.
[27] Elkins, Guzman, and Simmons 2006.
[28] Lupu and Poast 2013; Neumayer and Plümper 2010.
[29] Elkins, Guzman, and Simmons 2006.

Finally, we come to the content – or design – of investment treaties. Here rationalist approaches would expect that 'states seek to identify the combination of relevant design elements that maximize the value of the agreement.'[30] Accordingly, if the 'value of the agreement' is to promote foreign investment we would expect that competitive dynamics should have gradually driven up the level of protection developing countries were willing to provide.[31] Similar to the example above, i may initially have been hesitant to offer too wide-ranging protections in its BITs, but once c agreed to 'investor-friendly' provisions i would follow suit in the fear of being considered a relatively more risky jurisdiction by market actors. And because c was facing the same strategic considerations, the end result would be a frequent 'upgrading' of treaties in the race to attract capital as long as transactions costs were not excessive. This would all be to the benefit of foreign investors.

Importantly, these predictions would be largely similar even if incorporating public choice considerations. For although some government officials may promote BITs for selfish reasons even if it doesn't help attract foreign investment, rational stakeholders losing out from the treaties would be expected to lobby against 'reckless' adoption and design strategies.[32] I'll return to this in the section on policy learning below.

For now, let's compare the aforementioned predictions with a competition model based on bounded rationality. Here, we would not expect that investment-hungry governments went through a careful cost–benefit analysis of different investment promotion policies. Instead, they would have focused excessively, if not exclusively, on particular salient policy solutions. In particular, search routines based on salience rather than efficiency would have made predefined policies pursued elsewhere and promoted by actors with perceived credibility, such as international organizations, particularly tempting.[33] BITs were perfect candidates. The treaties had been around for decades and were promoted by international organizations, developed countries, and other actors. They provided a short, simple, and standardized blueprint for governments worried that political risks were keeping foreign investors away. And although the treaties were perhaps not optimal, they were tempting for bounded rational policy-makers by providing an 'easy fix' to attract foreign capital. Rather than the result of a rigorous assessment of their

---

[30] Guzman 2008, p. 132. On rational design of international institutions, see Koremenos, Lipson, and Snidal 2001.
[31] Neumayer, Nunnemkamp, and Roy 2014.   [32] See generally, Lake 2009, p. 226.
[33] Weyland 2006, pp. 52–4.

34   Bounded rationality and the spread of investment treaties

functional utility, investment treaties may thereby have become popular simply because they were effectively promoted as a salient solution to an immediate problem. Note also that the treaties were much easier to adopt than a multilateral investment treaty. For why engage in costly, and risky, institutional innovation if BITs were 'good enough'?

When assessing whether investment treaties actually 'worked', bounded rational policy-makers would also have relied excessively, if not exclusively, on particularly salient information. More specifically, they would have been biased by a 'feature-positive effect', which refers to the fact that inferences are often disproportionally influenced by events and acts rather than 'non-events' and omissions.[34] The latter naturally have crucial diagnostic value to assess co-variation, yet they are less salient and therefore often ignored. This could have skewed conclusions towards confirming BITs were important for investment flows. An anecdote about a political risk insurer or investor saying BITs were important for their decision to invest may have been the *only* information used to make a general inference about the relationship between investment flows and BITs, whereas the thousands of investors who did not care about the treaties would have been forgotten.

In some cases, of course, people explicitly look for disconfirming rather than confirming evidence. What explains the difference? The answer often comes from motivated reasoning, where preferences impact information processing in ways actors may not realize. Accordingly, policy-makers desperately seeking foreign capital would unintentionally seek confirming information that policies designed to attract foreign investment did in fact work as intended.[35] The same would be the case for bureaucrats or politicians with more selfish motives to promote the treaties. In both cases, even dubious claims by external actors about the treaties' ability to attract investment would be accepted with little scrutiny. By contrast, we would expect that when developing countries tried to distance themselves from Western policy prescriptions during the post-colonial era, policy-makers should have been inherently suspicious of arguments that the treaties were economically useful. Developed country governments will have had a hard time convincing developing countries to sign on to BITs and may in extreme cases have had to consider resorting to coercion.

But after policy-makers in developing countries began regarding investment treaties as useful tools to promote investment, bounded rationality could have prevented sophisticated adoption strategies. If

[34] Newman, Wolf, and Hearst 1980.
[35] On prior political attitudes and information processing, see e.g. Taber and Lodge 2006.

the economic benefits of the treaties were vastly overestimated, there would be little reason to pay much attention to competitors or to be selective in choosing treaty partners. Even 'strange' South-South BITs could have been considered reasonable in the expectation that they would have promoted greater investment flows between developing countries themselves, also if the best available information at the time suggested otherwise.

Similarly, governments wouldn't continually search for ever more optimal treaty designs, as expected in rationalist frameworks. Instead, they would be inclined to simply stick with whatever templates were the default as long as they seemed 'good enough'.[36] In contract negotiations, for instance, random manipulation of initial template agreements has been found to have a considerable impact on decision-makers' subsequent choices.[37] Also, a recent observational study of treaty design found that when the default dispute resolution clause provided for ICJ jurisdiction, states were far more likely to agree to ICJ jurisdiction than if the default was that states had to opt in to accept it.[38] Without qualitative evidence it is difficult to assess whether this is mainly due to an irrational preference for default terms or for other reasons, but the strong correlations do fit remarkably well with previous experimental studies:

This result closely resembles the opt-in versus opt-out differences in individual behaviour on organ donation, 401(k) plan enrolment, and so forth. Just as the individuals in these studies exhibit status-quo biases, so states seem to be exhibiting status-quo biases in the course of treaty ratification. They tend to embrace the default terms of the negotiated treaty.[39]

A parallel occurrence could have transpired when developing countries considered the design of BITs: a preference to rely on the status quo may have made policy-makers anchor excessively to previous treaty provisions, even if information was available to suggest that alternatives were more effective in attracting investment. Unlike governments who seek to optimize their investment treaty designs, bounded rational policy-makers would have an excessive preference for simply copying and pasting provisions from standardized templates, and particularly those that were easy and simple to adopt.

Learning

Depending on whether policy-makers were fully or bounded rational, we would also expect markedly different behaviour when it comes to how

---

[36] Sunstein 2013.   [37] Korobkin 1998.   [38] Galbraith 2013.   [39] Ibid., p. 352.

36   Bounded rationality and the spread of investment treaties

governments learned about the risks of the treaties. Recall that the main risks of BITs are associated with investment treaty arbitration. Although investment treaties solely backed up by inter-state dispute resolution can have important implications for contracting parties, the potential costs are bound to be higher if investors can file claims themselves, as this radically increases the potential number of claimants.[40] Once claims are filed, costs for the host state could be monetary damages, legal costs, reputation costs, or even political costs such as negative political fallouts from controversial disputes. Also, the mere possibility of claims could potentially result in reductions of wanted 'policy space' for a government fearing international disputes.

Policy-makers considering whether to adopt BITs would need to assess the probability and scale of these costs associated with investment treaty arbitration.[41] And if policy-makers were rational, they would have been in no doubt by the early 1990s that signing up to BITs could entail significant liabilities, as there was ample information that the treaties included both potent and enforceable protections. I'll clarify this in a later chapter. For now, it suffices to say that if governments assessed information about the treaties in ways we would expect from rationalist models, they must have entered into BITs fully appreciating that it could involve some risks, such as constraints on their sovereignty. According to Montt, "governments knew and accepted [the potential costs] when they decided to join the BIT-network."[42]

That said, even fully rational governments could have underestimated the scope of several vague treaty provisions enshrined in BITs. As late as 1984, the Dutch branch of the Committee on Legal Aspects of a New International Economic Order noted about BITs that "[t]heir significance, even their existence and certainly their abundance, seems to be largely unknown to international lawyers."[43] The reason, of course, was

---

[40] An additional consideration is that investors may be less concerned with 'adventurous' legal reasoning that inflate the scope of the treaties beyond the initial intention of the parties. With inter-state dispute settlement, such as in the WTO, a government acting as a claimant will have to consider whether its legal arguments could backfire if the same arguments are used in future claims against itself. Since investment treaties do not allow governments to file treaty-based claims against investors, this is arguably not a concern for investors seeking to persuade arbitral tribunals.

[41] Note that throughout I treat the risks of investment treaties in a 'Knightean' sense. This implies that it is possible in principle to assign a measurable probability – or range of probabilities – to the potential adverse outcomes of the treaties. This seems appropriate. For although the risk of an investment dispute involves a range of elements hard for sovereigns to control (such as sub-national regulatory entities), it is difficult to argue that it is a case of extreme uncertainty where both potential outcomes and probabilities are entirely unknown.

[42] Montt 2009, p. 128.   [43] Peters, Schrijver, and de Waart 1984, p. 113.

Bounded rationality and the spread of investment treaties 37

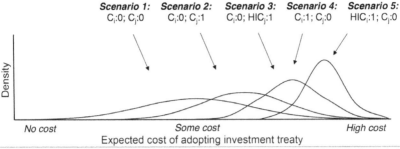

Figure 2.1 Rational learning about risks
Note: C:0 also implies HIC:0.

that no investor claims had actually been filed pursuant to investment treaties at this point. That began only a few years later and up through the 1990s and early 2000s international lawyers were surprised time and again about some of the more adventurous interpretations by arbitrators. This makes imperfect information crucially important for any account of the international investment regime.

Even governments in countries such as Canada and the United States were taken by surprise by the expansive interpretations of the vague provisions included in NAFTA's investment protection chapter. Policymakers in both countries reacted by revising their model BITs and issuing interpretive notes seeking to limit the discretion of tribunals.[44] This is uncontroversial, generally accepted, and entirely possible to explain using a rational learning framework: after arbitrators 'filled in the blanks' of imprecise treaty obligations, subsequent calibrations of treaty-practice ensued. For as in so many other areas of "incomplete contracting", not even Western experts could have accurately predicted how investment treaties were to be interpreted by arbitrators.[45]

Figure 2.1 illustrates the basic expectations if developing countries went through a similar learning process about the costs of BITs. To keep

---

[44] Gantz 2004, 740–2; Vandevelde 2009; Note of Interpretation of the NAFTA Free Trade Commission, 31 July 2001. See also US Intergovernmental Policy Advisory Committee 2004, pp. 14–15 ('The Methanex and Loewen cases in particular have reinforced concerns that the provision [on dispute settlement] will be abused by investors who simply hope to circumvent established legislative and judicial procedures.').
[45] Van Aaken 2009. On rational choice theory and unanticipated consequences of international legal obligations, see generally Martin and Simmons 1998.

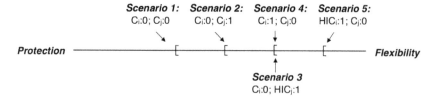

Figure 2.2 Rational learning and the zone of agreement
Note: C:0 also implies HIC:0.

it simple, it includes only five scenarios along two dimensions: whether claims were against the country itself, i, or other countries, j, and whether claims had a potential for very significant costs, HIC, or not, C. The final option is if no claims have been filed, which in this case is scenario one. Here, we see that the understanding that BITs can be costly is understood all along, but in the absence of claims the expected risks are not only very uncertain (note the high variance of the graph) but also quite moderate (note the small mean of the graph). So once other countries became subject to claims from the late 1980s, policy-makers gradually updated their risk assessments as arbitrators interpreted the treaties as providing greater investor protections than initially expected (scenario two). Governments now saw the treaties as entailing higher costs and were also more certain in their assessments than they were previously. Particularly, claims with a high impact would be important by providing important clues on the potential scope of the treaties (scenario three).[46] Finally, because the probability of a claim depends on country-specific factors, learning effects could have been somewhat stronger – both in terms of expected costs as well as their variance – for comparable claims against i (scenarios four and five).[47]

A similar process would have transpired when it comes to learning about the risks of different treaty designs. To illustrate, Figure 2.2 outlines a uni-dimensional continuum for a developing country trying to strike a balance between investor protection and regulatory autonomy in the scope of the fair and equitable treatment clause. The government's

---

[46] On Bayesian policy learning from high-impact cases, see generally, Meseguer 2006.
[47] I make the simplifying assumption that a high-impact claim against j entails as much information as a low-impact claim against i.

'resistance points' – or reservation values[48] – are marked as '[' and refers to the worst possible deal it could accept without walking away from the negotiation. Although based on a zone of agreement, the figure is otherwise similar to Figure 2.1, and the expectations are again straightforward. Starting from the left-hand side, an absence of claims could have made i underestimate the importance of the fair and equitable treatment provision and thereby have been willing to accept more generous protections than if information was available from arbitral practice (scenario one). Returning to the context of NAFTA, for instance, it was clear that even North American officials were surprised when some arbitrators decided the provision provided protections over and beyond the international minimum standard enshrined in customary international law.[49]

As mentioned, this type of learning process about 'incomplete contracts' is not irrational in itself, and in Figure 2.2 we see that once there is information from the claims the resistance point of i moves to the right, indicating a preference for a less broadly drafted provision (scenarios two and three). But again, because the probability of claims is dependent on country-specific factors, claims against i itself have a greater impact on its risk assessment, which in turn result in a larger movement of its resistance point than comparable claims against other countries (scenarios four and five).

Now let's see how policy-makers would have learned about the risks of the treaties if they were not constrained just by imperfect information but also by imperfect processing of information. As a starting point, it is worth recalling that even though investment treaty claims can have considerable implications, they have rarely occurred for individual countries – at least until recently. And for such low-probability risks, bounded rationality often leads to bimodal responses.[50] Some greatly exaggerate low-probability risks whereas others assume they can ignore them completely, and salience bias means the choice between the two depends on the extent to which people can bring salient examples to mind. If they can, it can lead to inflated concerns. Deaths from accidents are often expected to be much more frequent than deaths from diseases.[51] When travellers are asked to price two flight insurance packages, one covering

---

[48] Raiffa 1982.
[49] Yannaca-Small 2008, ftn. 9 (North American officials and politicians had not 'entirely grasped the real nature of the standard. Some had rarely given a second thought to its potential breadth ... As was the case with the majority of BIT provisions, second thoughts only began to arise when arbitral tribunals began to shed light on these provisions'.)
[50] McClellan, Schultze, and Coursey 1993.
[51] Licthenstein, Slovic, Fischhoff, Layman, and Combs 1978.

40   Bounded rationality and the spread of investment treaties

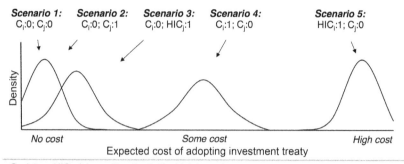

Figure 2.3 Bounded rational learning about risks
Note: C:0 also implies HIC:0.

'terrorism' and one covering all causes, the latter tends to be cheaper (despite also covering terrorism).[52] And so on. If people *cannot* bring a salient example to mind, however, overreaction tends to be replaced by complacency. Out of sight, out of mind.

This is important for negotiations. When considering contract designs, for instance, negotiators often fail to appreciate low-probability risks if they are not salient. Korobkin is worth quoting at length:

> Many of the terms commonly specified in standard form contracts govern what will happen if a low-probability risk comes to pass ... If these possible but unlikely outcomes are not readily 'available' to buyers, they are likely to respond to the risk of these harms by treating them as if they do not exist at all ... [Buyers] might allocate their attention elsewhere, rendering the form terms that concern low-probability risks non-salient ... A form term calling for arbitration of disputes in an inconvenient state, for example, is likely to be non-salient to the vast majority of buyers unless the type of contract in question commonly results in disputes.[53]

There could be important parallels in the international investment regime. To illustrate, Figure 2.3 includes the aforementioned five basic scenarios but with learning based on bounded instead of unbounded rationality. The first crucial point lies in scenario one. For whereas the rationalist learning framework could explain if policy-makers underestimated some of the disciplining effect of BITs due to an absence of claims, salience-induced errors would imply that many officials *ignored* the risks entirely. So although in rationalist frameworks officials who are constrained or who lose out from BITs should be vigilant about considering the potential liabilities of consenting to investment treaty arbitration, salience bias

[52] Johnson, Hershey, Meszaros, and Kunreuther 1993.   [53] Korobkin 2003, pp. 1233–4.

Bounded rationality and the spread of investment treaties 41

could have made stakeholders fail to realize they should take an interest in the treaties. In turn, this would have given actors with a private interest in promoting BITs a free hand to sign them without much deliberation, if any. Because if the economic benefits of the treaties were overestimated and the risks ignored, there would be little reason not to adopt them right, left, and centre. Diplomats, for instance, may have been given a carte blanche to promote the treaties, which could explain why diplomatic links have been such strong predictors of investment treaty adoption in quantitative studies.[54] More broadly, the failure to appreciate the risks of the treaties could also provide yet another reason for the hundreds of otherwise 'strange' BITs among countries with no economics links.[55]

Now look at scenarios two, three, and four. Whereas rational governments would gradually update their risk assessments when claims were filed against other countries, bounded rational policy-makers would fail to adequately factor in experiences abroad and therefore continue to entirely ignore the risks of BITs in the absence of dramatic and vivid claims (scenario two). This again follows from the salience bias, since bounded rational decision-makers tend to focus primarily on their own experiences when making inferences as these are more salient.[56] Relying on one's own experiences can be prudent in some situations but not when it comes to low-probability risks, as they are by definition unlikely to be part of decision-makers' immediate past. This means bounded rational decision-makers often fail to consider such risks until 'lightening strikes'. Along the same lines, policy-makers in developing countries could also have been 'prisoners of their own experience' when learning about the risks of BITs.[57] So although high-impact claims against other countries could result in slight adjustments in risk assessments if they were sufficiently salient (scenario three), learning effects about the 'strength' of the agreements would only really materialize after claims against i (scenario four). In short, just as people tend to insure themselves against low-probability events *after* they have already taken place, bounded rational governments could have had completely haphazard investment treaty policies until they found themselves on the receiving end of a claim.[58]

---

[54] Allee and Peinhardt 2010, ftn. 37; Elkins, Guzman, and Simmons 2006.

[55] Note that even these treaties can entail costs as their MFN provision can allow arbitrators to 'export' their provisions into other agreements.

[56] See Jervis 1976, p. 240; Kaufmann 1994. See generally, Keller, Siegrist, and Gutscher 2006, p. 632; Weinstein 1989.

[57] The term is from Kates's classic study of risk-adjustments to low-probability hazards; Kates 1962, p. 142.

[58] Another way to think of the same mechanism comes from experimental and field evidence indicating that people display unwarranted optimism when it comes to judging possible future risks; Wakslak and Trope 2009, pp. 52–3, 57; see also, Shelley 1994. As delayed losses are much more heavily discounted than delayed gains, long time horizons do not

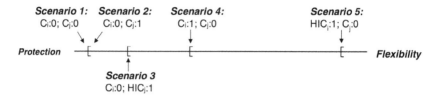

Figure 2.4 Bounded rational learning and the zone of agreement
Note: C:0 also implies HIC:0.

Yet, even at this point bounded rational policy-makers would still fail to factor in all relevant experiences from abroad and therefore have lower risk perceptions than if they based their policies on a balanced search for relevant information (compare scenario four in Figures 2.1. and 2.3). Combined with their strong preference for the status quo, this will make reactions to claims against themselves highly incremental, as the treaties will still be considered 'good enough'. After realizing that BITs actually have some 'bite', i may slow down its adoption of the treaties and perhaps seek minor changes in content (see below); otherwise policy-makers will be hesitant to seek more extensive reforms departing from the status quo. Only if claims against i have a high perceived impact (scenario five), or at least the potential for a high impact, would we expect bounded rational policy-makers to react very strongly as the risks of the treaties now appear particularly salient. In such cases, treaties previously signed as a matter of routine could be seen as outright dysfunctional and thus prompt policy-makers to consider undertaking significant and re-anchoring reforms, for instance by considering leaving the regime altogether.

Similar expectations arise when looking at treaty design. This is illustrated in Figure 2.4, which again includes the bargain over the fair and equitable treatment provision. Unlike the comparable figure in the fully rational model, contracting choices are here influenced not only by imperfect information, but also by imperfect processing of information. For whereas bounded rational decision-makers are still expected to

necessarily decrease risk-tolerance. This type of optimism bias can in turn facilitate agreement where we would otherwise expect none, as negotiators become less concerned with the long-term costs of maintaining cooperation; Krebs and Rapport 2012. For a traditional view of time horizons and investment treaties making the opposite prediction (i.e. long time horizons make negotiators much more careful), see Blake 2013.

Bounded rationality and the spread of investment treaties 43

consider whether provisions help achieve strategic goals, their understanding of the implications of different treaty designs is less than assumed in traditional rationalist approaches. One result is that the initial resistance point of the bounded rational government is much more generous towards foreign investors than had it been perfectly rational (scenario one). This follows from the observations already made. If both negotiators and stakeholders entirely failed to realize the potency of the agreements, they were likely to accept provisions that officials with better information processing skills would steer clear of. This could imply that certain provisions may have diffused throughout the global BIT regime, not because developing countries found them representative of their national interests after carefully considering alternatives, but rather because they relied excessively on default rules and failed to appreciate the potential risks of different treaty designs.[59]

Also, if i is bounded rational then the additional information from claims against other countries, j, does not lead to a gradual reconsideration of treaty drafting (scenario two). Although high-impact claims against other countries may have a slight impact on what i is willing to offer (scenario three), it ultimately has to take a claim against i itself before considering treaty revisions, as only then do the risks become immediately available and vivid for policy-makers (scenario four). Yet because of status-quo bias, the government still anchors to previous choices and the resistance point therefore remains considerably more 'investor-friendly' than had i been fully rational (compare with scenario four in Figure 2.3). In this particular case, governments may be more attentive about clarifying the scope of the fair and equitable treatment provision by copy-pasting from slightly more restrictive models already available in the status quo, but the basic design will remain intact as it still appears 'good enough'.[60] For only in cases where a claim against i is perceived as particularly costly would bounded rational policy-makers consider significant, and re-anchoring, changes to the default rules included in Western template agreements (scenario five). We should, in other words, expect considerable path dependence in treaty design: even if governments signed up to provisions without appreciating the

---

[59] See generally Weyland 2006; 2008. A similar outcome could follow from prospect theory: if governments are concerned about losing FDI from competitors, loss aversion could lead them to take considerable risks by accepting obligations, which would not otherwise suit their national interest. Yet, the causal mechanism would differ, as this would require actors to actually realize the risks involved. See generally, Kahneman and Tversky 1979.

[60] On 'institutional selection' under conditions of bounded rationality, see Jupille, Mattli, and Snidal 2013, pp. 43–5.

44   Bounded rationality and the spread of investment treaties

implications, and other treaty designs were more optimal, bounded rational governments will keep anchoring to Western default rules except if they appear to be outright dysfunctional.

These predictions are radically different from those based on fully rational learning. But recall the boundary conditions of the argument: the limitations on policy-makers' rationality should depend at least in part on their levels of expertise and experience. This means that whereas developed countries with highly skilled and experienced officials may have behaved closer to the rational ideal, the bounded rational learning process should be particularly relevant for developing country governments. For only few developing countries had officials with any legal expertise in international investment law during the 1980s and 1990s,[61] which could have exacerbated the failure to appreciate the risks of the agreements. As noted by Neale and Bazerman in the context of negotiations, it is 'not the expert's ability to process more information that gives him or her the edge. Rather it is the ability to know which information is important and to which cues to attend in selecting a successful course of action.'[62] These 'cues' are far from intuitive when it comes to traditional BITs. For while most officials would be able to appreciate the relevance of certain intuitive provisions, such as national treatment or transfer of capital, vague provisions such as 'indirect expropriation' or 'fair and equitable treatment' could pass unnoticed by generalists. In the experience of a former American BIT negotiator, the result could be that 'the receiving party will have had perhaps only the most general notion of what it was accepting.'[63]

Another contributing factor to salience-induced biases is the high turnover in many developing country bureaucracies. Because when risk perceptions are strongly associated with personal experiences of risk, bureaucrats shifting in and out of offices may often fail to incorporate previous experiences with low-probability risks within their new task domain. Appreciating the potential sovereignty costs of BITs requires an understanding of technical questions, such as how certain regulatory conducts can breach different provisions or, more fundamentally, what investor–state arbitration is in the first place. In the absence of experience with investment treaty claims such knowledge may not be immediately available, which should make 'novice' negotiators and stakeholders even more likely to ignore the risks of the treaties and different treaty designs until hit by a claim themselves.

---

[61] UNCTAD 2008.   [62] Neale and Bazerman 1991, p. 96.
[63] Vandervelde 1988b, p. 301.

Conclusion

Finally, an absence of expertise and experience should also be important for the status quo bias. As noted by Sunstein, 'Many people appear to think that the default was chosen by someone sensible and for a good reason. Especially if they lack experience or expertise, they might simply defer to what has been chosen for them.'[64] The implication is that generalist bureaucrats should be much less likely to opt out of default treaty designs. When negotiating BITs developing country officials may thereby have been particularly prone to relying on European models simply because they failed to appreciate the implications. Consider the experiences of a Korean official:

> Until recently most Korean experts of international litigation ... were found only in the private sector and not in the government. ... negotiators were often unable to adequately address the complex procedural issues surrounding investor–State dispute resolution. As a result, they often resorted to using the same simple provisions as in previous investment agreements.[65]

Conclusion

This chapter has offered a new – and simple – theory to explain why and how developing countries signed investment treaties. By introducing a few key insights from behavioural psychology and economics we have derived a number of predictions that are distinct from those in traditional rationalist models. The core argument is that although governments may have tried to pursue their own preferences when using investment treaties to compete for capital, systematic information processing biases among policy-makers could have resulted in predictably irrational behaviour both in terms of adoption patterns and treaty designs. We would expect that officials considerably overestimated the economic benefits of investment treaties by relying on wishful thinking rather than carefully seeking and processing information about the functional utility of the agreements. Second, we would expect that the risks of the treaties were ignored entirely until governments were hit by their first claim. As a result, embassies and investment promotion officials could have had a free hand to promote the treaties wherever possible with no objections from stakeholders potentially constrained by the agreements. Finally, we would expect that in the absence of expertise and experience, developing country policy-makers were often unable to adequately assess the implications of different treaty designs and

---

[64] Sunstein 2013, p. 20.   [65] Kim 2012, p. 68.

therefore decided to simply rely on European templates, as they were easy to adopt and seemed 'good enough'.

The rest of the book will be spent testing these claims. As a starting point, however, we first need some historical context. For although many may find the modern rules of international investment protection entirely intuitive and obvious, they were born out of a long power struggle between developed and developing countries going back to the colonial era. It was in response to this conflict that Western governments developed brief and simple bilateral templates for investment protection during the 1950s and 1960s, which have served as focal points of the international investment regime ever since. So in order to analyze how developing countries negotiated around these 'default rules' in later decades, we need to first understand where the templates came from and why they were rejected by most capital importing states during the post-colonial era.

3 A difficult beginning

This chapter will begin by describing why, and how, Western template investment agreements emerged. On that basis two important features from the early investment treaty negotiations will be highlighted. First, whereas European investment treaty models were signed off by developing countries in a rush during the 1990s, this was not the case during the post-colonial era. On the contrary. Unlike in later years, European governments had significant difficulties getting developing countries to the negotiating table, as only few believed the treaties would help attract investment. Governments that were not outright opposed to negotiations often insisted on significant changes being made to European templates, and even small and weak developing countries managed to resist Western pressure.

Second, even though developing countries proved to be difficult, archival records from negotiations with the United Kingdom indicate that those countries that did agree to negotiate rarely engaged in sophisticated cost–benefit analyses of the treaties. Governments already subscribing to Western investment protection standards were easily persuaded that the treaties would attract investment, although a balanced search for information would probably have led them to think otherwise. Also, not only did several governments appear to ignore the crucial innovation in 'modern' investment treaties - the broad and prospective consent to investor–state arbitration - their negotiation teams also suffered from an absence of expertise.

This broadly corresponds with the predictions of the bounded rationality framework outlined in the previous chapter, at least according to the scarce records available. This is an important caveat. For whereas macro-level organizational theories of bounded rationality can be tested by focusing mainly on outcomes,[1] an emphasis on individual cognition constraints requires inputs from decision-makers themselves or, at a

---

[1] See e.g. Jupille, Mattli, and Snidal 2013.

48 A difficult beginning

minimum, detailed historical records. We have neither from the early days of the investment treaty movement, and this chapter will therefore refrain from making strong causal inferences about the role of information processing strategies. Instead, the main aim is a descriptive account of the investment treaty movement's difficult beginning.

Investment protection after empire

The protections enshrined in the modern international investment regime have long historical roots. Based on principles developed between major European trading powers in the seventeenth century, international investment protection became part of the broader 'civilizing mission' of international law during the colonial encounter. Western powers ensured that assets of trading companies and private investors were protected through a combination of treaties, concessions, political pressure, and military intervention.[2] In the absence of colonization, where investment disputes were simply resolved within imperial legal systems, justification was ensured by making foreign investment protection part of the legal doctrine on the diplomatic protection of aliens. Eventually, companies abroad had to be treated and protected according to international minimum standards – such as the right to compensation for expropriation – a breach of which could justify home state intervention. If developing country governments refused to submit investment disputes to international arbitration, they would have to face Western gunboats along their shores.

Under constant threat of Western intervention triggered by commercial disputes, Latin American countries began to embrace a different set of ideas about a just international economic order. Argentinean legal scholar Carlos Calvo suggested that the notion of state sovereignty made it illegal for foreign powers to intervene in the affairs of other sovereign states by diplomatic or more forceful means. And instead of being favoured with independent standards, aliens solely had the right to be treated as well – or as poorly – as citizens or companies of the host state. National treatment should replace international minimum standards, and disputes should be settled in domestic courts rather than through international arbitration. These ideas were incorporated into laws, contracts, and even certain constitutions in Latin America, yet they were fiercely opposed by the United States and European countries. By 1914, as the 'long nineteenth century' came to an end, Western powers

[2] Miles 2013.

Investment protection after empire

continued to insist that the international law governing foreign investors rested on the key principles of international minimum standards and diplomatic protection.

The fall of the Imperial Order made it difficult for Western powers to sustain the international regime for the protection of foreign investment. European governments rarely had the leverage needed to defend their interests abroad, and although the United States continued to intervene on behalf of its investors, aggressive diplomatic protection often came at the expense of broader foreign policy concerns.[3] More benign means of protection had to be found. But when Western states proposed to enshrine international minimum standards into multilateral agreements during the interwar years, developing countries – and particularly Latin American states – refused.[4]

After the Second World War, an attempt was made yet again. At the Bretton Woods conference in 1944, Washington reached an agreement with its allies to set up three multilateral organizations: the International Monetary Fund (IMF), the International Bank for Reconstruction and Development (World Bank), and the International Trade Organization (ITO). The latter was intended to govern international trade flows, but because American business wanted it to include protections for foreign investment as well, Washington proposed enshrining provisions similar to those in its bilateral treaties for Foreign, Commerce, and Navigation (FCN).[5] This would entail national treatment, most favoured nation (MFN) treatment, and – importantly – the Hull standard of compensation for expropriation. The latter was named after US Secretary of State, Cordell Hull, who after Mexico nationalized American investments in 1938 wrote to his Mexican counterpart that the international minimum standards on expropriation required 'prompt, adequate and effective compensation'.

Yet, the proposal met resistance from capital-importing states and the resulting compromise failed to please anyone. American business was dissatisfied with an agreement failing in ambition, whereas organized labour saw it as too far-reaching. This undermined support for the treaty in Congress and it was never ratified. So whereas the ITO could have played important roles for international investment governance (it was, for instance, charged with promoting bilateral and multilateral investment agreements)[6] this never happened. Instead, the General Agreement

---

[3] Maurer 2013.   [4] Newcompe and Paradell 2009, ch. 1.
[5] Wilcox 1949, pp. 145–64; Bidwell and Diebold 1949, 208-212.
[6] Art. 11(2) of the Havana Charter for an International Trade Organization.

50   A difficult beginning

on Tariffs and Trade (GATT) became responsible for regulating international trade relations, yet GATT did not include provisions on foreign investment protection.

The German plan

The ITO experience was a reminder of the contested nature of international investment protection, and over the coming years the North-South divide grew ever larger. Many post-colonial states began to see foreign multinationals as the face of Western hegemony and associated mandatory compensation for expropriation and international arbitration of investment disputes with continued foreign domination and control over their resources.

This was especially unsatisfactory for Germany. German investors had an increased appetite for overseas activities, but they wanted protection after having lost almost all of their assets abroad in the aftermath of the Second World War. Yet with a highly constrained foreign policy, no colonial ties, and a membership of the European Economic Community (EEC), which took away the ability to unilaterally impose trade sanctions, it was impossible for the German government to aggressively defend its investors abroad. A solution was proposed by Herman Abs, chairman of the Deutche Bank, personal adviser to Germany's minister of economics, and one of the most influential spokesmen for post-war Germany. He suggested a 'Magna Charta' for the protection of foreign investment, which should operate 'in the same way as we are defending ourselves in the military field'.[7] Private investors were too weak when pitted against sovereigns seeking to expropriate their capital, Abs argued, and diplomatic protection was inadequate not just for Germany but also for other European states. Either Western politicians 'are falsely afraid that counteractions would drive the offending States in the arms of Eastern powers', he said, 'or they feel obliged, in order to prove they are through with colonialism, to suffer interferences with private rights'.[8] Abs therefore proposed an investment protection treaty based on international minimum standards backed up by investor–state arbitration and sanctions in case of non-compliance.

When Abs presented his idea at a conference in San Francisco in 1957, Cuba's representative attacked it as a 'return to the gay nineties' of imperial exploitation during the late nineteenth century, and the

---

[7] 'Colonialism dispute: speakers argue role of investors', *San Francisco Chronicle*, 16 October 1957.
[8] 'Magna Charta for investment interests asked', *American Banker*, 16 October 1957.

The German plan

governor of the Central Bank of the Philippines warned that it would grant excessive powers to foreign investors over developing countries.[9] By contrast, Vice-President Nixon supported the idea,[10] and the American Bar Association also thought the United States should take up Abs' proposal.[11] But the State and Commerce Departments didn't agree. The failure of the ITO had made clear that a multilateral agreement along Western principles couldn't be reached, and it was more practical instead to expand the network of FCN treaties, which increasingly included investment protection provisions.[12] Back in Europe, Abs also failed to convince the six EEC members to initiate a joint European investment treaty – intended by Abs 'first and foremost [as] an instrument of pressure for inducing third countries' to protect Western investment.[13]

His plan did appeal to Hartley Shawcross, however, a former attorney general of Britain and then director of Shell who was working on a similar proposal.[14] In a letter to the Foreign Office in 1957, Shawcross had noted that given the risks of expropriation for British oil interests in the Middle East, the flow of capital 'will break down unless it is possible for the Governments concerned to provide some sort of umbrella treaty protection'.[15] So when learning of Abs' ideas, Lord Shawcross was excited. Unlike FCN agreements Abs' multilateral treaty would protect all Western investors, which in turn would benefit capital importing countries by receiving more investment.[16] For Shawcross, as for Abs, the Magna Charta was a win-win. Talks between the two began in 1958, which resulted in an international study group backed by European banks and industries,[17] and the year after Abs convinced the German government to introduce his proposal to the Organisation for European Economic Co-Operation.

---

[9] 'The capitalist Magna Carta', *Time*, 28 October 1957.

[10] PA, AA, B56, 60; 'A good idea for foreign investment', *Time*, 28 October 1957.

[11] PA, AA, B56, 61 (ABA President Charles Rhyne told the American Bankers Association that '[h]ere, we have a field where bankers and lawyers can promote such growth by cooperative effort in so developing a mechanism of world law to govern world investment as to make it possible to use the genius of free enterprise to pave the road to peace under law').

[12] Protection of private investments overseas, US Congress, House, hearings before an Ad Hoc Subcommittee of the Committee on Foreign Affairs on H.J. Res 160, February 23 to March 13, 1957, p. 14. See also; Wilcox 1949, pp. 145–64; Walker 1956, p. 244.

[13] The plan was that even non-members who didn't execute arbitral awards or refused to submit investment disputes to international arbitration in the first place should have European loans and investment guarantees withheld; European League for Economic Co-operation (ELEC) 1958.

[14] Fatouros 1961.   [15] FO 371/127210.   [16] PA, AA, B56, 61.

[17] Shawcross 1995, pp. 307–8; PA, AA, B56, p. 60.

52   A difficult beginning

The OECD, as it was renamed in 1960, took up the proposal, but parallel suggestions came from other members and it was clear that even if agreement could be struck among OECD countries it would be a long process. The German government therefore decided to complement the multilateral track with a bilateral instrument, the BIT. The initiative was tied to a new state-backed investment insurance programme of DM2 billion,[18] which would require a BIT in place if the host state could not be expected to protect German investments according to certain minimum standards and agree to international arbitration in case of disputes. A similar approach was pursued by the United States, which negotiated brief inter-governmental agreements with most developing countries during this period (including most Latin American states) to facilitate guarantees by the American Investment Guaranty Program, the precursor to the Overseas Private Investment Corporation (OPIC).[19] But whereas the American guarantee agreements were put in place solely to allow Washington to recover losses on insured projects through interstate arbitration, the new German BIT was more closely related to FCN agreements. Although almost as brief as American guarantee agreements, the BIT followed Abs' proposals of including substantive investor rights for a very wide range of investments. Whether insured or not, German investors should be entitled to non-discrimination, full compensation for expropriation, limited restrictions on capital transfers, and protections against contract breaches as well as losses due to war or civil conflicts. The treaty included no obligations for German investors operating abroad, only rights.

These substantive rules were not just reflective of prior international legal norms, but also formative for the international investment regime as the German model became the focal point for practically all investment treaties ever since.[20] Unlike 'modern BITs', however, the template was backed up only by inter-state dispute resolution. If German investors found a host state was in breach of the treaty, they had to convince their government to take up a claim on their behalf. This was in contrast to Abs' Magna Charta, but the German government feared that binding investor–state arbitration could politicize investment

---

[18] 'The promotion of the international flow of private capital: progress report by the secretary-general, UNESCO, 1960, UN Doc E/3325, pp. 65–6.

[19] 'Intergovernmental agreements under the United States investment guaranty program,' *Indiana Law Journal*, 43 (1967–1968), p. 429. Agreements with Peru, Argentina, and Chile did not include arbitration provisions. Note that business interest in the programme waned in the 1960s as only few guarantees were authorized by USAID.

[20] On reflective and formative events in the context of human rights law, see Elkins, Ginsburg, and Melton 2014.

The German plan 53

disputes by turning 'every case of expropriation into an international litigation with political relevance'.[21]

Bonn introduced the BIT around the world. But whereas the intention with the treaties had been to 'substitute' for unfavourable domestic investment regimes, negotiations primarily proceeded in countries already committed to attract foreign investment. The first agreement with Pakistan, for instance, fitted well with the liberalization programme initiated by General Ayub Khan trying to revive a faltering economy. '[F]rom the first day of independence we have been very keen to develop economic relations with Germany',[22] said the Pakistani finance minister, and the treaty was thought to be of 'paramount importance' to promote German investment in Pakistan.[23] The Dominican Republic also signed in 1959, during the rule of Trujillo, a devoted anti-communist supported by the United States, and Malaysia signed the year after while working on similar proposals of investment protection it wanted introduced in the United Nations.[24] Similarly, the 1961 treaty with Morocco was signed only months after King Hassan II took over from his father and began market-led reforms; and Liberia's President Tubman also pursued Western-oriented liberal reforms when agreeing to the German treaty the same year.

But most countries were sceptical. Although German officials tried to convince their counterparts that its new instrument of economic diplomacy could be signed as 'a means of stimulating German private capital investment in developing countries',[25] several Latin American governments opposed German proposals because they contradicted the Calvo doctrine.[26] Libya refused as well taking the view that its own investment law was sufficient to encourage investment,[27] and while important markets such as Chile, India, Kenya, and the Philippines all signed in 1964, they later refused to ratify.[28] The same was the case with the 1965

---

[21] PA, AA, B56, 61.
[22] 'Pakistan W. German investment accord: way cleared for basic industries' growth', *DAWN*, 27 November 1959.
[23] Ibid.; 'Investment in Pakistan', *Civil and Military Gazette*, 26 November 1959.
[24] Combined with the fact that the Malaysian proposal didn't include sanctions in case of non-compliance, this was a non-starter for Shawcross who worked together with Abs and John Foster Dulles to get the Malaysian suggestion buried in a sub-committee; PA, AA, B56, 62.
[25] PA, AA, B84, 409.
[26] Negotiations were tried with Brazil, but failed, and Argentina and Mexico resisted as well; PA AA, B33, 322; PA, AA, B33, 312; PA, AA, B33, 418.
[27] PA, AA, B36, 295.
[28] In the case of Kenya, ratification was blocked in the 1970s after initiating a more restrictive policy towards foreign investment (PA, AA, Zwischenarchiv, 121333), the Philippines later objected to the national treatment provision (PA, AA, Zwischenarchiv,

54   A difficult beginning

Table 3.1 *The first decade of the BIT movement, German and Swiss treaties*

Year of signature	Germany	Switzerland
1959	Pakistan (1962), Dominican Republic (NA)	
1960	Malaysia (1963)	
1961	Greece (1963), **Togo (1964)**, **Morocco (1968)**, **Liberia (1967)**, Thailand (1965)	**Tunisia (1964)**
1962	**Guinea (1965)**, Turkey (1965), **Cameroon (1963)**, **Madagascar (1966)**	**Nigeria (1962)**, **Guinea (1963)**, **Ivory Coast (1962)**, **Senegal (1964)**, **Congo (1964)**
1963	**Sudan (1967)**, Sri Lanka (1966), **Tunisia (1966)**	**Cameroon (1964)**, **Liberia (1964)**, **Rwanda (1963)**
1964	**Senegal (1966)**, Korea (1967), Chile (–), **Ethiopia (–)**, India (–), **Niger (–)**, **Nigeria (–)**	**Togo (1966)**, **Madagascar (1966)**
1965	**Tanzania (1968)**, **Sierra Leone (1966)**, Colombia (–), Ecuador (1966), **Central African Republic (1968)**, **Congo (1967)**, Iran (1968)	Malta (1965), **Tanzania (1965)**, Costa Rica (1966)
1966	**Ivory Coast (1968)**, **Uganda (1968)**, **Zambia (1972)**	**Benin (1973)**, Honduras (–)
1967	**Chad (1968)**, **Rwanda (1969)**, **Ghana (–)**	**Chad (1967)**
1968	Indonesia (1971)	Ecuador (1969)
1969	**Zaire (1971)**, **Gabon (1971)**	**Burkina Faso (1969)**

Note: Year of entry into force in brackets. African countries in bold.
Source: UNCTC 1988

Colombia agreement, even though President Muñoz, a conservative, had initially stressed that he wanted to do everything necessary to protect foreign investments.[29] In the end, most partners were newly independent African countries of minor commercial interest, so looking back at Germany's experiences a British official wasn't too off the mark when stating that Bonn could get BITs 'only where they were not necessary, because where they were necessary they could not be negotiated'.[30] The same was the case for Switzerland's BIT programme, which began in 1961 and pursued treaties very closely following those of Germany (Table 3.1).

121350). Note that the Philippines came out in strong support of the ICSID Convention the same year as signing the German BIT; ICSID History vol. II, p. 547.
[29] PA, AA, B84, 391.   [30] FCO 59/1444.

ICSID and the emergence of modern investment treaties

From the beginning of its investment treaty programme, the German government had seen BITs as stepping stones for ongoing multilateral efforts.[31] After some redrafting the Abs-Shawcross proposal provided the basis for a 1962 OECD Draft Convention, but Washington was sceptical about the OECD project and so were capital-importing members Greece, Portugal, and Turkey. Also, even if there had been strong political buy-in within the OECD, there was still the problem of how to get developing countries to sign on. German bureaucrats had expressed concerns early on that developing countries saw the OECD initiative 'as a continuation of an imperialist and colonialist policy and considered it as an intervention in their sovereignty'.[32] So to get the support of the developing world, OECD asked the World Bank if it would take over the project.

Unfortunately for Germany, the Bank was 'not prepared to touch' the OECD undertaking.[33] This was not because it didn't support the underlying principles of OECD's draft, which it did, but because many developing countries were still unlikely to agree. As noted by the US Supreme Court in 1964, '[t]here are few if any issues in international law today on which opinion seems to be so divided as the limitations on a state's power to expropriate the property of aliens'.[34] With this in mind, the World Bank decided it wasn't worth the effort. Discussions were ongoing about a World Bank agency for political risk insurance, but even that was opposed by some developing countries as an investment protection treaty in disguise.[35]

Although OECD's proposal was unfeasible, the World Bank was not opposed to some form of multilateral investment framework. The Bank had increasingly become involved in settling the growing number of investment disputes in the developing world and the executive board occasionally blocked loans to countries not providing adequate compensation for expropriation.[36] This was partly for reasons of self-interest as most of the Bank's resources came from private capital markets and

---

[31] This was made clear early on to the Deutche Bank for instance; PA, AA, B56, p. 61.

[32] PA, AA, B56, 61.   [33] Schwarzenberger 1969, p. 153.

[34] Harlan J in *United States* v. *Sabbatino*, 374 US 398 (1964).

[35] Shihata 1988, pp. 40, 54–5. See further in St John 2014. The agency only materialized with MIGA in the 1980s; see Chapter 4.

[36] IBRD 1969, p. 31; Mason and Asher 1973, ch. 11. Note that on a number of occasions home states of aggrieved investors explicitly decided not to block World Bank lending fearing it would not only be counterproductive but also conflict with broader foreign policy considerations; FCO 59/941.

56   A difficult beginning

would therefore risk higher lending rates if its funds went to governments with outstanding expropriation claims.[37] But having the Bank's development policies subdued to concerns about investment disputes was clearly unsatisfactory, and the Bank had a long-standing wish that such disputes should be dealt with by an 'impartial body of technical experts.'[38] So rather than creating an agreement with substantive investment protection rules, as suggested by the OECD, the World Bank suggested one solely dealing with dispute settlement. If foreign investors could be given direct recourse to international arbitration when running into disputes with host states, they no longer had to ask their home states (or the World Bank) for assistance. In other words, whereas German officials feared that investor–state arbitration could further aggravate political tensions, the World Bank expected the opposite: a de-politicization of investment disputes.

The United States backed the proposal. Not only would a convention on procedure be easier to obtain than one on substance, the resulting arbitral decisions could also create 'a new body of international law' in favour of Western standards.[39] Moreover, the US Congress regularly twisted the arm of the White House to involve itself in investment disputes on behalf of American corporations by sanctioning expropriation states until full compensation was provided.[40] Much to the dismay of American presidents, Congress even managed to make it a statutory requirement that countries not providing American companies full compensation should have their aid flows withheld and trade preferences suspended. The end result was a success for expropriated American firms, who almost always managed to receive compensation at fair value, but a failure for American foreign policy as ardent protection of American corporate interests often contradicted broader strategic considerations.[41] Along with investment insurance, the World Bank's proposal for a multilateral agreement on investor–state arbitration could potentially alleviate such pressure.[42]

The chief architect of what was to become the International Centre for Settlement of Investment Disputes (ICSID) was the general counsel of the Bank, Aron Broches.[43] Although ultimately successful, the drafting

---

[37] St John 2014.   [38] IBRD 1946–1947 *Annual Report*, p. 13.
[39] Meeker quoted in St John 2014.   [40] Maurer 2013.
[41] Maurer 2013. See also Lipson 1985.
[42] It is not entirely clear how big a role de-politicization played for the US thinking on ICSID. Maurer (2013) suggests it was crucial, but St John (2014) points out that neither Cold War foreign policy concerns nor past investment disputes were mentioned during the US ratification process.
[43] For detailed accounts, see Parra 2012; St John 2014.

ICSID and the emergence of modern investment treaties   57

stage was an uphill battle for Broches as he received significant pushback from a number of developing countries, particularly in Latin America. Following the Calvo doctrine, experts nominated by Brazil, Ecuador, and Argentina complained in 1964 that the proposed convention would grant foreign investors a 'privileged position' by giving them direct access to international arbitration against host governments.[44] The expert from India expressed similar concerns and the representative from Ceylon (Sri Lanka) feared ICSID might 'enable pressure to be brought to bear on the developing countries'.[45] Representatives from Jordan and Thailand were also sceptical and asked Broches to provide evidence for his claim that the convention would help developing countries attract investment. He couldn't, as no economic analyses were made by the Bank.[46] In the end all the governors from the 19 Latin American World Bank members voted against the convention as investor–state arbitration was 'contrary to the accepted legal principles of our countries'.[47] When ICSID was finalized, its membership among developing countries was therefore limited to African countries and parts of Asia.[48]

Partly for that reason, hardly any claims were raised under ICSID in the first decades of its existence, which led to repeated questions about its relevance as an organization. British officials pointedly told Broches in 1971 'that ICSID appeared to be a Convention without teeth',[49] and awareness of the organization among major Western firms was minimal.[50] So with no cases to administer, ICSID instead became involved in influencing international investment policy. Apart from getting developing countries to sign up to the ICSID Convention itself, Broches urged governments to consent to ICSID arbitration and conciliation in contracts, domestic investment laws, and – importantly – BITs. Even though a multilateral investment treaty was out of the question by then – Germany had finally given up its efforts in 1967[51] – other

---

[44] Quoted in Parra 2012, p. 55. Note that Latin American members of the board were not lawyers but bankers; Szasz 1971, p. 257.

[45] Quoted in Parra 2012, pp. 55–6.   [46] St John 2014

[47] Governor of Chile speaking on behalf of Latin American colleagues, quoted in Parra 2012, p. 67. Two other countries voted against the resolution: Iraq and the Philippines.

[48] Among the critics, India and Ecuador were about to sign BITs with Germany, and Sri Lanka had already done so. But recall that the German treaties didn't include reference to investor–state arbitration. Note that it was Ecuador, not Germany, that initiated the 1966 BIT; FCO 59/1449.

[49] FCO 59/633.

[50] In a 1976 survey of legal counsel in Fortune 1000 companies, Ryans and Baker (1976) found that there was a 'dramatic lack of knowledge' about ICSID as only 15 per cent of respondents were familiar with the organization.

[51] Dolzer and Kim 2013, p. 294. 'In light of several developing countries' ambitions to reject international legal protections of foreign investors,' the German government noted

58   A difficult beginning

European countries had begun signing investment treaties following Bonn's lead. The negotiating templates closely resembled the German draft, but Broches wanted them 'upgraded' by also including consent to investor–state arbitration.[52] The Dutch government, Broches' former employer, followed his advice in a 1968 economic cooperation agreement with Indonesia.[53] Shortly after, Broches and his staff published a set of template clauses ready to be inserted into laws, contracts, and treaties. Italy was the first country to include an ICSID clause in a BIT in the 1969 agreement with Chad, and several other European governments soon followed suit.

This was an important achievement for ICSID, as it laid the groundwork for the investment treaty regime we know today. By combining substantive provisions similar to those in the German model and procedural provisions following the advice of ICSID, practically all the features of the 'modern' BIT was now in place.

But it didn't solve the immediate problem of how to get developing countries to sign the treaties. Broches regularly told developing country governments that adopting BITs with ICSID clauses was a useful way to de-politicize investment disputes and attract investment.[54] But as Germany had come to realize, it was mainly countries already committed to foreign investment protection who signed on to the agreements and Bonn faced increasing difficulties in the early 1970s when developing countries were becoming ever less enthusiastic about foreign investment and began a wave of expropriations. Although Germany had signed 36 BITs during the 1960s, Bonn only managed to sign half that in the 1970s. The United States, as well, found it increasingly difficult to conclude its FCN treaties.[55] After the last agreements with Thailand and Togo in the late 1960s, the United States was unable to get other countries to sign the agreements.

Other major capital-exporting states had the same experiences. As an illustration, the following section will focus on those of the United Kingdom, which give us important clues on the nature of the early BIT negotiations. The UK is also a particularly important case. It was the largest capital exporter in Europe with the most to lose when developing countries began expropriating Western assets, and it was one of the

---

some years later, 'the Federal Government will strive to obtain such protections by concluding another [type of] agreement.'; PA, AA, Zwischenarchiv, 121319, own translation.

[52] St John 2014.   [53] Parra 2012, p. 133.

[54] See e.g. Broches 1995, pp. 263, 457. See generally, St John 2014.

[55] Vandevelde 1988, pp. 207–8.

Early negotiations: the case of the United Kingdom

first – along with France and Belgium – to include a broad and binding consent to ICSID arbitration in its model BIT.

Early negotiations: the case of the United Kingdom

Like in the United States, frequent rifts occurred during the Cold War between British overseas commercial interests, concerned about expropriation, and policy-makers concerned about maintaining British influence post-empire and keeping newly independent nations outside the orbit of the Soviet Union.[56] But unlike the US, broader geostrategic interests typically trumped the defence of British business, and by the mid 1970s British investors had experienced expropriation in a total of 42 countries.[57] Sanctions were used only when it didn't hurt broader strategic foreign policy concerns,[58] and aid funds were rarely withheld to induce settlements as Whitehall feared it would not only subordinate public interests to those of private firms but also further deteriorate investment climates in the long run.[59] With limited willingness to intervene on behalf of British investors abroad and a multilateral investment agreement out of the question, it seemed the bilateral instruments negotiated by Bonn could be useful for British investors. Apart from establishing a political risk insurance programme, the British government therefore developed a model investment treaty, which, like other

[56] Stockwell 2000; Tignor 1998; White 2000. [57] FCO 59/1685.

[58] This was the case in Egypt after the Suez crisis (FCO 59/699); the 1971 Libyan nationalization of BP (FCO 59/699); and the CIA-implemented but MI6-orchestrated coup in Iran after the Anglo-American Oil Company had its concessions cancelled; Maurer 2013, ch. 7.

[59] FCO 59/633 (UK opposing an American proposal for a joint OECD statement on using 'aid as a weapon' after expropriation); FCO 59/951 (FCO opposing a suggestion that the EC should make preferential market access by African ex-colonies contingent on treating foreign investors fairly in the Yaoundé Convention; the predecessor to later Lomé agreements. 'The Americans have made considerable trouble for themselves through the legislative constraints under which they operate ... We have set our face firmly against such a course as a matter of policy'). See also FCO 59/949 (aid flows not cut after expropriations in Bangladesh, India, and Pakistan as it could hurt diplomatic relations); FCO 59/941(World Bank aid not opposed after expropriation of Iraq Petroleum Company, as it would have been counterproductive for the settlement negotiations); FCO 59/1295 (as the 1975 BIT with Egypt didn't help with past disputes, Lord Killearn and an MP write FCO requesting aid to be withheld until all British investors have been compensated after the Suez campaign. FCO refused.); FCO 59/1199 (when British companies asked for a similar approach to the Americans, the response was clear: 'Her Majesty's Government were not prepared to do this'). Exceptions included Sudan in 1970 (FCO 59/1685); Ghana in 1973 (FCO 59/1685) (see Chapter 4); and Tanzania in 1971 (FCO 59/941; FCO 59/1199). Although aid was also cut to Uganda and Sri Lanka in early 1970s, this was seen by several companies as counterproductive to reach settlements (FCO 59/949).

60   A difficult beginning

European programmes, was inspired by the OECD draft agreement – though with an accommodation for British foreign exchange controls. Unlike the German programme, however, it included a reference to binding ICSID investor–state arbitration.[60]

Given the rising opposition to multinationals in the developing world, a large number of countries were ruled out as impossible beforehand. Even countries willing to negotiate were expected to ask for significant revisions to the model as a British investment treaty would often be far more important than one with Germany given the amount of British capital abroad.[61] Even so, if negotiations should fail the British government would at least have stated for the 'record our views on the duties of foreign governments to protect overseas investment and to pay proper compensation in the event of expropriation'.[62] This was important for Western states at the time as Latin American governments were in the process of convincing developing countries to take advantage of their majority vote in the General Assembly of the United Nations to promote their version of international investment law. Here, they proposed a New International Economic Order allowing them 'Permanent Sovereignty over Natural Resources' and agreed to the 1974 'Charter of Economic Rights and Duties of States'. The charter challenged the Hull standard of compensation and questioned the very concept of an international minimum standard by basing foreign investment disputes on domestic law to be settled in the courts of host states. This was unacceptable to London, as it was to many other capital exporters, and the BIT programme was one attempt to offer its own vision of the proper protection and treatment of foreign investors.[63]

But although the Foreign and Commonwealth Office (FCO) approached 'the easiest countries first in order to lay a foundation for our subsequent approaches',[64] negotiations that did proceed were typically 'rather confrontational',[65] 'disappointingly slow',[66] and several failed entirely. A summary is provided in Table 3.2. Countries such as Iran and India told London that an agreement was out of the question as domestic legislation was sufficient to protect foreign investment, and Kenya simply asked whether the Brits could send a 'new and less obviously pro-British

---

[60] FCO 59/625; FCO 59/630; FCO 59/633; FCO 59/1295. Note that in 1970, Broches had encouraged the United Kingdom to include ICSID clauses into economic cooperation agreements with the Ivory Coast and Congo; FCO 59/631.

[61] FCO 59/698 ('No doubt the Germans have found it easier to conclude bilateral agreements than we are likely to do because their existing investment at the time was unimportant'.).

[62] FCO 59/948.   [63] Denza and Brooks 1987.   [64] FCO 59/943.

[65] UK official II.   [66] FCO 59/1449.

Early negotiations: the case of the United Kingdom   61

Table 3.2 *The early BIT programme of the United Kingdom, 1971–1979*

Bangladesh	Ongoing negotiations in 1979, treaty signed and entered into force in 1980.	59/1685
Barbados, Jamaica, and West Indies Ass. States	Failed negotiations in 1974. Barbados and Antigua suggested subrogation agreement instead. But their comments 'virtually identical' to those of Jamaica, who took the lead and found that the treaty would result in 'large, imprecise and unquantifiable obligations [which] might constitute a serious impediment to . . . social and economic objectives. . . . [I]f Jamaica were to conclude one with Britain, all other investing countries would seek similar Agreements and Jamaica would be unable to resist such requests. Jamaica was therefore in their view being asked to undertake immense obligations in relation to all foreign investment in Jamaica.' St Vincent and Dominica were more receptive as they expected an agreement could help attract investment.	59/944 59/1197 59/1198 59/1200
Brazil	Brazil expressed interest in 1972, but unclear whether it merely wanted subrogation agreement. No trace of negotiations.	59/700
Chile	Approached after signing US subrogation agreement, but no trace of negotiations.	59/1449
Ecuador	Approached after signing BIT with Germany, but no negotiations.	59/1449
Egypt	BIT initiated in connection with other integration agreements, one of which was a credit arrangement to finance British participation in Egyptian development projects worth £40 million. This agreement was important to the Egyptians and 'formed a helpful background for . . . negotiations'. Treaty signed in 1975; entered into force in 1976. Transfer clause subject to domestic laws.	59/1294 59/1295
Fiji	Ongoing negotiations in 1979, but no result.	59/1685
India	Considered unlikely. Draft handed over in 1976 but India argued 'foreign investors adequately protected under the Constitution, and accordingly bilateral investment protection agreements are not required'.	59/632 98/213 59/1449
Indonesia	Treaty signed in 1976; entered into force in 1977. Treaty excludes national treatment provision and applies only to specifically approved investment. Indonesia became difficult when their oil revenue trebled and attitudes towards	59/1190 59/1191 59/1192

62 A difficult beginning

Table 3.2 (*cont.*)

	foreign investment deteriorated during the negotiations. An unidentified British firm in Indonesia complained about lacking progress on negotiations.	
Iran	Considered unlikely. Iran rejected UK approach in 1974 'as foreign investment in Iran was fully covered by the protection given in the country's domestic legislation'. The matter was dropped after British investment guarantee agency noted they didn't care whether a BIT was in place.	59/1192
Kenya	No further talks after Kenya asked to get 'a new and less obviously pro-British draft' in 1973.	59/1195
Korea	Treaty signed and entered into force in 1976. Korea easily convinced to almost entirely sign off on British model as foreign investors were already given preferential treatment.	59/1293
Malawi	Approached in 1974 after signing BIT with Denmark and subrogation agreement with US. But just as Malawi had resisted German and Swiss BITs as 'they were complex and appeared to offer no positive advantage to Malawi', the government did not want to limit it's ability to discriminate and expropriate and wanted actual evidence that UK treaty promoted investment. Negotiations dropped.	59/947 CAOG 22/33
Malaysia	Failed negotiations in 1974 and 1975. Treaty signed in 1981; entered into force in 1988. BP and other British investors pushed for signature in 1975 to protect their existing investments given the change in investment climate.	59/1194 50/1296
Pakistan	Approached in 1974 and ongoing negotiations in 1979, but no treaty until 1994.	59/1449
Papua New Guinea	Negotiations initiated in 1979. Treaty signed and entered into force in 1981.	59/1685
Philippines	Discussions begin in 1976. Treaty signed in 1980; entered into force in 1981.	59/1449
Romania	If UK didn't finalize treaty before a Romanian state visit to London in 1976, 'the Romanians would stall on Concorde overlying rights, the purchase of further British aircraft and the joint venture agreements that are in the pipe-line'. Treaty signed and entered into force in 1976. Transfer clause subject to domestic laws, no national treatment, and only	59/1446 59/1447

Early negotiations: the case of the United Kingdom

Table 3.2 (*cont.*)

	disputes regarding compensation for expropriation can go to arbitration after exhaustion of local remedies.	
Singapore	Treaty signed and entered into force in 1975. Smooth negotiations, but Singapore insisted on restricted national treatment clause and application only to specifically approved investment.	59/943 59/1196
Thailand	Negotiations at advanced stage in 1975. Treaty signed in 1978; entered into force in 1979. No investor–state arbitration and application only to specifically approved investment. Negotiation history unavailable.	59/1293
Tunisia	Tunisia approached in 1975, but no progress in spite of UK reminders.	59/1449
Yugoslavia	Exchange of drafts in 1975, but no trace of further negotiations.	59/1449
Zaire	Made a high-priority country upon urging of the British American Tobacco Company, who had investments there. Negotiations failed in 1974 after Zaire began expropriations of Western assets and sent a much watered-down counter-draft. As treaty was thought to be irrelevant for the expropriations and commercial interest was small, FCO dropped negotiations.	59/700 59/1193

Notes: Third column gives FCO archival references. Summary is subject to usual caveats about the silence of archives. The following countries were considered unlikely to negotiate by the FCO and were seemingly not approached: Algeria, Argentina, Iraq, Lebanon, Libya, PDR Yemen, Sierra Leone, Sri Lanka, Sudan, and Tanzania. For further details, see Poulsen, Paparinskis, and Waibel 2015. Note that in parallel with early BIT negotiations, the UK played a key role in negotiating investment protection rules in the Euro-Arab dialogue, though the EC initiative later failed for political reasons; UK official I; Denza and Brooks 1987.

draft.' Even Caribbean countries proved impossible, as the British team was met with 'a stern, and occasionally hostile, examination by the negotiating teams'.[67] In Jamaica, for instance, British investors were looked upon with suspicion – the British team was told that 'managers must not kick workers!' – and the obligations of foreign investors were considered a more important issue than their additional protection. It soon became clear to British officials that 'the days of special privileges for foreigners were over', and an 'attempt to "freeze" customary

[67] FCO 59/947; FCO 59/1200.

64   A difficult beginning

international law as understood by HMG in our favour ... did not fit comfortably into the changing Caribbean scene'.[68] The FCO had been overly ambitious. On expropriation:

We knew we were asking for much more than our companies had ever secured in the past and we were seeking to write this formulae into an agreement which we hoped would last 30 years. In the case of Commonwealth countries we were seeking to persuade them to accept obligations on this question of compensation which we had not secured in the Constitutions we negotiated with them before they obtained Independence. Really this was never on.[69]

British and German officials regularly exchanged experiences about BIT negotiations, and London would typically initiate negotiations with countries where Bonn had been successful, and vice versa. This could be an effective strategy, but the early British attempt of securing a wide BIT network was by and large a failure. Whereas a country such as Romania went so far as to threaten London with sanctions if a BIT wasn't finalized quickly, most developing countries were more than sceptical towards BITs. All in all, London only managed to sign seven BITs during the 1970s. Although several governments were ready to sign on to American-style subrogation agreements, as they had with Washington, they didn't see the need to give British investors treaty-based protections. And those that did often insisted on significant changes to the British model. Yet despite these difficulties, Whitehall didn't want to use coercive means to secure more agreements.[70] London was aware that the Netherlands had used its aid programme as an incentive for some of its early BITs,[71] but the Ministry of Overseas Development found the suggestion of using 'essentially extraneous aid considerations' to be 'undesirable'.[72] This line was followed, as had been the case in Germany when similar suggestions were made in Bonn.[73]

Although many developing countries opposed the treaties – or at least didn't see the need to sign them – the content and process of negotiations

---

[68] FCO 59/1200.   [69] Ibid.

[70] FCO 59/1449 ('Since we are the demandeurs, there is little we can do if a chosen target does not respond'.)

[71] The 1965 Cameroon BIT was linked to a £4 million credit line for developmental projects, and the Ivory Coast entered into a BIT the same year expecting that the Netherlands would fund a major schooling project; NA, AOK, AZ, KMP, 2.03.01–3514; NA, AOK, AZ, KMP, 2.03.01–3537. In Tunisia, as well, the Netherlands linked investment treaty negotiations to the provision of financial assistance; NA, BZ, 2.05.118-10864; NA, BZ, 2.05.118-10510; NA, MF, 2.08.53–603.

[72] FCO 59/1685.

[73] FCO 59/1449; FCO 59/1685; PA, AA, B33, 15164. See comments on Egypt BIT in Table 3.1.

Early negotiations: the case of the United Kingdom   65

that did take place had some puzzling characteristics. With respect to content, the very thing making British BITs far more potent than those of Germany – the broad and binding consent to investor–state arbitration – was not a core issue during negotiations. Involving ICSID was the one part of the agreement that was 'applauded' by Jamaica, for instance, and the fact that investors could sidetrack their domestic courts received a 'particularly warm welcome'.[74] In negotiations with Egypt the arbitration provision wasn't even discussed,[75] and in Malaysia it was one of the few clauses with which Kuala Lumpur agreed.[76] Countries such as Singapore and Korea were happy to sign off on the British draft despite having previously signed agreements with the Netherlands requiring exhaustion of local remedies,[77] and Indonesia was not concerned about the unconditional consent to arbitration either.[78] Instead, most of the focus was on the more 'familiar' – and salient – issues, such as expropriation, national treatment, and capital transfers.

There were some exceptions of course. Romania raised concerns that 'trivial or inflated' claims could go to international arbitration 'with attendant ill-publicity for the State even if the claims were wholly unmeritorious'.[79] Remarkably, the UK only found investor–state arbitration a 'desirable but not essential' element of their model,[80] so a watered-down compromise was produced in the last 20 minutes of the negotiation. With Thailand, London even agreed to exclude the clause entirely. But otherwise, investor–state arbitration was not at the centre of negotiations. For whereas most Latin American states were consistent in their rejection of international arbitration it wasn't a matter of principle for many other developing countries who seemed to have been concerned mostly with displaying developing country solidarity when following Mexico's call to promote the Calvo doctrine in the UN in

---

[74] FCO 59/1200.
[75] This could be because Egypt had already given advance consent to ICSID in its 1974 investment law. A minor issue that came up with Egypt was whether it might lead to double-compensation for insured investors (which it couldn't); FCO 59/943.
[76] FCO 59/1194.
[77] The Korean negotiating team initially asked to follow the Dutch example, but it wasn't a matter of principle; FCO 59/943; FCO 59/1192; FCO 59/1293
[78] FCO 59/1292. Indonesia solely had troubles with the length of the British provision and the absence of conciliation as an additional option to resolve disputes; see also ICSID Case No. Arb/12/14 and 12/40, Decision on Jurisdiction, 24 February 2014, par. 212 and 225.
[79] FCO 59/1446.
[80] See also FCO 59/1446 (FCO officials noting that the most important difference with the German approach, was that unlike London the Germans insisted on national- and most-favoured-nation treatment. The difference in dispute settlement provisions – interstate versus investor–state – was not mentioned).

66   A difficult beginning

1974.[81] As a result, the core feature of modern investment treaties often passed unnoticed in the early BIT negotiations. Although the records are too scarce to make any hard conclusions, the observation by Korobkin quoted in the previous chapter appears relevant: 'Many of the terms commonly specified in standard form contracts govern what will happen if a low-probability risk comes to pass ... A form term calling for arbitration of disputes in an inconvenient state ... is likely to be non-salient to the vast majority ... unless the type of contract in question commonly results in disputes.'[82]

The process of negotiations was surprising as well. For even though talks were often difficult due to the growing resistance towards foreign investment, the UK regularly had to deal with poorly informed negotiating teams. The Egyptian legal adviser, for instance, didn't understand the concept of incorporation and 'confused it both with "amalgamation", "merger", and even "multinational corporation"'.[83] In Singapore, British negotiators had to remind their counterparts that one of Singapore's proposals would have taken away Singapore's ability to block undesirable investment – the opposite of what the Singaporean team had asked for.[84] In Korea, as well, negotiators mistakenly included North Korea in their initial definition of 'Korea' and failed to realize that their definition of Korean companies would have covered Korean-controlled firms established anywhere in the world. After a puzzled British team explained to the Koreans the implications of their suggestions, they reflected overnight 'upon their liberality' and withdrew their suggestions.[85] Although the BIT was signed, it was more the result of a training session than a negotiation. The troubles continued in Indonesia. Apart from the fact that 'it was as difficult to persuade Indonesian departments to co-operate with each other as to arrange a blood transfusion between two Egyptian mummies',[86] some of the Indonesian suggestions on the arbitration clause, for instance, were outright 'meaningless' and quickly

---

[81] Voss 1981. It is notable just how few countries, other than Latin American states and India, took strong positions on Article 2(c) of Chapter II in the charter. See also comments by the Thai delegation, for instance, stating that while voting for the charter the country was still very much interested in attracting, rather than expropriating, foreign investment; Singapore noting that it would continue to adhere to ICSID; Kuwait which was 'not at ease' with the promotion of local remedies in Article 2; and Indonesia noting that the article didn't preclude peaceful dispute settlement by means other than national tribunals; Schrijver 2008, pp. 108–9.

[82] Korobkin 2003, pp. 1233–4.

[83] On the other hand, the Egyptians did concede national treatment for British investors in Egypt, as they had also done with the German and French treaties.

[84] FCO 59/1196.   [85] FCO 59/1192; FCO 59/1293.   [86] FCO 59/1192.

Early negotiations: the case of the United Kingdom 67

discarded after the British team explained the implications.[87] Also in Malaysia, the approach to the treaties was everything but sophisticated. The Malaysian team had initially told London that all negotiations could probably be finished in one day and the FCO later learned Malaysian negotiators had arrived in Paris in 1975 wanting to sign off on the French model in its entirety without any negotiations.[88] French officials were surprised, but jumped on the opportunity. Negotiations with London turned out to be more difficult, probably because of the higher levels of British investment in Malaysia, but it was still 'inexplicable' to the FCO why Malaysia would just sign off on a French agreement with such broad, binding, and – at the time – controversial obligations.[89] Not all partners were this haphazard of course. The Jamaican team was particularly impressive and managed to explain 'the difficulties they foresaw more forcefully and clearly' than other Caribbean governments.[90] Generally, however, the British teams spent much time in the early negotiations simply explaining basic provisions and concepts. As we shall see later in this book, this problem continued throughout the 1980s and 1990s.

It is equally puzzling that among those who agreed to negotiate with the UK there are no traces that they conducted even superficial economic impact analyses or requested evidence that British investors actually took the treaties into account when determining where, and how much, to invest. When initiating negotiations, British missions sent out a letter, as follows:

British industry and British investors have represented to the British Government that, in their view, bilateral investment protection agreements could assist significantly in the creation of a climate of confidence, which would encourage further substantial investment in the Third World. ... [We wish to] encourage our investors to play an even larger part in the strengthening of your economy. It is our hope that the conclusion of agreements of this kind will play a part in promoting a greater flow of resources from developed countries to the developing Third World within a framework of law, which will be to the advantage of both.[91]

This message was repeated time and again.[92] And if developing countries proved difficult during negotiations, London would reiterate the investment promotion potential of the British draft provisions.[93] Yet, apart

---

[87] Indonesia suggested combining language from earlier agreements, which in the aggregate meant the arbitration would have been strengthened (by *requiring* investors to consent to arbitration; something the FCO found curious) and weakened at the same time (by excluding most foreign investors from coverage); FCO 59/1292.
[88] FCO 59/1194; FCO 59/1294; FCO 59/1296.   [89] FCO 59/1296.
[90] FCO 59/1200.   [91] FCO 59/701.
[92] E.g. FCO 50/943; FCO 50/947; FCO 59/1192.
[93] This happened in Zaire for instance; FCO 59/1193.

68   A difficult beginning

from the Jamaican team, which was again prudent to ask London for actual evidence to sustain this claim,[94] the few governments willing to negotiate simply took the British promise at face value.

The only real debate seems to have been within the British government itself. The British High Commissioner of Singapore, for instance, initially objected to the FCO's request for negotiations because investors were going to Singapore in the absence of the BIT. The considerable obligations combined with few expected benefits seemed to him as 'a good example of an unequal treaty' as Singapore 'would be giving guarantees with nothing in return'.[95] This view was not shared by the Singaporeans themselves, however, and after the High Commissioner was put in place by the FCO, the Singaporean team agreed to most of the British model treaty (Table 3.2).

It was fortunate for the British government that it didn't have to back up its claims about the investment promotion impact of the treaties. FCO officials themselves realized that although a BIT would 'be very much in our interests, it might not serve the interests of developing countries equally well. In particular we could not confidently promise them a substantial increase in new British investment were they to conclude such Agreements.'[96] Whereas Germany and the Netherlands could reasonably argue that their treaties mattered on at least a couple of occasions, due to statutory requirements making them a condition for insurance in risky jurisdictions,[97] BITs had no implications for insurance pricing or coverage in the UK.[98] In practice, the Export Credits Guarantee Department (ECGD) found it 'unrealistic to expect an individual investor to be greatly concerned about [BITs]' and for the underwriters, the treaties were 'unlikely to transform an unacceptable risk into an acceptable one, except possibly in a few highly marginal situations'.[99] When considering that the few British investors who seem to have taken

---

[94] FCO 59/1200.   [95] FCO 59/943.   [96] FCO 59/699.

[97] This occasionally made German and Dutch investors push hard for negotiations. A number of major German firms encouraged the German government to enter into a BIT with China in the late 1970s, for example, so as to allow investment guarantees for joint venture projects; PA, AA, Zwischenarchiv, 121316. Also, in Papua New Guinea the German firm Metallgesellschaft lobbied for the 1980 agreement to facilitate a guarantee for the largest raw materials project in the country, Ok Tedi; PA, AA, Zwischenarchiv, 121346. In the Netherlands, a contracting firm pushed for a BIT with Tunisia in the early 1960s to obtain an investment guarantee, though other Dutch investors went ahead with Tunisian investments even without the treaty, including Shell and Unilever; NA, MF, 2.08.53–603; NA, BZ, 2.05.118-10510; NA, BZ, 2.05.118-10864.

[98] The same was the case in France; FCO 59/1444 (UK official notes that the French did not consider BITs 'as a firm prerequisite for conferring investment guarantees. They seemed to be ready to extend guarantees without any legal protection'); FCO 59/698.

[99] FCO 59/1572.

Conclusion 69

notice of BITs had already made their investments – most notably in Zaire and Malaysia (Table 3.1) – it is remarkable just how easily British officials managed to convince some of their counterparts that the treaties were important to attract British investment. We shall see that this was not an isolated incident either, but a hint of what was yet to come.

Conclusion

The majority of investment treaty claims pursued against developing countries in recent years have been based on treaties very similar to the templates crafted in Europe and 'perfected' by ICSID during the 1950s and 1960s. The United States had its own treaty practice, but its subrogation agreements didn't include substantive investment protections, and by the late 1960s Washington was no longer able to conclude its preferred investment treaty – comprehensive FCN agreements covering both trade and investment liberalization as well as investment protection. Instead, it was Europe that led the way for the modern investment treaty regime by creating and negotiating short and simple bilateral treaties focused solely on investment protection.

But whereas European templates later became uncontroversial 'default rules' often adopted swiftly and with little deliberation, this was not the case during the first decades of the investment treaty movement. For although the origin of Western investment protection rules may have been imposed on the developing world during the colonial encounter, power asymmetries were rarely crucial in investment treaty discussions during the Cold War. Just as numerous developing countries refused to sign up to the ICSID Convention, European negotiators had difficulties in expanding their networks of BITs. In the face of developing country opposition, European governments were tempted to use quasi-coercive means to induce treaty adoption but mostly refrained from doing so, and developing countries were therefore more than capable of resisting Western pressure. By the late 1970s only 165 BITs had been signed as most Latin American states refused and other developing countries often caused European BIT negotiators a hard time as well. Some European countries, such as Denmark, had even given up, finding the agreements 'not worth the candle, because they can only be exceptionally achieved, and then only after long and difficult negotiations'.[100]

Negotiations that actually did proceed were rarely as sophisticated as we might have expected. This may not be overly surprising in a country

---

[100] FCO 98/213.

70   A difficult beginning

such as Somalia, for instance, where German officials had doubts in 1981 as to whether their Somali counterparts had even read the German model treaty Mogadishu signed,[101] but even British talks with countries such as Egypt, Korea, and Indonesia often had a character of training sessions rather than rigorous and informed negotiations. Also, whereas governments that were suspicious of Western investment protection standards wanted more evidence that the treaties could help them attract foreign capital, more liberal economic regimes took British promises of more investment at face value. It appears both the scepticism and optimism were politically motivated – the same information was assessed differently depending on pre-existing preferences. Finally, there are indications that the very design element that gave modern BITs significant 'bite' – private recourse to arbitration – was rarely even considered during negotiations. As there were no claims at the time, the arbitration clause was not sufficiently 'salient' to warrant much attention, compared with national treatment clauses for instance. So although archival records are too scant to draw any significant conclusions about the role of cognition constraints, these patterns do provide a first hint that perhaps developing country governments were not as rigorous and careful when negotiating investment treaties as has been assumed in previous accounts of the international investment regime.

[101] PA, AA, Zwischenarchiv, 121370.

4 Promoting investment treaties

With the rise of the Washington Consensus the suspicious attitude towards foreign investors was a thing of the past and developing countries began looking for policy instruments to lure multinationals to invest. Among investors themselves, BITs were very low on the priority list – as discussed in Chapter 1 – and it is therefore not obvious why the treaties became so remarkably popular in the developing world. This chapter will provide part of the answer. It will show how Western actors invested significant efforts in making sure BITs were particularly salient on the radars of developing country policy-makers. Rather than strong-arming governments into adopting the treaties, international organizations and Western advisers successfully brought attention to BITs as easy instruments to adopt and spread the causal belief that they were important to attract foreign investment.[1] Developing countries were also persuaded to enshrine BIT-like protections into domestic laws, which made the treaties become even more attractive as a seemingly low-cost addition to complement ongoing domestic reforms. This much could be explained by most models of economic diplomacy. But apart from outlining these supply side factors, the chapter will also present a first set of illustrations indicating that the way in which developing countries responded to Western advice is difficult to account for without reference to bounded rationality.

The World Bank

In the wake of the 1980s debt crisis, developing countries increasingly had to adjust their economics in exchange for receiving debt relief and foreign aid from the international financial institutions. This meant that at exactly the same time the BIT movement took off, the World Bank and the IMF had become deeply involved in shaping investment policy

---

[1] Causal beliefs are ideas about cause–effect relationships deriving authority from a shared consensus among recognized elites; Goldstein and Keohane 1993, p. 10.

72   Promoting investment treaties

regimes around the world. Not surprisingly, the two developments are related. Focus will here be on the World Bank. For although the IMF was a staunch promoter of investment liberalization reforms, investment protection was not a core issue for the fund and BITs therefore never played any considerable and sustained role for its oversight or financing functions. Another reason was that the treaties' capital transfer provisions often conflicted with IMF obligations by failing to include exceptions for serious balance of payments difficulties, which meant the international financial order promoted by the Fund was somewhat undermined by investment treaties.[2] The World Bank, on the other hand, was a staunch promoter of the treaties. And although attaching BIT adoption to lending conditions was never really an option for the Bank – as it is not a unilateral decision to negotiate a treaty – its technical assistance programmes often paved the way for BITs.

ICSID

As described previously, the development of the International Centre for the Settlement of Investment Disputes (ICSID) was always closely connected to the spread of modern investment treaties. In 1968, Robert McNamara – then President of the World Bank – told the ICSID Administrative Council that the Centre was 'helping to ease and accelerate the process of negotiating investment agreements',[3] and up through the 1970s and 1980s ICSID succeeded in a 'further harmonization of bilateral investment treaties'[4] by convincing developed countries to include ICSID clauses into their BIT models. Whereas hardly any BITs concluded by Germany and Sweden included ICSID clauses, the Netherlands, France, and the UK had included them in most of theirs.[5] Many, though not all, of these clauses entailed a comprehensive and binding consent to investor–state arbitration, often without having to exhaust local remedies. And by the late 1980s, such 'strong' arbitration provisions were commonplace in investment treaties[6] – not in small measure due to the policy work by ICSID. As noted by Broches' successor in the early 1980s, the dozens of ICSID clauses, which were being

---

[2] Siegel 2013. Investment treaties and investor–state arbitration hardly ever came up in the detailed policy priorities outlined in IMF's 'Letters of Intent' and 'Structural Adjustment Facility Framework' papers; Poulsen 2011. For a rare exception, see comments on US BIT in IMF, *Uruguay: Letter of Intent and Technical Memorandum of Understanding*, 12 November 2004; IMF, *Uruguay*, IMF Country Report No. 04/172, June 2004.
[3] Quoted in St John 2014.   [4] Delaume 1985, p. 20.   [5] St John 2014.
[6] Yackee 2008.

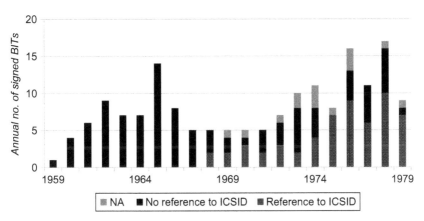

Figure 4.1 Reference to ICSID in bilateral investment treaties

Note: Figure shows annual number of signed BITs with and without a reference to ICSID. A reference to ICSID does not necessarily imply a legally binding consent to ICSID arbitration.

Sources: Compiled by author based on revised version of Allee and Peinhardt 2010 dataset using ICSID's Annual Reports 1981–1982 and UNCTAD's online BIT database

included in investment agreements, had become a good 'yardstick [to] judge the efficiency of ICSID'.[7]

ICSID also continued to promote investment treaties in the developing world. Here, Broches and his successors repeatedly stressed to developing countries that the treaties provided 'an incentive for investors to assume long-term commitments'[8] and ICSID began working on a handbook for investment treaty negotiators in 1985.[9] Long delayed, the volume was published 10 years later and repeated the message that the treaties would assist developing countries in sending 'an important signal to the international business community'.[10] In addition, BITs also played an important indirect role in promoting investment, as the provision of political risk insurance was:

in most instances conditioned on the existence of a BIT between the insuring State and the host country of the insured investment ... the BIT should help reduce the 'risk profile' of a covered investment to a level where it can be prudently insured by the investor's home State or investment guarantee agency.[11]

---

[7] Address by Golsong to ICSID's Administrative Council at its 16th Annual Meeting, 8 September 1982.
[8] See e.g. Broches 1995, p. 263; Shihata 1987, p. 685.   [9] Parra 2012, p. 154.
[10] Dolzer and Stevens 1995, p. 12.   [11] Ibid., p. 156. Italics added.

74   Promoting investment treaties

This latter message was not entirely accurate, as only few public insurance agencies have found the treaties crucial,[12] but may have been influenced by the fact that one of the authors of the volume was a senior bureaucrat from Germany, the country most closely tying its investment and insurance programmes. In any case, the overall lesson from ICSID to developing countries was clear: if they wanted to convince foreign investors to commit for the long term, it would be prudent to adopt investment treaties as part of their governing apparatus.

But although the ICSID secretariat actively and consistently pushed for the spread of investment treaties, ICSID remained a minor outlet in the Bank's legal department, which provided no input to conditions attached to Bank loan programmes as this would conflict with its role as an independent forum for the settlement of disputes.[13] Nor did it have the capacity to run an extensive policy-advisory programme, as its budget was well below one million in today's dollars and the secretariat had very few staff members – still only 11 at the end of the 1990s.[14] Instead, it was the Multilateral Investment Guarantee Agency (MIGA), which after its establishment in 1988 became the focal point within the Bank to promote foreign investment protection reforms.

MIGA and FIAS: paving the way for investment treaties

The idea of a multilateral organization providing investment insurance against political risks in developing countries had been on the World Bank agenda since the 1950s, but it was not until the 1980s that a compromise gained widespread support.[15] The result was an agency that had two purposes. First, and foremost, the organization should issue guarantees to foreign investors against non-commercial risks, and second it should carry out complementary activities assisting in promoting investments into the developing world.[16] Although the convention did not include substantive investment protections – much to the frustration of Germany and France – the Agency had a duty to 'promote and facilitate the conclusion of agreements, among its members, on the promotion and protection of investments'.[17] In the words of Ibrahim Shihata, the architect of the convention, this meant that instead of undermining BITs or other investment treaties, which some developed countries had feared, the Agency was 'to play a catalytic role in enhancing such attempts'.[18]

---

[12] Poulsen 2010.   [13] Parra 2012.   [14] Ibid., p. 128.   [15] Shihata 1988.
[16] MIGA Convention, Art. 2(a), (b); Shihata 1988.
[17] MIGA Convention, Art. 23(b), (i).
[18] Shihata 1988, p. 228. Shihata was general counsel and senior vice president of the World Bank as well as secretary general of ICSID.

The world bank

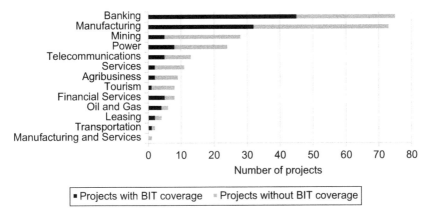

Figure 4.2 Investment projects with MIGA guarantees, 1990–1999
Note: A project is assumed to have BIT coverage if one or more investor countries have a ratified BIT with one or more host countries before or one year into the project start. Note that some projects could still be covered by other investment treaties, such as the Energy Charter Treaty. Five power projects with investors from Cayman Islands not included, as it was not clear whether UK BIT extended coverage. Sector classifications are from MIGA.
Sources: Compiled by author from MIGA and UNCTAD

MIGA could do this in two ways. One option was to withhold investment insurance if developing countries didn't sign up to BITs. Developing countries expressed concerns about this possibility during the establishment of the convention,[19] but it didn't happen. For even though the treaties have always been relevant to MIGA's underwriting process, it is only in exceptional circumstances that the absence of a treaty has had a considerable impact on the availability of insurance or premium rates. This is confirmed in interviews with current and previous MIGA staff,[20] and MIGA ultimately ended up providing guarantees for more projects without BIT coverage during the 1990s than projects with BIT coverage (Figure 4.2). In fact, in several sectors where at least some investors would be expected to concern themselves with the treaties, the share of MIGA projects covered by BITs was very small up through the 1990s: 18 per cent in mining and 33 per cent in the power sector. So although the treaties were undoubtedly important on occasion, foreign investors overall had equal access to MIGA insurance with or without BITs in place.

---

[19] Ibid., p. 220.   [20] Poulsen 2010.

76   Promoting investment treaties

Rather than quasi-coercive means, the more decisive role MIGA played in spreading support for the treaties was through its policy-advisory functions. A particularly important project was Shihata's involvement in drafting a set of legal guidelines for the treatment of foreign investment to be used for inspiration in foreign investment legislation. The project began in the late 1980s after Germany and France had asked the Bank to initiate a multilateral investment treaty, now that they failed to get substantive standards included in the MIGA convention itself.[21] Within the United Nations there had also been significant, but failed, efforts during the 1980s to reach consensus on a Code of Conduct on Transnational Corporations (see below) and the two European countries therefore pushed for a new attempt.

Yet, Shihata feared that negotiating an actual treaty would either fail or merely reflect the lowest common denominator.[22] Instead, he recommended a soft-law approach by proposing specific provisions to be included in foreign investment laws. This wouldn't just achieve the aim of Western governments – investment protection – but also complement broader developments within the Bank to involve itself with judicial reforms in the developing world. For whereas law reform had never been a core part of the Bank's work – lawyers were quite absent from Bank activities during the Cold War – this all changed after Shihata convinced the executive directors in 1991 that the Bank's increasing focus on 'good governance' and private sector development had to be accompanied by an emphasis on legal reform.[23] And with respect to foreign investment, his guidelines could be for domestic investment reforms what ICSID clauses and BIT models were for investment treaty negotiations: a set of readily available 'default rules' easy to include in domestic laws by governments seeking to attract investment.

Drafting the guidelines was a balancing act. On the one hand, Shihata and his staff couldn't depart too far from state practice as this could result in yet another failure of a multilateral compromise. But on the other hand, the World Bank's Development Committee had explicitly defined his task as one of investment promotion, which meant Shihata pushed the envelope in favour of developed countries' favoured standards.[24] Focus was squarely on protection, however, much to the frustration of

---

[21] Shihata 1993, pp. 31, 40.   [22] Ibid., p. 40.
[23] Shihata 1991, p. 230; Ofusu-Amaah 2002.   [24] Shihata 1993, pp. 64, 85.

the American government as well as Lawrence Summers, then chief economist at the World Bank, who both wanted greater emphasis on liberalization. But Shihata managed to convince the United States to support the project nevertheless, and the final draft was anonymously adopted in 1992. Developing countries provided hardly any comments throughout the process but welcomed the non-binding and adaptable instrument. The chairman of the Third World Forum commented that 'for once, I will be defending the views of the Bretton Woods Institutions'.[25]

The guidelines were not just intended to push forward, and standardize, investment laws, but also to pave the way for investment treaties. Apart from borrowing from state practice, the drafting process had benefitted 'in particular from the conclusions of [a] study on bilateral investment treaties',[26] which meant key investment treaty standards found their way into the guidelines as well. And just as MIGA had a mandate to promote BITs, the World Bank Development Committee similarly noted that the guidelines were an instrument to:

promote fair and equitable international standards for the general treatment of all foreign direct investment in the absence of applicable treaties, and should be of particular value for developing countries. Ministers expect the Guidelines to serve as an important step of the progressive development of international practice in this area and *hope that they will facilitate further developments through bilateral treaties and similar instruments.*[27]

This is exactly what they did. During the 1990s an increasing share of the World Bank's lending was to so-called core investment climate projects relating to investor-friendly judicial and legal reforms.[28] Here, again, MIGA played a key role as it had joined the International Finance Corporation (IFC) in managing the World Bank's Foreign Investment Advisory Services (FIAS).[29] After its establishment in

---

[25] Shihata 1992, p. 147.   [26] Shihata 1993, p. 63.
[27] Development Committee, 'Communiqué of the Development Committee', in: Shihata 1993, p. 144. Italics added.
[28] World Bank OEU 2004, fig. 4.3.
[29] Note that independently of FIAS, the IFC also promoted international arbitration in its loan agreements, and in one investment treaty claim before ICSID, the IFC – itself a World Bank agency – had shares in the investment enterprise pursing the claim; ICSID Case No. ARB/03/19, Petition for transparency and participation as *amicus curiae,* available at www.ciel.org/Publications/SuezAmicus_27Jan05_Spanish.pdf. The petition mentions a range of other multinationals funded in part by the IFC, which have also pursued claims under ICSID, p. 14, ftn. 39.

78   Promoting investment treaties

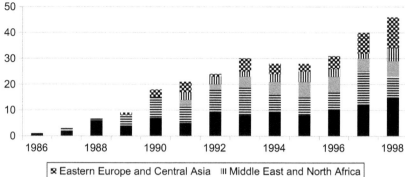

Figure 4.3 FIAS advisory projects, 1986–1998
Note: The following projects involved drafting, revising, or implementing investment legislation: China (1987), Ghana (1987), Papua New-Guinea (1989), Togo (1989), Cameroon (1990), Madagascar (1990), Vietnam (1991), Czechoslovakia (1991), Hungary (1991), Guinea-Bissau (1991), Honduras (1992), Malawi (1992), Namibia (1992), Cote d'Ivoire (1993), Equatorial Guinea (1993), Zambia (1993), Ghana (1993), Cambodia (1994), Fiji (1994), Russia (1994), Dominican Republic (1994), Jordan (1995), Kazakhstan (1995), Guinea (1996), Guinea-Bissau (1997), Lesotho (1997), Sierra Leone (1997), Solomon Islands (1997), Swaziland (1997), West Bank and Gaza (1997), Bosnia (1998), China (1998), Costa Rica (1998), Dominican Republic (1998), Fiji (1998), Kuwait (1998), Kyrgyzstan (1998), Marshall Islands (1998), Mongolia (1998), Romania (1998), Russia (1998), Uganda (1998), and Ukraine (1998).
Sources: Adapted from Weigel 1997, Appendix C; and World Bank Operations Evaluation Group 1998, Attachments 3 and 7.

1985 FIAS was increasingly called upon to offer advice to developing country governments, and during the 1990s its activities took off. Only five years after the guidelines were adopted 150 FIAS projects had been initiated throughout the developing world (Figure 4.3).

It is beyond the scope of this chapter to review these programmes in any detail. But the key point is that FIAS's efforts made it easier for developed countries to initiate BIT negotiations with developing countries. Although in some cases the economists at FIAS encouraged BIT

The world bank 79

adoption directly,[30] and a few countries were encouraged to include language from BITs into domestic laws,[31] FIAS's main policy was to focus on enshrining the World Bank Guidelines into domestic laws.[32] But because the guidelines had been directly inspired by BIT obligations, they provided the enabling conditions to make the treaties obvious complements to domestic reforms. We shall see a clear example of this towards the end of the chapter, but for now a few brief examples can serve as illustrations.

In Zambia, the Bank became deeply involved in law reform after the country underwent a structural adjustment programme starting in 1991.[33] The package included a new investment act, which provided prompt compensation for expropriation at market value, free repatriation of capital, and the establishment of an investment promotion agency. The act was updated with the assistance of FIAS in 1993, and the same year the Zambian government decided to sign a BIT with Switzerland – its first since 1966. Zambia signed yet another with China two years later. Another example is Gabon, which since 1995 implemented investment protection reforms attached to an IMF–World Bank structural adjustment programme. An investment charter was prepared in collaboration with the Bretton Woods institutions, which embodied 'the commitments and reforms being put in place'.[34] Finalized with the assistance of FIAS in 1998,[35] the charter made explicit reference to the fact that Gabon had begun signing BITs in 1995 – its first since 1979.[36]

Zambia and Gabon were somewhat unique by having investment acts directly attached to structural adjustment financing – something FIAS was opposed to[37] – but the pattern was similar elsewhere. Honduras, for instance, signed its first-ever BIT in 1993 one year after FIAS made

---

[30] See e.g. FIAS reports to Iran (1999c) (encouraging BITs with OECD countries) and Brazil (2001a) (encouraging adoption of ICSID, the New York Convention, a DTT with the United States, as well as BITs). In Albania (2001b) BITs were mentioned as 'further evidence of Albania's strong legislative commitment' to FDI.

[31] See e.g. FIAS reports to Jordan (1997a) and Sierra Leone (1997b). Bulgaria (1994) was encouraged to include recourse to arbitration in domestic law as network of BITs was not enough.

[32] Interviews with previous FIAS staff members. For instance, not a word was mentioned about BITs in reports to Yugoslavia (1998), Honduras (2001c), Bosnia and Herzegovina (2001d), or Grenada (2004). FIAS reports are classified except if released by the host state, and the author would also like to thank FIAS staff for declassifying a number of reports for the purpose of this section.

[33] Ofusu-Amaah 2002.   [34] World Bank 1997, p. 4.

[35] Statement by Ali Bourhane, World Bank board meeting, 15 October 1998.

[36] Gabon Investment Charter of 1998.

[37] World Bank Operations Evaluation Group 1998, p. 14, available at http://ieg.worldbank.org/Data/reports/fias_evaluation.pdf.

80   Promoting investment treaties

Table 4.1 *World Bank programmes and BIT adoption*

	(1)	(2)	(3)
WB technical assistance programmes	0.107*		0.135**
	(0.064)		(0.068)
WB structural adjustment programmes		−0.045	−0.073
		(0.052)	(0.054)
GDP	−0.000	−0.000	−0.000
	(0.001)	(0.001)	(0.000)
Constant	0.826***	0.876***	0.860***
	(0.151)	(0.153)	(0.153)
Year dummies	Yes	Yes	Yes
Country fixed effects	Yes	Yes	Yes
Observations	2180	2181	2180

Note: Standard errors in parentheses. $*p < 0.10$, $**p < 0.05$, $***p < 0.01$.

Dependent variable is the annual number of BITs signed by 127 developing countries from 1980 to 1999. Table reports coefficients from negative binomial estimation. The model includes a full set of year dummies to control for time-specific shocks shared by all countries – such as the end of the Cold War or changing global norms towards foreign investment. To control for time-invariant effects specific to individual countries – such as geography or legal culture – the model also includes country fixed effects. Apart from year dummies, all covariates are lagged one year to avoid simultaneity. World Bank project data is from Boockmann and Dreher (2003) and takes the value of one when country participated in a World Bank programme in a given year and zero otherwise.

recommendations on its investment law. Similarly, in 1994 FIAS drafted Cambodia's investment law and reviewed the investment legislation in the Dominican Republic. In the same year Cambodia signed its first BIT, and the year after the Dominican Republic followed suit. These were no coincidences. Table 4.1 shows that although there is no substantial or significant increase in BIT adoption for countries participating in World Bank's structural adjustment programmes, the Bank's technical assistance activities were associated with an 11 per cent to 15 per cent increase in subsequent BIT adoption.[38]

Causality could of course go both ways as countries willing to sign BITs were also more likely to invite World Bank advisers, and in several cases BIT adoption would have taken place even without World Bank involvement. But to the extent the association picks up the efforts of FIAS and other World Bank staff involved in investment-related technical assistance, this was exactly the sort of dynamic initially intended by Shihata

---

[38] exp(0.107)=1.113; exp(0.135)=1.145.

American advisers 81

when drafting the guidelines. For rather than coercing developing countries into adopting the treaties, the Bank made them appear as 'cheaper' instruments after promoting BIT-like standards into domestic laws and regulations. As Charles Brower noted in 1999, the year Shihata left the World Bank:

[S]ince he arrived on duty in Washington, no less than 1,235 bilateral investment treaties have been concluded around the world ... the masterful missionary, Ibrahim Shihata, may disclaim responsibility, but the world knows better.[39]

American advisers

Apart from their influence in the World Bank, Western states also played important roles in promoting investment treaties through bilateral efforts. Focus will here be on the United States which, although a latecomer to the investment treaty movement, spent considerable resources on shaping investment protection regimes in developing and transition economies after the Cold War. Similar to the policy work of MIGA and FIAS, these efforts also helped lead the way for investment treaty adoption during the 1990s.

The American BIT programme

As a starting point, let us briefly take a step back to provide some context to the American investment treaty programme. While initiated in the final years of the Carter administration, it was soon after Reagan took office that the United States began its BIT programme in order to affirm Washington's commitment to Western compensation standards increasingly under pressure in the United Nations.[40] Although espousal worked rather well for American investors abroad,[41] industry groups also supported the initiative as a useful alternative to the lingering American FCN programme.[42] Combining language from European templates with American FCN treaties Washington developed a BIT model, which was not only long and complex but also more ambitious in scope than European agreements by including binding market access provisions and constraints on performance requirements.

---

[39] Brower 1999, pp. 82–3. [40] Vandevelde 1988. [41] Maurer 2013.
[42] U.S. Policy Toward International Investment, Hearings Before the Subcommittee on International Economic Policy of the Committee on Foreign Relations, United States Senate, 30 July, 20 September, and 28 October 1981; Vandevelde 1988, pp. 208–9, ftn. 67.

82   Promoting investment treaties

Yet, the early efforts of getting developing countries to sign were unsuccessful. Unlike the more flexible Europeans, who managed to sign a growing number of BITs during the 1980s, the State Department only wanted treaties almost identical to the American BIT model, as deviations could question American positions on customary international law on investment protection.[43] A former American negotiator described the 'negotiations' as 'an intensive training seminar conducted by the United States, on U.S. terms, on what it would take to comply with the U.S. draft.'[44] In the case of Grenada, for instance, talks about a BIT began in 1985, two years after the US invasion, and concluded after one hour of discussions with the Grenadian prime minister while he was getting medical treatment in a Washington DC hospital.[45] But Grenada was one of the only countries willing to sign on to the American model, and most other US treaty partners during the 1980s were also of limited commercial importance.[46] Instead, Washington tried to include comprehensive investment rules into the GATT, though mostly focusing on liberalization, but this largely failed as well as even other developed countries were hesitant at the time.[47] Not a flying start for the American investment treaty programme.

This all changed after the end of the Cold War. Whereas the Reagan administration at one point considered using aid and trade preferences to get developing countries to sign on to BITs,[48] a growing number of partner countries were now ready to sign on to the American model. Washington itself also became more flexible, as the Bush administration began using investment treaties as political symbols.[49] As long as investment climates were *eventually* going to reflect the American BIT model, the United States was now ready to enter into BITs with a wide range of

---

[43] Vandevelde 1992. China, for instance, insisted on excluding national treatment and investor–state arbitration at the time which meant an agreement with Washington was unfeasible.

[44] Alvarez 1992, pp. 552–3.   [45] Vandevelde 1992, p. 539.

[46] Panama (1982), Senegal (1983), Haiti (1983; never came into force as a result of military coup in 1986), DR Congo (1984), Morocco (1985), Turkey (1985), Cameroon (1986), Egypt (1986), Bangladesh (1986), and Grenada (1986).

[47] Christy III 1990–1991.

[48] On the plans of making BIT adoption part of the 1982 Caribbean Basin Initiative, which provided market access and economic assistance to stem anti-American and communist sentiments in the region, see comments by John Bolton in *The Caribbean Basin Policy: Hearings Before the Subcommittee on Inter-American Affairs of the House Committee on Foreign Affairs*, 97th Cong., 1st Sess. (1981), p. 142. See also US Department of State, *Background on the Caribbean Basin Initiative*, March 1982, pp. 2, 5; Newfarmer 1985, p. 70. The plans never materialized and BIT negotiations failed in El Salvador, Honduras, Costa Rica, and the Dominican Republic.

[49] Vandevelde 2009.

American advisers 83

countries. Adopting investment treaties with Argentina (1991) and Ecuador (1993), for instance, was a useful way to show that Hull had finally won over Calvo and Latin America was ready to tie neoliberal reforms to the mast of international law. The treaties showed what European negotiators had also noticed a few years earlier, namely that the attitude in Latin America was 'softening and a number of Latin American countries are coming to accept that there is no incompatibility between sovereignty and the acceptance of international adjudication of disputes.'[50]

American advisers

Yet, the main focus of the American BIT programme was in the former Soviet bloc and Eastern Europe. This was no coincidence. After the end of the Cold War, the Bush administration funded an army of American consultants and advisers to promote economic and legal reforms in the region. The scheme has been described by Janine Wedel as a 'Marshall Plan of Advice',[51] and American lawyers played a key role. Funded by the US Agency for International Development (USAID), they promoted investment protection reforms through the Eastern European Democracies programme and the Commercial Law Development Program run by the Commerce Department. Most important in this context, however, was USAID's support to the Central and Eastern European Law Initiative (CEELI).[52] Organized by private lawyers of the American Bar Association (ABA), the CEELI programme facilitated more than 4,000 American lawyers going to more than 20 countries in the former Communist block to advise governments, bar associations, and NGOs seeking to build legal institutions to support capitalist democracies (Table 4.2).[53] Countless laws and several constitutions were drafted partly, or in whole, by CEELI lawyers, and one of their areas of focus was the protection of foreign investment.

Most CEELI lawyers were aware of the pitfalls of simply exporting American investment laws and regulations into the region. They were highly critical, for instance, of an overwhelmingly complex investment

---

[50] Denza and Brooks 1987, p. 923. See also 'Argentina and UK improve ties,' *Financial Times,* 12 December 1990 (Argentinean foreign minister stressing that UK BIT was seen as part of a broader move by Argentina to make its relations with the UK a 'symbol of Buenos Aires' desire to play a responsible international role'.)

[51] Wedel 1998, p. 30.

[52] See generally DeLisle 1999; Moyer, Ellis, and D'alemberte 2009. I would like to thank Philippe Sands, QC, for drawing my attention to this program.

[53] Judge O'Connor 1997–1998.

84   Promoting investment treaties

Table 4.2 *CEELI operations by 1994*

Country	Year of first project	Number of major assistance areas
Albania	1991	17
Armenia	1992	8
Azerbaijan	1992	7
Belarus	1992	13
Bulgaria	1991	17
Croatia	1994	10
Czech Republic	1990	13
Estonia	1992	15
Hungary	1991	14
Kazakhstan	1992	16
Kyrgyzstan	1993	10
Latvia	1992	13
Lithuania	1992	16
Macedonia	1992	11
Moldova	1993	9
Poland	1991	12
Romania	1991	19
Russia	1992	21
Slovakia	1993	5
Ukraine	1993	7
Uzbekistan	1992	6

Source: *ABA Journal*, May 1994, vol. 80

law drafted for the Lithuanian government by the United Nations Development Programme, which was almost exactly similar to Canada's investment act and had been drafted it in such a hurry that UN staff forgot to remove Commonwealth references to 'Her Majesty'.[54] But despite CEELI's founding principles to be 'policy neutral', 'without an agenda', and not 'to advance a policy',[55] the organization had a very particular view of the rule of law when it came to investment protection: international minimum standards and recourse to investor–state arbitration. As a result, CEELI lawyers routinely promoted investment codes with BIT-like protections, and to support the effort the American BIT negotiating team forwarded copies of their model BIT as inspiration.[56]

To complement the investment law reforms, CEELI lawyers encouraged governments to enter into BITs with the United States and other countries. In the case of Lithuania, for instance, a CEELI lawyer told the

[54] CEELI 1993a.   [55] Moyer, Ellis, and D'alemberte 2009, p. 309.
[56] Vandevelde 1993, p. 634.

American advisers

Chambers of Commerce and Industry in 1993 that to 'be successful in attracting foreign capital', Lithuania should continue to 'enter into BITs with the U.S. and other Western States'.[57] That same year CEELI sent another adviser to Vilnius, Kenneth Vandevelde – a former US BIT negotiator. Vandevelde spent six weeks there to analyze past and proposed BITs, revise the Lithuanian model BIT, and develop a 96-page single-spaced negotiation manual.[58] The manual went through clause by clause in considerable detail and highlighted the inconsistencies of the early Lithuanian BITs. The message from Vandevelde was clear: these were important agreements that should be negotiated carefully. Lithuania's previous model was 'a cut and paste arrangement of provisions taken from other agreements that they already have signed or are in the process of negotiation ... [But] the Lithuanians have not always chosen wisely among the variations'.[59] So although Lithuania wanted an investor-friendly model, Vandevelde warned the government to not simply sign off on European models. He did, however, strongly support the core design features of the treaties. On arbitration: 'The investor-to-state disputes provisions generally [are] superior to litigation in local courts or espousal'.[60]

CEELI's advice on BITs to other countries was less comprehensive, but equally favourable of the treaties. One of the lawyers who promoted BITs became involved in CEELI explicitly to spread 'libertarian ideas and practices',[61] and included references in his reports to writers such as Hans-Herman Hoppe and Murray Rothbard.[62] The standard justification of CEELI, however, was that the treaties were important as strategic instruments to attract investment. This was also the stated view of the American Bar Association itself.[63] 'In order to attract investments from abroad', another CEELI lawyer notes, 'developing countries need to enter into BITs and be signatories to the ICSID convention, so this naturally played a role in the advice I gave'.[64] Albania, for instance, was urged to negotiate BITs by CEELI lawyers, and they forwarded the text of several US BITs for inspiration.[65] After Albania signed its first in 1991, the government in Tirana signed more than 20 during the next four years – including one with the United States.[66] An ABA adviser on leave from the Internal Revenue Service praised this development because the treaties fitted well with Albania's broader FDI reforms, which addressed 'the bulk of the issues that

---

[57] Kinsella 1993, pp. 2–3.   [58] CEELI 1993c.   [59] Ibid., p. 462.
[60] Ibid., pp. 502–3.   [61] CEELI lawyer I.   [62] CEELI 1996, ftn. 19.
[63] See e.g. Rovine 1987, pp. 274, 277.   [64] CEELI lawyer II.   [65] CEELI 1992.
[66] See also Sands 2006, p. 118.

86   Promoting investment treaties

international lawyers, Western ones in particular, have concluded are crucial for a successful foreign investment law'.[67]

Romania was also encouraged to sign up to the treaties. Although Romania had adopted BITs since the 1970s – the first was with the UK described in Chapter 3 – many of its early treaties offered only limited recourse to investor–state arbitration. As one of the tools necessary to attract FDI, CEELI therefore encouraged Romania to 'strengthen the protections ... provided in BITs and other treaties'.[68]

In some cases, BIT negotiations resulted in investment laws inspired by BIT-like provisions rather than the other way around.[69] One American negotiator noted that Central and Eastern European countries were 'faced with the task of building a modern investment regime from the ground up ... So our BIT negotiations play a useful role in this process. When writing their investment laws, many of these countries incorporated the basic provisions provided by the BIT'. At the same time, however, the BITs also 'served to anchor their economic reform efforts in these areas', thus locking in domestic obligations.[70]

Whether the treaties were used to push forward reforms, lock in existing reforms, or both, it suffices to say that having American lawyers encourage foreign governments to sign BITs with the United States was a model ripe for conflicts of interest. In some cases, American lawyers even advised on actual negotiations. This was the case with the 1992 US–Bulgaria BIT, for instance, where a CEELI lawyer advised the Bulgarian government on the negotiations, which had begun the year before and ended up closely following the 1991 US model BIT.[71] A CEELI lawyer also advised the Albanian team negotiating a BIT with the United States, and Lithuania was assisted by Vandevelde when preparing for its negotiations with the United States.[72] The State Department didn't want too informed negotiating partners, however, so the American team noted that although 'the Lithuanians did not understand BIT negotiations very

---

[67] Carlsson 1995.   [68] Kinsella 1997.

[69] Vandevelde 1993, p. 634; Dan Price in Hearing of the International Economic Policy, Export and Trade Promotion Subcommittee of the Senate Foreign Relations Committee, 30 November 1995.

[70] Daniel Tarullo in Hearing of the International Economic Policy, Export and Trade Promotion Subcommittee of the Senate Foreign Relations Committee, 30 November 1995.

[71] CEELI 1993b.

[72] CEELI 1993c. Despite his overall favourable view of the treaties, it is important to mention that Vandevelde underwent great efforts to prevent Lithuania from unduly exposing itself from expropriation claims by American investors dating back to the Soviet occupation.

The United Nations 87

well' Vandevelde could not be allowed into the room during negotiations, much to his frustration.[73]

CEELI lawyers were not unaware of the potential conflicts of interest, and particularly the involvement of a former American BIT negotiator was discussed by Vandevelde and the CEELI administrators.[74] But overall, the CEELI programme illustrates what the literature on American legal assistance pointed out long ago: 'International and national interests, professional and self-interests, developmental and humanitarian interests – the various motives for American legal assistance worked together'.[75] Even if conflicts of interest were acknowledged, they were 'pushed aside by the implicit celebration of American legal ways'.[76]

Whether this conflation of interests was real, as opposed to merely potential, is outside the scope of this study to determine. For our purpose, the key point is that entrepreneurial American advisers played a crucial rule in alerting attention to investment treaties as a salient and standardized instrument ready to adopt as part of ongoing efforts to attract investment. This was convenient for the American government, not least because political concerns with outgoing investment meant the administration could not state publicly that the treaties promoted FDI.[77] But CEELI lawyers did and along with other American advisers in the region (see below) their activities were at least partly responsible for making the former Socialist block one of 'the most fertile source of new BIT-partners'.[78] With the exception of Hungary, the United States thus managed to complete BITs with all 13 former Communist states included in Figure 4.4.

---

[73] Ibid., p. 459.   [74] Ibid.   [75] Gardner 1980, p. 285.   [76] Ibid

[77] Vandevelde 1992a. On several occasions, USTR officials did highlight the investment promotion potential of the treaties, however. See e.g. comments by Harvey Bale Jr. ('US China investment talks,' *New York Times*, 26 May 1983) and Clayton Yeuter ('Tourism, investment treaties signed with Morocco,' *Associated Press*, 22 July 1985). Similarly, when trying to get Pakistan to sign a BIT in 2008, the American ambassador in Islamabad said that 'This Government believes that one of the foundations for such increased investment is a BIT that provides appropriate protections for American investors'; Letter from Anne Patterson, 30 August 2008; on file with author.

[78] Vandevelde 1993, p. 703. See also Daniel Tarullo, Assistant Secretary of State, Hearing of the International Economic Policy, Export and Trade Promotion Subcommittee of the Senate Foreign Relations Committee, 30 November 1995.

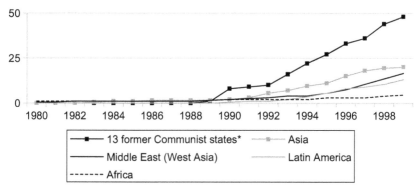

* Albania, Bulgaria, Croatia, Czech Republic, Estonia, Hungary, Latvia, Lithuania, Poland, Romania, Russia, Slovakia, Ukraine.

Figure 4.4 The rush to BITs in Central and Eastern Europe, median total number of BITs by region

The United Nations

I turn now to a third 'BIT entrepreneur', perhaps one more surprising than the World Bank, OECD governments, and Western investment lawyers, namely the United Nations. Starting with its Centre on Transnational Corporations (UNCTC), the UN played a central role in the development of the modern international investment regime. Established in 1974, UNCTC evolved directly out of the movement for a New International Economic Order and was as such primarily concerned with protecting the interests and sovereignty of developing countries in their engagement with foreign investors.[79] On the part of developed countries, UNCTC was seen as a useful instrument to tame 'their' investors abroad amidst widespread popular criticism against multinationals in Western capitals.[80]

UNCTC and other UN institutions became involved in drafting investment laws in a large number of developing countries. Highest priority, however, was given to achieve a multilateral investment agreement in the shape of a Code on Transnational Corporations initiated in 1975. Apart from standards on the rights of multinationals vis-à-vis their host states (as in BITs), the code was intended to incorporate obligations for foreign

---

[79] Sagafi-Nejad 2008, ch. 5. The UN's Industrial Development Organisation (UNIDO) was also involved in the promotion of industrial projects by foreign investors in developing countries, for instance, by establishing a network of Investment Promotion Services; see Shihata 1991, pp. 493–4.
[80] Sauvant 2015.

The United Nations 89

investors (unlike BITs).[81] Most of the code's investor obligations were agreed to relatively quickly, as they were expected to be voluntary, and Western states had already signed on to similar voluntary guidelines in the OECD and the ILO. Yet, fundamental disagreement remained on whether foreign investors should be granted protections tied to international minimum standards and given recourse to international dispute settlement. The Calvo doctrine remained the priority among Latin American states, much to the frustration of Western governments and private arbitration lawyers.[82] An additional problem was a lack of expertise. As the United Kingdom had also experienced in BIT negotiations at the time, many countries sent representatives to negotiate 'having but the faintest idea of the practical issues to be tackled'.[83] Combined with the large number of countries involved, this significantly slowed down the process. Momentum dropped through the 1980s, and the initiative was overtaken by events as the rise of the Washington Consensus made the code appear as 'a relic of another era, when foreign direct investment was looked upon with considerable concern' and did not 'reflect the current investment policies of many developing countries'.[84]

As the code steadily faded away from the international agenda, UNCTC not only shifted its attention to BITs but also became more favourably inclined towards the treaties.[85] For whereas some UN delegates criticized UNCTC for being unduly sceptical of BITs in the early 1980s,[86] the message began to change towards the end of the decade. BITs were no longer presented as unbalanced legal instruments (due to the absence of investor obligations), which were unlikely to entail any real economic benefits to developing countries.[87] Instead, their 'alleged one-sidedness' was now subject to important caveats and the treaties would in some cases be a 'decisive element in attracting foreign capital to a country where it would not otherwise go'.[88] By the early 1990s, UNCTC presented BITs as

---

[81] The Code was moreover envisioned to be an umbrella treaty to cover a wide range of issue-specific UN codes of conduct negotiated at the same time, including on illicit payments, consumer protection, restrictive business practices, and the transfer of technology. This section is based on Sauvant 2015.

[82] Arbitrator William Park, for instance, urged UNCTC to include reference to ICSID arbitration in the code; letter quoted in St John 2014

[83] Chair of the working group, Sten Niklasson, quoted in Sauvant 2015.

[84] US government *demarche* from 1991 quoted in Braithwaite and Drahos 2000, p. 193.

[85] UNCTC official I ('BITs were all that was left, so this is where we focused our attention'). Delegations noted in 1983 that UNCTC had overlooked the treaties in its work on international investment rules, which prompted an annual UNCTC update on issues pertaining to international investment agreements, including BITs; UNCTC, E/C.10/1983/15, p. 15.

[86] UNCTC, E/C.10/1984/20, p. 20. [87] UNCTC, E/C.10/1984/8.

[88] UNCTC 1988, pp. 11, 75–6.

90   Promoting investment treaties

'a routine backdrop to a more positive focus on the economic environment for foreign direct investment'.[89] This change in tone was not because UNCTC staff had undertaken extensive research on the economic and political implications of the treaties or learned from such work elsewhere. On the question of FDI promotion, for instance, UNCTC backed up its claims with references to publications, which themselves presented no actual evidence.[90] Rather, the changing position was part of the Centre's broader effort to reorient itself towards Western investment policy principles.[91] And according to the head of the organization at the time, 'it became increasingly difficult for us to advise against the bilateral treaties, as we suddenly didn't have much of an alternative to offer'.[92]

That said, although some UNCTC staff members were highly in favour of the treaties,[93] the organization primarily supported BITs to conform to international trends and did not actively try to persuade developing countries into signing them, like the World Bank.[94] And when offering to produce a model BIT in the late 1980s, some members – most likely the United States – strongly opposed it so as to limit UNCTC's influence in the area.[95] The Centre was not even invited to contribute to the development of the World Bank Guidelines, but was merely kept informed on an ad hoc basis by Shihata.[96] So after having taken centre stage in discussions on international investment protection in the late 1970s and 1980s, UNCTC was slowly but securely put on the sidelines. And in the early 1990s, the United States managed to facilitate

---

[89] UNCTC 1992, p. 61. See also; UNCTC, E/C.10/1993/8, p. 21.
[90] Burkhardt 1986 (quoted in UNCTC 1992); OECD 1985, p. 24 (quoted in UNCTC 1988). Similarly, UNCTC's claim that BITs were 'very often' a pre-condition for PRI seem to have been driven by the practice of just a few states, such as Germany; UNCTC 1986, p. 23; UNCTC 1988, p. iv.
[91] Sagafi-Nejad 2008, pp. 209–11; Rothstein, 1979.   [92] UNCTC official II.
[93] Thomas Wälde, for instance, advised more than 60 developing countries while working at UNCTC until 1991 and was a very strong supporter of BITs. For his later writing, see Wälde 2000, p. 16 ('the absence of a BIT with the relevant investor home state ... will attract a higher risk rating and therefore higher borrowing costs ... Therefore, it is advisable to encourage host states to negotiate BITs with relevant home states'); Wälde 2007 (justifying BITs as part of a broader international law effort, 'to create equal rules for all, to tame the natural asymmetry of sheer power with rules and procedure' and 'to create prosperity and peace to prevent a new Hitler or Stalin from emerging'.)
[94] In 1988, for instance, the year before the Soviet Union began adopting BITs, UNCTC produced a 138-page report with analyses and recommendations, yet it hardly even mentioned BITs when noting the wide range of policy instruments available for the Soviet Union to attract foreign investments; UNCTC 1988b.
[95] UNCTC, E/C.10/1991/9, pp. 7–8; UNCTC, E/C.10/1987/16, p. 25. On Washington's long-standing resistance towards the organization; see Taylor and Smith 2007, p. 69; Sagafi-Nejad 2008, pp. 119–20.
[96] Shihata 1993, pp. 44–5.

The United Nations   91

an organizational shift within the UN system with the UN Conference on Trade and Development (UNCTAD) taking over to handle all research and capacity building activities pertaining to FDI promotion and protection.[97] This was yet another use of American power, which proved to have important implications for the international investment regime.

UNCTAD

After the Cold War UNCTAD had embraced foreign investments as a necessary part of the package to promote economic development.[98] This was partly due to a change in management and partly based on the broader realization that a neoliberal bend was the only way the organization could survive.[99] Sceptics even began referring to UNCTAD as the 'Global OECD',[100] and the organization quickly became the leading international agency dealing with FDI regulation in developing countries. Particularly, the discussions for a Multilateral Agreement on Investment (MAI) in the actual OECD made UNCTAD's services relevant.[101] For although developing countries were not part of the negotiations, several went as observers and all were eventually intended to sign up to the treaty. And whereas UNCTAD would have preferred a multilateral framework based on the 'opt-in' approach of WTO's services agreement, which included some investment disciplines, pragmatism made it engage with, rather than oppose, the MAI negotiations – much to the frustration of NGOs.[102]

But when developed countries failed to 'go it alone' by agreeing to the MAI,[103] UNCTAD shifted its focus to BITs. In line with its commitment to Western investment protection principles, UNCTAD saw the treaties as part of an 'appropriate FDI framework' for developing countries.[104] For although they did not always have much to say about FDI incentives,[105] UNCTAD staff expected that when combined with other reforms, BITs sent 'important signals concerning a country's investment climate'.[106] This message was repeated time and again during the 1990s and early 2000s, where UNCTAD became the only international organization to offer extensive capacity building services pertaining directly to

---

[97] See generally Sagafi-Nejad 2008, pp. 121–2.   [98] See e.g. UNCTAD 1992, p. iii.
[99] Taylor and Smith 2007.   [100] Finger and Ruchat 2000, 9.
[101] Wilkie 2001, pp. 137–9; Fredriksson and Zimny 2004.   [102] Hormeku 1998.
[103] On go-it-alone power in international relations, see Gruber 2000.
[104] UNCTAD 1996a, p. 61.   [105] UNCTAD 1995, p. 302.
[106] UNCTAD 1996a, p. 147; UNCTAD 1996d, p. 6. See also; UNCTAD 1997c, p. xxi (BITs could contribute to successful FDI 'performance'); UNCTAD 1998a, p. 2 (together with other reforms, BITs partly responsible for 'the strong growth of FDI').

92   Promoting investment treaties

BITs.[107] For its part, FIAS was happy to leave specific advice on BITs to UNCTAD, as the UN position on the treaties had largely converged with that of the World Bank.[108] As an African negotiator notes:

> UNCTAD did create the feeling that by signing these investment treaties we could make the exporters of investments comfortable and they would increase their export of investments to the host countries ... The reasoning was that Africa was perceived as high-risk area and you need to have something that would make those people who have the capital to export investment to your country. That came up quite a lot.[109]

Even more than the World Bank, UNCTAD itself actively facilitated the signing of BITs. While not itself participating in negotiations, UNCTAD promoted the process by bearing the costs of travel, full board, and lodging for developing country officials as well as organizing the necessary facilities and substantive support.[110] The process began in 1999, when UNCTAD organized a negotiation round after G-15 governments had encouraged UNCTAD to help them conclude BITs to 'further promote economic cooperation and FDI'.[111] The round was sponsored by the Swiss government and the United Nations Development Programme (UNDP) and held at the four-star Hotel Victoria on the shores of Lake Geneva. In advance, UNCTAD had received feedback from participating countries to prepare a 'negotiation matrix' (Table 4.3) to make the process as smooth as possible.[112] The end result of the session was three fully finalized BITs (India-Zimbabwe, Sri Lanka-Zimbabwe, and Egypt-Jamaica), two consolidated texts with agreement on all key issues (Indonesia-Jamaica, Jamaica-Zimbabwe), and three consolidated texts with agreement on most provisions (India-Jamaica, Jamaica-Malaysia, and Jamaica-Sri Lanka). As noted by UNCTAD in the closing statement of the sessions, 'taking the already existing BITs into account, each of the seven participating countries will have a BIT with every other participating country if all BITs completed at the meeting enter into force – the maximum that could be achieved by this initiative'.[113] In the words of the Secretary General of UNCTAD, the

---

[107] See e.g. UNCTAD's encouragement of BIT adoption in reports to: Ecuador (UNCTAD 2001a, pp. 57, 92); Ghana (UNCTAD 2003a, p. 28); Nepal (UNCTAD 2003c, p. 31); Lesotho (UNCTAD 2003b, p. 23); Kenya (2005b, p. 58); Rwanda (UNCTAD 2006e, p. 34); Nigeria (UNCTAD 2006d, p. 27); Colombia (UNCTAD 2006c, p. 22); Botswana (UNCTAD 2006b, p. 29); Zambia (UNCTAD 2007b, p. 62); and Sierra Leone (UCTAD 2010a, p. 25).
[108] Interviews with current and former FIAS officials.   [109] Kenya official I.
[110] Karsegard, Bravo, and Blom 2006.
[111] Joint Communique, VII summit of the heads of state and government of the group of 15, Kuala Lumpur, Malaysia, 5 November 1997.
[112] Zimbabwe official I.   [113] UNCTAD 1999e.

Table 4.3 *UNCTAD's negotiation matrix for G-15 countries*

	Jamaica	Zimbabwe	India	Egypt	Indonesia	Malaysia	Sri Lanka
Day 1							
Morning	Egypt	India	Zimbabwe	Jamaica	–	–	–
Afternoon	Malaysia	India	Zimbabwe	–	–	Jamaica	–
Day 2							
Morning	Egypt Malaysia	Sri Lanka	–	Jamaica	.	Jamaica	Zimbabwe
Afternoon	Indonesia	Sri Lanka India	Zimbabwe	–	Jamaica	.	Zimbabwe
Day 3							
Morning	Malaysia Indonesia	India	Zimbabwe	–	Jamaica	Jamaica	–
Afternoon	Sri Lanka	Sri Lanka	–	–	–	–	Jamaica Zimbabwe
Day 4							
Morning	India	Egypt	Jamaica	Zimbabwe	–	–	–
Afternoon	India	–	Jamaica	–	–	–	–
Day 5							
Morning	Zimbabwe	Jamaica	–	–	–	–	–
Afternoon	Malaysia Indonesia	Egypt	–	Zimbabwe	Jamaica	Jamaica	–
Day 6							
Morning	India	–	Jamaica	–	–	–	–
Afternoon	Zimbabwe	Jamaica	–	–	–	–	–
Day 7							
Morning	Finalize	Finalize	Finalize	Finalize	Finalize	Finalize	Finalize
Afternoon	Sign	Sign	Sign	Sign	Sign	Sign	Sign

94   Promoting investment treaties

initiative was an example of 'how UNCTAD provides concrete practical assistance to developing countries in an area of great importance to their development efforts'.[114]

But when announcing this to the world UNCTAD had to confront the (undoubtedly uncomfortable) fact that the organization had just made the first publicly available econometric attempt to estimate the investment impact of BITs – and found none.[115] The implications of the analysis were played down,[116] however, and UNCTAD stressed that by 'signing BITs between themselves, developing countries are sending a strong signal of their commitment to provide a predictable, stable and reliable legal environment for foreign direct investors, to stimulate investors´ confidence, and boost FDI flows'.[117] This understanding was shared by participating governments as well. The representative from Jamaica, for instance, noted of the initiative that the 'conclusion of BITs will facilitate FDI between member countries of the G-15, in the mutual interest of promoting our development'.[118]

After the success in Geneva, nine further events between June 2000 and July 2005 led to an additional 160 BITs signed between 60 developed and developing countries – almost one fourth of all BITs signed between 2000 and 2005. Several governments noted that many of the treaties would not have been signed without UNCTAD's assistance (see Table 4.4).[119] 'In our two weeks here we managed to finalize five agreements', said the head of the Philippine delegation during the 'Sapporo round' for instance, 'which is far more than we could otherwise have done in two years'.[120] Not only UNCTAD, but also its external evaluators highlighted these sessions as a great success at the time due to the economies of scale involved in having BIT negotiations centralized leading to considerable cost-savings for the countries involved.[121]

Apart from facilitating a large number of BITs, the UNCTAD sessions also sent a clear signal from the leading international organization involved in advising developing countries on investment treaties: while BITs may not have been optimal, they were 'good enough' and could be negotiated easily and quickly by relying on standardized OECD

---

[114] Ibid.   [115] UNCTAD 1998b, ch. 4.

[116] UNCTAD 1999d ('BITs are nevertheless increasingly regarded by foreign investors as an expected component of a country´s investment environment. In many cases, they have become a sine qua non for the availability of political-risk insurance ... all other conditions being equal, the presence of a BIT can help tilt the balance in investors' locational decisions.')

[117] UNCTAD 1999c. See also UNCTAD 1999d.   [118] UNCTAD 1999d.

[119] Karsegard, Bravo and Blom 2006, pp. 4, 14.   [120] Quoted in UNCTAD 2000e.

[121] UNCTAD 2002b, p. 9; Karsegard, Bravo, and Blom 2006, p. 14.

The United Nations 95

Table 4.4 *UNCTAD's BIT facilitation rounds and signing ceremonies*

Date	Activity	Place	Participating countries
8–14 Jan. 1999	Facilitation round for G-15	Glion, Switzerland	Egypt, Indonesia, India, Jamaica, Malaysia, Sri Lanka, Zimbabwe
19–30 Jun. 2000	Facilitation round	Sapporo, Japan	Cambodia, Colombia, Croatia, Egypt, Ghana, India, Indonesia, Iran, Lao, Myanmar, Peru, Philippines
15–19 Jan. 2001	Facilitation round for Kyrgyzstan	Geneva, Switzerland	Austria, Denmark, Kyrgyzstan, Latvia, Sweden
24 Jan. – 3 Feb. 2001	Facilitation round for Francophone LDCs	Geneva, Switzerland	Belgium, Benin, Burkina Faso, Burundi, Cameroon, Chad, Comoros, Egypt, Ghana, Guinea, Libya, Madagascar, Mali, Mauritania, Mauritius, South Africa, Switzerland, Zambia
29–28 Feb. 2001	Facilitation round for India	New Delhi, India	China, Croatia, Ethiopia, India, Yemen
19–28 Apr. 2001	Facilitation round for Croatia	Dubrovnik, Croatia	Belarus, Croatia, Latvia, Malta, Moldova, Pakistan
18 May 2001	Signing ceremony	Brussels, Belgium	Belgium, Benin, Burkina Faso, Burundi, Cambodia, Cameroon, Chad, Comoros, Croatia, Ghana, Guinea, Mali, Mauritania, Mauritius
1–6 Oct. 2001	Facilitation round for LDCs	Bonn, Germany	Belgium, Cambodia, Eritrea, France, Malawi, Mozambique, Netherlands, Sudan, Sweden, Uganda, Zambia
4–13 Nov. 2002	Facilitation round for LDCs	Geneva, Switzerland	Belgium, Benin, Burkina Faso, Burundi, Cambodia, Cameroon, Canada, Chad, Egypt, France, Gabon, Guinea, Guinea-Bissau, Korea, Lebanon, Mali, Mauritania, Netherlands, Senegal, Togo
30 Jun. – 4 Jul. 2003	Facilitation round for LDCs	Geneva, Switzerland	Barbados, Belgium, Botswana, China, Egypt, Ethiopia, Finland, France, Ghana, Italy, Kenya, Lesotho, Malawi, Mauritius, Switzerland, Tanzania, Uganda, Zimbabwe
2–6 Feb. 2004	Facilitation round for Francophone LDCs	Brussels, Belgium	N/A
15 Jun. 2004	Signing ceremony	Sao Paulo, Brazil	Benin, Chad, Guinea, Lebanon, Mauritania, Switzerland

96   Promoting investment treaties

templates. As one participant recalls: 'The OECD model was actively promoted during this session, and no real negotiations actually took place. Treaties were just signed off in a rush in two or three hours'.[122]

Not surprisingly, developed countries were pleased with UNCTAD's efforts. In a 2005 external evaluation report, two thirds of developed country negotiators noted that because of UNCTAD's work over the years, they had witnessed 'a positive change in their developing country negotiation partners' ability to engage in discussions and/or negotiations of IIAs over time'.[123] Here, they were not only referring to greater quality of decision-making, as a result of UNCTAD's technical assistance programmes, but also a more positive attitude towards the treaties. For up until recently, UNCTAD kept spreading the message: 'sign BITs to get FDI'.

As the number of investment treaty arbitrations increased, UNCTAD shifted its focus to assisting developing countries with managing and preventing disputes. To compensate for staff constraints, Western private arbitration lawyers were brought in. As we saw above, this was not the first time private lawyers got involved in advising developing countries on investment treaties. But the rise of investment treaty arbitration prompted the arbitration community to get increasingly involved in advising developing countries on their investment treaty policies. And the most common denominator was that most major firms and arbitration chambers sent lawyers to act as experts in UNCTAD's technical assistance programmes (Table 4.5). Some even wrote UNCTAD's training modules for developing countries.[124]

Apart from their experience in private practice, several of the lawyers had the added advantage of having advised on or negotiated investment treaties before joining the arbitration community.[125] Yet, it is nevertheless notable that part of UNCTAD's technical assistance strategy was to give Western investment lawyers yet another stage to be co-architects of an international legal order providing the market for their own legal services.[126] And given the often-repeated message from arbitration lawyers that investment treaties are necessary to attract investment,[127]

---

[122] South African official VIII.   [123] Karsegard, Bravo, and Blom 2006.
[124] See e.g. UNCTAD 2003e (prepared by Christoph Schreuer).
[125] For an NGO critique of 'swing-door' problems in the international investment regime, see Eberhardt and Olivet 2012.
[126] For a parallel development in the field of international commercial arbitration, see Dezalay and Garth, 1996; Hale forthcoming.
[127] See e.g. Dolzer 2005, pp. 953–4; Juillard 2001, p. 6; Paulsson 2005, p. 240; Paulsson 2010, p. 347; Price 2009; Weiler 2002, p. 435; comments by Orrego-Vicuna and Gaillard in Ross 2010.

The United Nations

Table 4.5 *Private lawyers as government advisers*

Firm/Chambers	Examples of policy advice to developing countries	Lawyers with background in government or IO as investment treaty adviser or negotiator (n)
20 Essex Street	AILA; member of advisory committee of Chile's Ministry of Foreign Affairs	US, Canada, Chile
Allen & Overy	UNCTAD; AILA; Allen & Overy course to Rwanda on investment arbitration; advised states in Europe, Central Asia, and Middle East on negotiation and drafting investment treaties	
Arnold & Porter	UNCTAD; advised 15 CARICOM countries on investment chapter for external PTAs	US, Colombia (n), Costa Rica, ICSID
Baker Botts	UNCTAD and AILA; advised Caribbean government on its arbitration law	ICSID
Clifford Chance	UNCTAD; IISD; AILA	Argentina
Crow. & Moring	UNCTAD; one co-director of ILI's International Investment Law Centre	US (n), Canada
Curtis	UNCTAD; one co-director of ILI's International Investment Law Centre	ICSID
DAP LLC	UNCTAD; advised Colombia on implementation of BIT obligations, Chile on its model BIT, and Morocco on investment provisions in US PTA	US (n)
Dechert	UNCTAD; ILI	Ecuador, ICSID
Essex Court	AILA; BHR; advised Pakistan and Mauritius on their arbitration laws; advised arbitration office of Thai Ministry of Justice; UNCITRAL delegate of Mauritius	US, UK (n)
Foley Hoag	UNCTAD; advised South Africa on its arbitration law	US (n), Canada (n), Ecuador, Argentina, Ukraine (n), Inter-American Development Bank, UNCTAD
Freshfields	AILA; advised Mexico on negotiation of NAFTA Chapter Eleven and South Africa on its arbitration law; UNCITRAL delegate of Bahrain	US

98   Promoting investment treaties

Table 4.5 (*cont.*)

Firm/Chambers	Examples of policy advice to developing countries	Lawyers with background in government or IO as investment treaty adviser or negotiator (n)
Hogan Lovells	UNCTAD; AILA	Austria
King & Spalding	UNCTAD	ICSID, Mexico (n)
Lalive	UNCTAD; UNITAR	
Matrix	UNCTAD; AILA; advised 'numerous Latin American governments' on their model BITs	Mexico (n)
McNair	UNCTAD	Germany
Salans	UNCTAD and AILA	US
Sidley Austin	UNCTAD; IISD; CEELI; ILI; advised several countries on investment treaty arbitration clauses	US (n), Bulgaria (n)
Shea & Sterling	UNCTAD; ILI; AILA	US (n)
Steptoe	Advised several countries, incl. one in Asia, on BIT and PTA investment chapter negotiations	
Weil	UNCTAD; advised on NAFTA arbitration provisions (unclear for which party)	US (n)
White & Case	UNCTAD; ILI; AILA	US (n), Germany (n)

Note: Apart from UNCTAD, list includes technical assistance for International Law Institute (ILI), African International Legal Awareness (AILA), International Institute for Sustainable Development (IISD), United Nations Institute for Training and Research (UNITAR), and CEELI. Countries identified when possible.
Sources: Arbitrator online profiles, ili.org, and aila.org.uk, all accessed in January 2013. UNCTAD technical assistance agendas for 2006–2012 were provided by UNCTAD secretariat. Note that many lawyers refrain from making their advisory work public.

the informal alliance between UNCTAD and the arbitration community can only have strengthened the message that for all their costs BITs were a useful part of developing countries' regulatory framework.

In short, through its global reach and proclaimed 'development-friendly' profile, UNCTAD was sine qua non in spreading support for BITs towards the latter half of the 1990s and early 2000s. It endorsed the causal belief that the treaties could promote investment, even among developing countries themselves, and UNCTAD's signing sessions indicated that BITs were instruments that could reasonably be signed off in a short span of time with few, if any, deviations from pre-existing OECD templates.[128]

Rule takers

Although it may be surprising that UNCTAD was such an ardent promoter of investment treaties, there is of course nothing puzzling about Western actors and organizations promoting BITs in the developing world. Turning now to the 'demand side', however, patterns begin to emerge that are difficult to account for with standard models of investment treaty adoption, where governments are expected to have negotiated BITs based on sophisticated cost–benefit analyses. In fact, UNCTAD's signing sessions have already indicated that as late as the early 2000s, a large number of governments seemed satisfied with quickly signing off on European BIT templates, even though a number of investment treaty claims had already indicated just how potent investment treaties could be (see Chapter 6). And this section will provide a first set of illustrations to show that the UNCTAD experience is not just important in itself but also an indication of the carelessness with which many developing countries consented to investment treaty arbitration up through the 1990s. It will describe three cases in which the World Bank, American advisers, and UNCTAD eased the way for investment treaties, but where developing country officials considered and negotiated the treaties based on what can only be described as a highly bounded rational process. We begin in Ghana.

The role of the World Bank: the case of Ghana

After Ghana's independence from the United Kingdom in 1957, President Nkrumah, one of the founders of the non-aligned movement, pursued socialist economic reforms. Yet, he listened to his economic advisers who saw foreign investment as instrumental for the country's industrialisation and invited legal experts from the UK, Ireland, and the United States to help with his legislative reforms, including Ghana's new business law.[129] Ghana was one of the first states to join ICSID in 1965, signed a BIT with Germany in 1967, and installed a favourable regulatory environment for the protection of foreign investment.[130] But after

---

[128] It should be mentioned that in very recent years UNCTAD has been more critical of BITs and tried to keep private arbitration lawyers at arm's-length in its activities – partly as a result of changes in staff; UNCTAD official II. See e.g. UNCTAD 2013c.

[129] See Decker 2012; Nkrumah 1964; Ofusu-Amaah 2002, pp. 554–7.

[130] Germany, for instance, kept issuing investment guarantees to Ghana even though the German BIT was never ratified; PA, AA, Zwischenarchiv, 121319. The UK also considered Ghana a likely candidate for a BIT; FCO 59/632.

General Acheampong assumed power in January 1972, he began to expropriate Western capital in extractive industries and repudiated Ghana's external debts. In response, all Western states except Canada withheld their foreign aid until reaching a satisfactory settlement in 1974.[131] Acheampong excelled in economic mismanagement so when Ghana was returned to civilian rule in the early 1980s the country was edging towards bankruptcy. This prompted the World Bank to make Ghana a test case for its new approach to economic crises – structural adjustment – and the Bank's staff became deeply involved in the day-to-day management of Ghana's economy.[132]

One aim of the adjustment package was for Ghana to attract foreign investment, and the involvement of the World Bank prompted a series of reforms gradually liberalizing Ghana's investment regime.[133] In 1985 this included an amended investment code, which guaranteed foreign investors' repatriation of their profits and other transfers as well as compensation for expropriation. The code was implemented in 1989 with the assistance of FIAS. So when the United Kingdom approached its former colony the same year to enter into an investment treaty, this seemed a useful tool to underpin that process. The agreement was quickly negotiated based on the British template and when it was signed the same year, Ghana's Secretary of Foreign Affairs noted that it would reinforce Ghana's 'program to attract private investment as a major catalyst in the economic recovery by creating the necessary investment climate'.[134] The treaty would 'enhance the effectiveness' of the incentives provided in Ghana's investment code in relation to British investors and he hoped 'the agreement would attract more British investments into the country'.[135]

A legal officer in Ghana's investment promotion agency 'realized this was a huge opportunity that we should latch on to'[136] and on that basis suggested Ghana should initiate an investment treaty program. This initiative was in line with the institutional reforms promoted by FIAS within the investment promotion agency, where its staff was encouraged by FIAS to move away from merely vetting investment projects to also play an active role in promoting investment policy reforms.[137] The initiation of the BIT programme was not, however, based on any extensive

---

[131] FCO 59/1685; FCO 59/1198; FCO 59/1199; Decker 2012, p. 8. Interestingly, both Ghana and the British government tried to convince British firms to settle the claims via ICSID, but the firms refused as their contracts had been 'obtained through unorthodox means'; FCO 59/1203.
[132] Decker 2012.   [133] Aryeetey, Harrigan, and Nissanke 2000.
[134] Quoted in *Daily Report: Sub-Saharan Africa*, FBIS-AFR-89–056, 24 March 1989.
[135] Ibid.   [136] Ghana official I.
[137] World Bank Operations Evaluations Department 1998, p. 48.

analyses of the treaties' potential costs and benefits. Anything akin to an economic impact analysis was never contemplated and no surveys of investors were made by FIAS or Ghanaian officials, however small. 'We didn't really study this in any way'.[138] Rather, the new treaty introduced by the British was seen as an easy, and simple, instrument to attract investment, and after the approval of the attorney general four more treaties were signed that year. Investment started flowing to Ghana after 1989 and although the official in charge did not attribute this trend entirely to the treaties it was generally accepted that they played an important role.[139] Yet, this was based solely on a hunch rather than on any analytical inputs.

FIAS and MIGA kept their involvement with Ghana – MIGA's first investment promotion conference was held there for instance – and helped revise the investment law in 1994, which included protections closely following those in BITs. Yet, Ghanaian officials never asked for assistance with analyzing the economic implications of its growing stock of treaties. As late as 2000, when Ghana signed BITs with India, Indonesia, and the Philippines at an UNCTAD's signing ceremony, it was justified by the Ghanaian negotiator as 'paving the way for increased FDI flows, particularly between developing countries'.[140] The treaties were seen as 'major instruments of investment promotion in addition to investment codes'[141] and were therefore useful for Ghana to 'vary her sources of investment capital ... and attracting investments from countries from the Far East'.[142] But instead of even rudimentary empirical assessments, these expectations were based on a predisposition: Ghanaian officials *wanted* to believe the treaties worked and never asked the World Bank or others to produce evidence that BITs played a role in foreign investors' establishment decisions.

The content of the treaties was not carefully analyzed either, but merely followed whatever was proposed by the other negotiating partner.[143] There were no attempts to create an optimal treaty design, as European templates seemed 'good enough'. The choice of treaty partners was also left largely to chance. Apart from proposing the treaties whenever the Investment Promotion Agency went on foreign visits, diplomats also promoted the treaties when possible.[144] 'In the 1990s, when ambassadors were appointed, they were informed about all sorts of

---

[138] Ghana official I.   [139] Ibid.
[140] Quoted in 'Ghana signs three investment agreements,' *The Dispatch*, 15 July 2000.
[141] 'Ghana: riding the investment storm,' *Accra Mail*, 17 July 2000. See again Chapter 6.
[142] Quoted in 'Ghana: riding the investment storm,' *Accra Mail*, 17 July 2000.
[143] Ghana official I.   [144] Ibid.

102   Promoting investment treaties

agreements they should keep in mind, including double-taxation agreements and BITs ... Ambassadors used this information and saw the treaties as an indicator of their performance'.[145] This resulted in a number of 'strange' treaties, such as those with Romania (1989), Bulgaria (1989), Cuba (1999), and Serbia (2000). No one in Ghana objected to such a haphazard policy, as the treaties were seen as instrumental to attract investment.

Finally, a very large share of Ghana's BITs was never ratified. But again, this was not because of standard political economy reasons – with governments making a sophisticated decision not to make their commitments binding due to domestic opposition.[146] Rather, it was because the Parliament didn't find BITs important enough to warrant attention, much to the frustration of negotiators who expected the treaties to be important investment promotion instruments.[147] It was not until Ghana itself became subject to disputes in the early 2000s – after more than 20 BITs had been signed – that it became clear to policy-makers in Ghana 'that we have to be careful and proper in our approach ... [because] there are implications of these treaties.'[148] Before then, the assumption had been that the treaties entailed only economic benefits with no associated costs.

Ghana was far from the only country pursuing investment treaties in this way. Let's turn now to Eastern Europe, where American advisers took a key role in shaping investment regimes after the end of the Cold War.

The role of American advisers: the case of the Czech Republic

The Czech Republic is a good illustration. Czechoslovakia didn't permit FDI up until 1986 and only seriously liberalized its investment regime in the early 1990s, when a team of senior officials was asked to come up with a plan for a transition of the Czechoslovakian economy. After having outmanoeuvred sceptics who wanted to prevent red-carpet treatment for foreign investors, Vaclav Klaus – then minister of finance and later president of the Czech Republic – installed fast-track liberalization. The sale of Czech enterprises to foreign investors was handled by technical advisers from USAID. They brought in investment bankers from Wall Street, who formed a deregulation team – referring to themselves as Crimson Capital Corporation – and the Ministry of Privatization was itself outsourced mostly to young American staff.[149] As noted by the *New York Times*, this 'Wall Street Brigade' was so influential

---

[145] Ibid.   [146] See e.g. Haftel and Thompson 2013.   [147] Ghana official I.
[148] Ibid.   [149] Meaney 1995.

Rule takers   103

that 'nowhere else have Americans managed to reach a position of such decisive influence in the conversion of an economy.'[150] USAID rewarded Czechoslovakia for its ambitious liberalization program by providing the government with half of all USAID funds for the region.[151]

Part of this rush towards neoliberalism involved a new Commercial Code in 1991. Drafted in cooperation with FIAS, it was based on Western company law and granted foreign investors protections against expropriation. The law was coupled with international legal protections as Czechoslovakia joined ICSID in 1992 and the Ministry of Finance began signing BITs. The first had been entered into with Belgium and Luxembourg in 1989, after Czechoslovakia had begun slowly liberalizing its investment regime, and was celebrated by the Czechoslovak minister of finance as an agreement creating 'favorable economic and political conditions for the development of mutually advantageous forms of cooperation'.[152] But the real take-off in the investment treaty programme started in the summer of 1990, after which nine BITs were signed in just six months. Eight agreements were signed the year after, and after the Czech and Slovak republics split into two states in 1993 both countries continued unabatedly. In the case of the Czech Republic, at least, the perception was that BITs were necessary because 'investors want guarantees for long-term investments that they will not be expropriated ... They were necessary for the Czech Republic to attract investments'.[153] As noted by Fecák, '[BITs] with capital exporting countries appeared to be an ideal tool to instantly raise the credit of the local environment in the eyes of foreign investors'.[154] So to complement the reforms pushed through by the Wall Street Brigade the Czech Republic had developed one of the largest networks of BITs in the world by the end of the decade – 45 in total.

But again, no economic impact analyses or investor surveys were conducted or even requested by any agency in the Czech Republic. 'There were no studies about those developments, but it was the prevailing idea that those agreements were instrumental and necessary for the Czech economy at the time.'[155] The belief that the treaties 'worked' was based on wishful thinking.

With respect to the content of the treaties the 1993 BIT with Hungary was used as a de facto model. It entirely mirrored the short and vague European templates. But if other parties wanted differently worded

---

[150] 'Czechoslovakia's Wall Street brigade', *New York Times*, 12 June 1992.   [151] Ibid.
[152] *Daily Report. East Europe*, FBIS-EEU-89-082, 1 May 1989; Fecák 2011.
[153] Czech official I.   [154] Fecák 2011, p. 235.   [155] Czech official I.

104   Promoting investment treaties

provisions, Czech officials agreed and thereby led the content of their BITs be determined 'almost fully by the other Contracting Party'.[156] In 1991, however, Czechoslovakia had signed a BIT with the United States that stood out.[157] President Bush noted to Vaclav Havel when visiting Washington DC at the time that the treaty would help assure 'an attractive investment climate for American firms that do business in your country'.[158] And for Vaclav Klaus, the treaty fitted perfectly with his dual agenda of liberalization and Western integration. He signed it on behalf of Czechoslovakia and by doing so, obliged Czechoslovakia to grant American investors national treatment both pre- and post-establishment, except for real estate ownership and insurance.[159] Performance requirements were also disallowed again following the US model (as well as the Foreign Investment Guidelines being finalized within the World Bank). These two elements of the US BIT stood out compared to traditional European models. Accordingly, if the Czech Republic wanted to engage in a competitive race to attract more capital, this was one area where the government could have tried to 'upgrade' its treaty content compared to standard BITs. Yet at no point after its independence in 1993 did the Czech Republic move towards the more encompassing US model. When signing BITs with EU members this was partly for legal reasons, as market access was within the 'competence' of the European Community, but even when adopting treaties with countries outside of Europe, Czech officials continued to sign agreements 'crafted in line with European Community norms' – as noted by the Czech minister of finance.[160] Not even in cases where the other party had also entered into BITs with the United States were liberalization obligations included.[161] Instead of pursuing ever more investor-friendly BITs, as expected in optimizing frameworks, the content of Czech BITs remained more or less the same throughout – anchoring to the simple, yet less 'competitive', BIT models of European states. As we shall see in the next chapter, the Czechs were not alone in this regard.

[156] Ibid; Fecák 2011, p. 240.
[157] 'Vaclav Havel, 'Getting down to business: at the White House dinner, Czechoslovak's labor of love,' *Washington Post*, 23 October 1991.
[158] 'White House arrival ceremony by President Bush for President Vaclav Havel of Czechoslovakia,' Federal News Service, 22 October 1991. See also 'White House readout on the visit of Czechoslovakian Vaclav Havel to the United States briefer,' Federal News Service, 22 October 1991.
[159] US-Czechoslovakia BIT, 1991, annex.
[160] Daily Report. East Europe, FBIS-EEU-93–010, 15 January 1993.
[161] Belarus (1996), Egypt (1993), Tunisia (1997), Mongolia (1998), El Salvador (1999), Mongolia (1998), Panama (1999), and Nicaragua (2002).

Rule takers

The preference for easy negotiations was amplified by the fact that Czech policy-makers didn't take the treaty obligations particularly seriously. Although there was an expectation that they would increase foreign investment, BITs were seen as more or less risk-free instruments. Fecák notes:

The extremely short time period needed for the conclusion and ratification of these agreements indicates how much attention was probably paid by Czechoslovak officials, at that time having only a small amount of experience with treaties of this kind, to their content and possible impacts.[162]

The memorandum to the Assembly for the approval of BITs with Denmark, Netherlands, Norway, and Greece, for instance, contained only the following:

The first article stressed the necessity of inflow of foreign capital and assumed that concluding the presented BITs may stimulate inward investments into Czechoslovakia. The second article briefly described (in 12 sentences) the content of all 4 treaties. The dispute settlement mechanism was not mentioned at all. The third article concluded that the treaties did not require changes to the legal order, that they were [in] compliance with other international obligations and would have no budgetary implications. The whole explanatory memorandum is barely one and half pages long.[163]

As Czech negotiators did not have 'any relevant knowledge of investment treaty protections',[164] stakeholders did not 'have a clear idea of what they were approving' either.[165] Czech officials didn't just fail to appreciate the finer nuances of different provisions, however, they entirely ignored the scope and potency of the protections enshrined in the treaties. 'Negotiators really didn't know that the treaties had any bite in practice', a senior official involved notes.[166] 'They were neither aware of the costs or the fact that it could lead to arbitration.' And as the attitude was similar in many other countries, negotiations were easy during the 1990s. The Czech Republic signed a BIT with Croatia in 1996, for instance, and because Croatia had not been subject to any disputes at this point either negotiators there also 'didn't think they [BITs] were that important'.[167]

It was not until the Czech Republic was subject to its first set of BIT claims, described further in Chapter 6, that officials began to appreciate the 'potential implications'.[168] Just as had been the case for Pakistan, the claims led to a rethink of the Czech investment treaty programme. Apart

---

[162] Fecák 2011, p. 235. [163] Fecák 2011, p. 236. [164] Veselá 2009.
[165] Fecák 2011, p. 237. [166] Czech official I. [167] Croatian official I.
[168] Czech official I.

106   Promoting investment treaties

from slowing down their rush to sign BITs, Czech officials became more careful with the ones they adopted. The cases illustrated, for instance, the risks of 'treaty-shopping' due to broad definitions of investors, which meant Czech officials began requiring a more substantial link between the investor and a state in order for it to be considered an investor of that party.[169] Similarly, one reason Prague initiated a renegotiation of its BIT with the United States – something Washington resisted – was the perception that it fuelled 'speculative foreign investments and indirect investments made with the sole goal of later launching legal proceedings'.[170] Yet, the important point here is that not only did Czech policymakers fail to make even simple assessments of the economic implications of their treaties, it had to take 13 years before they began to take BIT obligations seriously – despite numerous other claims having already been filed against other states.

The role of UNCTAD: the case of Zimbabwe

Finally, I turn to the role of UNCTAD in spreading support for, and facilitating, investment treaties. Here, Zimbabwe is a particularly illustrative case. After having discouraged foreign investment since Zimbabwe's independence in 1980, the Mugabe government announced a new investment code in 1989 to attract foreign investors.[171] While attacked by Mugabe's fellow-Marxists as Zimbabwe's 'Satanic Verses',[172] the economy was collapsing and Mugabe began travelling abroad to encourage Western investment to his country.[173] Zimbabwe also joined MIGA in 1989, and the year after Zimbabwe signed its first BIT. Rather than an instrument of investment promotion, however, the first BIT was signed at the behest of Zimbabwean investors wanting to invest in Mozambique. The civil war in Mozambique in the late 1980s made them concerned about political risks and when discussing this with their government, an official from Zimbabwe recalled an UNCTAD report sent to his office and suggested that the treaties described in there might be a useful tool.[174] His suggestion was approved and a treaty was signed between the two countries which, according to the Zimbabwean finance minister, 'would facilitate cross-border investment and the

---

[169] Compare e.g. the Czech BITs with Jordan (2009) and Bulgaria (1999), and the Croatian BITs with Azerbaijan (2007) and Hungary (1996).
[170] Shabu 2011.   [171] For details on the code, see Dashwood 2000.
[172] 'Zimbabwe shifts investment rule', *New York Times*, 15 May 1989.
[173] See e.g. 'White House readout on the visit of President Robert Mugabe of Zimbabwe', Federal News Service, 24 July 1991.
[174] Zimbabwe official I.

Rule takers

107

formation of joint-venture partnerships'.[175] Subsequently, a policy decision was made in Zimbabwe that the treaties would be important to not just protect their own investments (as in Mozambique), but also attract investments from abroad. Zimbabwe thereby began to follow the calls of European states, which in the 1984 and 1990 Lomé agreements with the Caribbean and African states had included provisions calling for member states to enter into BITs.[176]

This was a policy reversal for Zimbabwe. Mugabe had previously refused to sign up to an OPIC agreement with the United States, for instance, arguing it was unnecessary to add any further protections against expropriation than what was provided in Zimbabwe's Constitution.[177] By the 1990s, the attitude changed. To underpin Zimbabwe's continuing investment liberalization, which was partly assisted by FIAS,[178] Zimbabwe joined ICSID in 1991 and government officials became keen to start a BIT programme. In his 1990 opening address to the Zimbabwean parliament, Mugabe noted that:

> The Government has now stepped up its efforts to increase investment, especially in the productive sectors. In addition to the protection of investment embedded in our Constitution, the Government will enter into multilateral and bilateral investment agreements with those countries whose nationals are willing to invest in Zimbabwe. These agreements should go a long way towards attracting investment into Zimbabwe.[179]

This set in motion a flurry of BIT signing activity up through the 1990s. 'We were negotiating treaties to promote investment', according to the architect of the BIT programme, 'we wanted to be the most competitive investment destination'.[180]

---

[175] 'Zimbabwe and Mozambique sign economic agreement', *Reuters*, 12 September 1990.

[176] The European Commission was keen on including comprehensive investment rules into association agreements with African, Caribbean, and Pacific (ACP) states. But Lomé II (1981) almost collapsed when the suggestion was made and the UK along with Germany and France eventually feared community-wide investment treaties would erode protections they had achieved bilaterally. Instead, London suggested a unique MFN principle in Lomé III (1984): once an ACP state had entered into a BIT with an EC member, it would be *obliged* to enter into similar BITs with other EC members with similar protections. This was, not surprisingly, rejected as infringing on partner countries' sovereign right to negotiate treaties, and investment protection provisions in Lomé III and IV therefore largely followed the hortatory character of Lomé II, where the parties were primarily encouraged to enter into BITs. This was also the case in other EC cooperation agreements, such as the 1980 agreements with ASEAN and Yugoslavia. See Denza and Brooks 1987; Voss 1981.

[177] Cokorinos and Mittelman 1988.   [178] Weigel, Gregory, and Wagle 1997.

[179] Quoted in 'Sub-Saharan Africa', *Daily Report*, FBIS-AFR-90–125, 28 June 1990.

[180] Zimbabwe official I.

108   Promoting investment treaties

But the process differed markedly from expectations based on rational competition dynamics, where Zimbabwean policy-makers are assumed to have made an informed and sophisticated choice when signing treaties, which in recent years have exposed Zimbabwe to expensive compensation claims. First of all, no analyses were ever made to determine whether UNCTAD had actually been right when saying the treaties were important tools to promote investment flows. 'We didn't make these sort of economic impact analyses or surveys. We haven't done that, though probably we should.'[181] Not only did the Zimbabwean government accept UNCTAD's message without question:

[A]ctually we didn't do anything at all. Occasionally, we would make a country profile to see the potential benefits of the partner – is it technological transfer, is it expansion of existing investments, and so forth – but that was the only sort of economic analysis we would engage in.[182]

Once Zimbabwe had decided to roll out the red carpet for foreign investors and UNCTAD had introduced investment treaties as a salient, easy, and useful tool in that process, the treaties were adopted with hardly any analysis of their functional utility.

On that basis, there was no need to engage carefully in long and hard negotiations. Apart from transfer provisions, where Zimbabwe drafted an exception – again based on inspiration from UNCTAD publications – the government generally signed off on model treaties of European states.[183] Although the pace of the negotiations were constrained by the lack of government resources – to the frustration of Bonn, for instance, as German investors needed their investment guarantees[184] – Zimbabwe was an easy negotiating partner. And although UNCTAD publications were used to inform officials about the availability of different clauses, at no point did Zimbabwe try to strategically 'strengthen' the content of its BITs so as to appear more investor-friendly than its competitor countries.[185] Zimbabwe never engaged in a continuous search for ever-more perfect investment treaties. Instead, it anchored to the short – but easy – 'default' models crafted by European states.

Finally, it is notable that despite the engagement with UNCTAD reports, Zimbabwe failed to learn about the risks of the treaties and different treaty provisions from the rise of investment treaty arbitration. As noted by a leading official involved:

---

[181] Ibid.   [182] Ibid.   [183] Ibid.
[184] 'Sub-Saharan Africa', *Daily Report*, FBIS-AFR-92–218, 11 November 1992.
[185] Zimbabwe official I.

Conclusion 109

I must be honest, that we didn't follow the disputes during the 1990s. We only started getting interested when we were taken to court – when we found ourselves on the receiving end so to speak … We were negotiating treaties to promote investment without paying much attention to the cases and not necessarily knowing the implications.[186]

Conclusion

After the end of the Cold War, advisers from international organizations and OECD countries promoted investment treaties as simple, standardized, and off-the-shelf solutions which could be effective to attract investment in conjunction with domestic investment reforms. Although advisers did occasionally highlight the importance of different treaty designs, the general message was clear: Western BIT templates were 'good enough' and easy to adopt. This much is straightforward. Yet, the three illustrations towards the end of the chapter indicate that developing countries may not have responded to this advice in ways we would expect if they were engaged in a sophisticated treaty-making process. Rather than trying to assess whether the treaties were in fact useful to attract investment, they took the recommendations by Western advisers at face value. Whereas policy-makers during the 1960s and 1970s were often sceptical about the promise of investment treaties' grand bargain – greater protection in return for greater investment – the neoliberal turn in the 1990s made governments in the three countries 'motivated optimists': they *wanted* to believe the treaties worked. And rather than conducting a meticulous and sophisticated search and processing of information about the risks of the treaties, as well as different treaty provisions, policy-makers were attracted to standard European BIT templates as seemingly satisfactory solutions without any significant risks. It had to take claims against countries themselves before the possible liabilities of the treaties became salient enough to warrant any attention.

This is very similar to the experiences in Pakistan described in the preface, and also exactly as we would expect from a bounded rationality framework. So were the three cases merely outliers or part of a broader pattern? Could it really be that a large share of developing countries signed up to investment treaties up through the 1990s without carefully considering the implications?

---

[186] Ibid.

5 A less than rational competition

Whereas most of Chapter 4 highlighted the 'supply side' of the modern investment regime, the remaining chapters will focus on the experiences of developing countries themselves. As a first step, this chapter will revisit the claim that developing countries used BITs as part of a sophisticated and informed competition for capital. That was clearly not the case for Ghana, the Czech Republic, and Zimbabwe; but what about other countries?

The first section will take a step back and show that when looking at the broad patterns of treaty adoption, the quantitative evidence usually quoted in favour of the rational competition dynamic is far from robust. Small, but justified, changes in model specifications make the findings disappear. This serves not just as a reminder that an exclusive reliance on econometrics can be a risky enterprise to assess how governments signed up to BITs, but also that the aggregate patterns of investment treaty adoption don't seem to fit the standard rationalist narrative. The same goes for the patterns of treaty design, where hardly any developing country governments appear to have been interested in departing from the short and simple European templates, even when alternative provisions could have given them an advantage in the competition for capital. While they did sign BITs to attract investment, most developing country governments 'satisfied' rather than 'optimized' when negotiating and designing their treaties. On this basis, the second section will complement the cases from the previous chapter with an additional set of country experiences, where policy-makers were as predictably irrational in their investment treaty policies.

Peculiar patterns

The most widely quoted account of the investment treaty movement is that of Elkins, Guzman, and Simmons (EGS), who argue developing country governments signed BITs as a strategic response to a standard collective action problem: policy-makers would have preferred to avoid

Peculiar patterns

the treaties as they realized the sovereignty costs involved, but had an individual incentive to sign them in their competition for capital.[1] They back this up with econometric evidence from 1960 to 2000 that shows developing countries signed BITs primarily in response to other countries signing them, and particularly those with which they competed for foreign capital. The conclusion arising from this pattern is obvious: developing countries carefully processed information about the costs and benefits of the treaties, yet signed them nevertheless in an approximately rational competition for capital. This account is not only popular, it also fits with standard expectations in international political economy literature assuming governments accurately assess available information about the impact of their economic policies.

Yet even on its own terms this narrative is unsatisfactory, as it builds on two basic assumptions that are misleading for most of the period covered in EGS's analysis. First of all, EGS assumes that developing countries were the ones initiating investment treaty negotiations in their competition for capital. Although this is true for the 1990s it was rarely the case during the early years of the investment treaty movement. As we saw in Chapter 3, most BITs during this period were initiated by developed countries seeking protection rather than developing countries competing for capital – it was driven by *source* rather than by *host* contagion.[2]

Secondly, following Guzman's previous work, EGS argue that BITs could reasonably be expected to act as credible commitment devices for foreign investors. Yet during the first decades of the investment treaty movement, the vast majority of BITs did not include consent to investor–state arbitration.[3] Although recourse to inter-state dispute resolution is far from useless for private actors – as observed in the context of the WTO for instance – it does make them dependent on governments willing to fight for their interests. For instance, Germany's early BITs were occasionally used by the German government to resolve disputes,[4] but not all German investors were so fortunate. In the case of Turkey, the German government was not willing to aggressively stand up for its investors, which meant the 1962 BIT did not 'have any practical impact

---

[1] Elkins, Guzman, and Simmons (EGS) 2006. Reprinted in EGS 2007a; EGS 2007b; EGS 2008; EGS 2010a; EGS; 2010b.

[2] Neumayer and Plümper 2010.   [3] Yackee 2008.

[4] As an example, in 1973 Zambia withdrew a fine on a German investor for taking hard currency out of the country after Germany had made the Zambian government aware that its transfer regime was incompatible with the German BIT; PA, AA, Zwischenarchiv, 121366.

112   A less than rational competition

[because] the Turkish have a wonderful way not to observe it'.[5] Had the BIT allowed German investors to take their dispute directly to international arbitration, the Turkish government would not have been insulated from claims just because it was politically inconvenient for the German government. This is a reminder that 'BITs as potential credible commitment devices are not created equal, and some treaties are likely to have far less value to investors than others'.[6] It is therefore inappropriate for EGS to simply group together 'old' and 'modern' BITs.

Perhaps, however, their theory does hold for the 1990s. That is when negotiations were often initiated by developing countries and most treaties combined their substantive protections with private recourse to arbitration. Honing in on the 1990s, in other words, provides the easiest case for EGS's account of BIT diffusion. Yet, when restricting their sample to this decade, EGS's main results are no longer statistically significant. Using their own updated dataset, Table 5.1 shows the results for the full sample (columns one and three) – which are significant – as well as those excluding 'old' BITs (columns two and four) which are not.[7] During the 1990s, BIT-adoption strategies of 'competitor' states appear to have been largely irrelevant for developing countries. This means the main quantitative evidence quoted to back up the rational competition dynamic is shaky exactly at the time when it should be strongest. And at least in the cases introduced in Chapter 4, the predictions of EGS are very far off the mark, as the behaviour of 'competitor' states had nothing to do with their BIT programmes. The response from a previous Czech negotiator is representative: 'This was our own initiative, not at all based on their [competitors'] behaviour. If Hungary or Poland signed a BIT with India or the UK, this had no impact on our strategy'.[8] In all three countries, the process was far more haphazard.

Another expectation from the rationalist account of the BIT movement is that developing country governments sought and carefully processed information about whether the treaties actually worked as intended. Rational policy-makers would not necessarily have to be

---

[5] PA, AA, 422, 41335, GRO, 1978–80. Own translation. In disputes with the Pakistani government during the late 1970s, the 1959 German BIT was also seen as ineffective by the German government; PA, AA, Zwischenarchiv, 121345.

[6] Yackee 2008, p. 422.

[7] The results were similar when replacing calculations in columns two and four with an interaction term between the competition measures and a dummy variable taking the value of one after 1989 (to ensure the different results are not caused by different sample sizes). I am grateful to Faisal Ahmed for this suggestion.

[8] Czech official I.

Peculiar patterns

Table 5.1 *Adoption patterns show no evidence of rational competition*

	EGS's Model 2		EGS's Model 3	
	(1)	(2)	(3)	(4)
Export product competition	1.128***	1.027		
	(0.033)	(0.032)		
Infrastructure competition			1.112**	0.977
			(0.035)	(0.036)
Years included	1960–2000	1990–2000	1960–2000	1990–2000
N	256,914	83,524	253,051	83,524
Log likelihood	−11,313.27	−8,571.06	−11,279.63	−8,571.21
Chi^2	1,741.64	885.13	1,719.09	884.83

Note: Standard errors in parentheses.

$* p < 0.10$, $**p < 0.05$, $***p < 0.01$

Table report results from Cox proportional hazards model. A hazard ratio of more than one indicates a positive effect on the odds of a BIT; less than one, a negative effect. Columns one and three reproduce the results of Model 2 and Model 3 of Table 2 in Elkins, Guzman, and Simmons (EGS) (2006) with updated, and larger, dataset provided by EGS. Full set of variables needed for EGS's Model 1 are not available in updated dataset. Variables are defined in EGS's article. Full set of controls included from EGS, but not reported. Columns two and four of this table restrict EGS's regression to 1990–2000.

'right' about the impact of the treaties, but merely be responding to the best available information at the time.[9] Although this didn't happen in Ghana, the Czech Republic, or Zimbabwe, it would have been prudent. For although Western states, international organizations, and the arbitration community promoted the idea that BITs were important to attract investment, the (very few) studies trying to assess the importance of the treaties during the time in which they proliferated concluded they had no real impact on investors' establishment decisions. Recall from previous chapters that the two main studies were published by the very organizations arguing that BITs were important instruments for attracting capital to the developing world: MIGA published a survey in 1991 and UNCTAD published an econometric analysis in 1998, and both concluded that BITs were unimportant for foreign investment flows. In a low-information environment this was surely relevant to consider. Yet, as noted by the authors of the UNCTAD report

---

[9] Peinhardt and Allee 2012.

114   A less than rational competition

(most of which were lawyers), the analysis by their economist colleagues should not be given too much weight:

[I]t would be incorrect to conclude, without further analysis based on much more comprehensive data than are currently available, that BITs have no influence at all on the size of FDI stocks of flows of countries.[10]

As there were strong reasons to expect the treaties had an impact on investment, it wouldn't necessarily have been irrational to follow UNCTAD's advice.[11] On the other hand, developing countries routinely told Western states and the World Bank during the 1960s and 1970s that they wanted evidence for the claim that BITs and ICSID would attract investment. By the early 1990s, no such evidence had come to light, so for instruments with high potential sovereignty costs it would have been rational to at least try to get some additional information on the economic impacts of the treaties.

One observable implication is that BIT adoption should increase in years when countries signing them appeared to benefit in terms of attracting FDI.[12] But although EGS's original article found evidence for this, it is no longer statistically significant when using their own updated dataset (Table 5.1, columns one and three). And when limiting their sample to the 1990s the effect becomes statistically significant but negative (hazard ratio less than one); that is, developing countries appear to have signed *fewer* BITs when the treaties seemed to 'work'. As EGS's results seem frail, it would be unwise to derive any hard and fast conclusions from the correlations, whether significant or not. Yet, the key point is that also on this dimension the absence of evidence for the rational competition narrative corresponds with the three cases in Chapter 4, none of which went through any effort to assess whether their treaties actually worked as intended.

Perhaps, however, the strategic and sophisticated competition for capital manifested itself not through patterns of adoption or learning processes, but rather through the content of the treaties. As mentioned in the case of the Czech Republic, European BIT models leave considerable scope to be far more 'investor friendly'. Two areas stand out. One is with respect to performance requirements, which have traditionally been a major concern for foreign investors.[13] Although prohibited in North American BIT models, traditional European BITs have

---

[10] UNCTAD 1998b, p. 142.
[11] On the role of strong 'priors' and scarce information for rational policy learning, see Meseguer 2005, p. 75.
[12] EGS 2006, pp. 832–3.   [13] World Bank Guidelines, II(3).

Peculiar patterns 115

Table 5.2 *Adoption patterns show no evidence of rational learning about economic benefits*

	EGS Model 2		EGS Model 3	
	(1)	(2)	(3)	(4)
Learning from success	1.349	0.194***	1.734	0.214***
	(0.520)	(0.086)	(0.665)	(0.092)
Years included	1960–2000	1990–2000	1960–2000	1990–2000
N	256,914	83,524	253,051	83,524
Log likelihood	−11,313.27	−8,571.06	−11,279.63	−8,571.21
Chi^2	1,741.64	885.13	1,719.09	884.83

Note: Standard errors in parentheses.

* $p < 0.10$, ** $p < 0.05$, *** $p < 0.01$.

Table report results from Cox proportional hazards model. A hazard ratio of more than one indicates a positive effect on the odds of a BIT; less than one, a negative effect. Columns one and three reproduce the results of Model 2 and Model 3 of Table 2 in Elkins, Guzman, and Simmons (2006) with updated, and larger, dataset provided by EGS. Full set of variables needed for EGS's Model 1 are not available in updated dataset. Variables are defined in EGS's article. Full set of controls included from EGS, but not reported. Columns two and four of this table restrict EGS's regression to 1990–2000.

typically been silent on the subject (to the extent that the requirements don't violate national treatment obligations).[14] Another area is with respect to pre-establishment rights, which are also absent from European templates. Accordingly, if developing country governments wanted to engage in a competitive race to attract ever more capital, here were two areas in which they could adopt treaties that would stand out compared to the norm.

Yet, few seemed interested in departing from the European models. Because apart from investment chapters in recent preferential trade agreements (PTAs), liberalization obligations and prohibitions on performance requirements have mainly been restricted to treaties entered into by the United States, Canada, and Japan.[15] One reason could be that liberalization provisions, in particular, entail higher negotiation 'costs' in terms of bureaucratic resources as the US BIT model requires the parties

---

[14] Note that several WTO agreements also prohibit various forms of trade-related performance requirements, and the draft MAI agreement included a clause prohibiting performance requirements as well.

[15] Newcombe and Paradell 2009, p. 422.

116 A less than rational competition

to review all the areas in which they do not want to grant foreign investors similar rights as domestic investors. Provided a country maintains some discriminatory measures – which most do – this 'negative list' approach can involve considerable administrative costs.[16] However, in cases where two countries have *both* entered into BITs with the United States before signing a BIT amongst themselves, and thus gone through the process of making exceptions schedules for their liberalization obligations, it is relatively simple to include liberalization obligations also in their own BIT. In a rational competition framework we would therefore expect US-type BITs to have had 'increasing returns' by making former US BIT partners more likely to include liberalization and other 'investor-friendly' provisions from the US model in their future agreements.[17] Yet, in the last chapter we saw that this didn't happen in the case of the Czech Republic and Table 5.3 shows that the Czechs were not alone in this regard.

Only two out of a total of 54 available treaties among countries which, at the time of signature, had signed a BIT with the United States include a provision on performance requirements: Argentina's BIT with Nicaragua (1997) and the BIT between Croatia and Azerbaijan (2004).[18] The only treaty including national treatment covering market access was between Argentina and Bulgaria (1993). Otherwise, the countries all chose to revert back to the simpler European BIT models, even though the administrative costs of following the more comprehensive US template would have been small. This is difficult to explain if developing countries were engaged in a sophisticated race to gain a competitive edge in their investment treaty programmes. It is exactly what we would expect, however, if governments were satisfied to anchor to easy and simple default rules, even if they weren't optimal to compete for capital.

Bounded rational competition

Just as the aggregate patterns don't fit well with the expectations of standard rationalist models, neither do inputs from decision-makers themselves. To complement the three illustrations from Chapter 4, this section will briefly describe the experiences of nine additional cases:

---

[16] Some countries, such as Sri Lanka and Poland, listed more than 20 industry- or activity-specific exemptions from their liberalization schedules in their BIT with the US. Others, such as Egypt, Bangladesh, and Bulgaria, listed slightly more than 10 exemptions, whereas countries such as Kyrgyzstan, Mozambique, and Tunisia listed none at all.

[17] For a similar argument in the context of the trade regime, see Kim and Manger 2013.

[18] The provision in the Azerbaijan-Croatia BIT does not correspond with the one included in US BITs, but seems to have been borrowed from Azerbaijan's agreement with Finland the year before.

Bounded rational competition 117

Table 5.3 *Subsequent treaties among US BIT partners*

Partner 1	Partner 2
Argentina	Armenia (1993); Bulgaria* (1993); Czech Republic (1996); Ecuador (1994); Egypt (1992); Jamaica (1994); Nicaragua* (1997); Panama (2004); Romania (1993); Russia (1998); Senegal (1993); Tunisia (1992); Ukraine (1995)
Bulgaria	Czech Republic (1999); Egypt (1998); Poland (1994); Romania (1994)
Croatia	Azerbaijan* (2004); Belarus (2001); Egypt (1997); Jordan (1999); Latvia (2002); Moldova (2001); Mongolia (2006); Romania (2010); Ukraine (1997)
Czech Republic	Belarus (1996); Egypt (1993); El Salvador (1999); Mongolia (1998); Nicaragua (2002); Panama (1999); Tunisia (1997)
Egypt	Armenia (1996); Belarus (1997); Cameroon (2000); Congo DR (1998); Georgia (1999); Kazakhstan (1993); Latvia (1997); Poland (1995); Russia (1997); Senegal (1998); Slovakia (1997); Sri Lanka (1996)
Jordan	Bahrain (2000); Poland (1997)
Mongolia	Poland (1995); Romania (1995)
Romania	Albania (1995); Slovakia (1994); Tunisia (1995)
Russia	Lithuania (1999); Ukraine (1998)

Note: Table includes 54 BITs where both parties had signed a BIT with the United States before signature and the full text of the agreement is available at UNCTAD's online BIT database in English, French, German, or Spanish. Year of signature is in brackets. Agreements where one party is a member of the EU at the time of signature have been excluded as EU countries are not allowed, as a matter of EU law, to follow the US model by including binding liberalization provisions in their BITs. Treaties with Turkey and Morocco not listed as their BITs with the US do not include national treatment obligations for market access. The three BITs marked with * stand out as either including national treatment for market access (in the case of Argentina-Bulgaria) or including a prohibition on performance requirements.

three from Latin America, four from Asia, and two from Africa. They'll show that the competition for capital in the investment regime corresponds much better with the predictions of a bounded rational framework. We begin in Latin America, where several countries were first introduced to investment treaties in their negotiations with the United States. But whereas the American BIT model has left its marks on the region, particularly after the rise in investment arbitration, Latin American governments preferred the much simpler and easier European models during most of the 1990s and early 2000s. And just as in Ghana, the Czech Republic, and Zimbabwe, policy-makers did not try and assess whether the treaties were useful to attract investment. Instead, they easily convinced themselves that the treaties simply *had* to work.

118   A less than rational competition

Latin America

From the early 20th century onwards, Mexico was at the heart of the North–South divide over which protections should govern international investment. Not only was it the 1938 expropriations in Mexico that resulted in the now famous Hull standard of compensation included in practically all BITs, Mexico was also the country leading the charge when the UN General Assembly voted in favour of the Calvo doctrine in 1974. Less than a decade after, however, Mexican policy-makers entirely changed course as the collapse of the Mexican economy made them open up to international trade and investment while undergoing a structural adjustment programme by the World Bank and the IMF.[19] US manufacturing and car firms slowly began shifting their production plants below the border, and in 1990 President Salinas initiated talks to join the Canada-United States Free Trade Agreement (CUSFTA). Along with his Harvard-trained economists in the administration, Salinas saw it as an opportunity to lock in liberal economic reforms to stabilize the economy and assist in attracting more foreign capital.[20]

During the course of the negotiations, Washington made clear it wanted BIT-like protections for American firms. Mexico agreed. One of Mexico's lead negotiators was Guillermo Aguilar-Alvarez, who later became an arbitrator. His view of the treaties was clear. As he later wrote: investment treaty protections 'enhance national welfare' and provide an 'aggregate gain to the public good through the type of broad cross-border investment fostered by arbitration'.[21] To advise on the investment protection chapter, Mexico also brought in Jan Paulsson, an arbitrator from Freshfields and one of the staunchest proponents of investment treaty arbitration. According to Paulsson, investment treaties can 'convince investors to invest for the longest time possible and for the lowest possible return'.[22] With such a team in place and strong political buy-in from the top, Mexico ended up asking for stronger investment protection disciplines than Canada: 'What Mexico wanted was more foreign investment', one negotiator notes, 'and while the constitution created limits, Mexico was open to strong disciplines'.[23] The constitutional 'limits' turned out not to be set in stone. For whereas the Calvo clause in the Mexican Constitution offered 'only' national treatment to foreigners, as did Mexico's relevant legislation and regulations, Mexico agreed with Washington to provide independent protections to

---

[19] Haber, Klein, Maurer, and Middlebrock 2008.   [20] Manger 2009.
[21] Aguilar-Alvarez and Park 2003, p. 399.   [22] Paulsson 2010, p. 347.
[23] Negotiator quoted in Cameron and Tomlin 2002, p. 101.

Bounded rational competition 119

foreign investors. This included recourse to international investor–state arbitration. And even though the terms *prompt, adequate,* and *effective* could not be used for the compensation standard in NAFTA, due to the specific history of the Hull formulation, government lawyers managed to find language to the same effect (compensation should be 'without delay', at 'fair market value', and 'fully realizable').[24] In the end Canada agreed, and NAFTA's Chapter 11 was a reality.

Building on this experience Salinas' successor, Ernesto Zedillo, decided to initiate a BIT programme. Zedillo was of the view that to attract investment, 'we don't have conditions for security; we don't have the rule of law that is required for Mexico to develop'.[25] Investment protection treaties were thought to assist with this problem, and officials proceeded to negotiate 20 BITs in 10 years.[26] Yet, 'nobody really questioned whether the strategy had results',[27] one official recalls, and no attempts of evaluating the economic implications of the treaties were sought. Instead of basing their inferences on a careful search for information, most Mexican officials *wanted* to believe the treaties somehow assisted with attracting investment. 'I devoted four years of my life negotiating them', one legal advisor notes, 'and I believe they are quite positive. BITs play a supplementary role within an overall package that is conducive to attracting FDI'.[28] This basic justification for the Mexican BIT programme was not based on any analytical inputs, however, and another former official notes that 'even today [in 2010] there is still not an awareness of the lacking impact between BITs and FDI'.[29]

When choosing negotiation partners there was a qualitative aspect, 'the relevance of the country to which Mexico had a specific interest, given its geographical location, geopolitical position or economic characteristics', and a quantitative aspect, 'that consider either the investment flows from the country concerned to Mexico, or from Mexico to such country, or both'.[30] As we shall see later, this was actually a rather sophisticated

---

[24] Ibid.

[25] President Ernesto Zedillo Ponce de Leon, Address at the 60th Mexican National Banking Convention, 7 March 1997, quoted in Yamin and Garcia 1999, p. 467.

[26] Mexican official I. See also justifications by Mexican officials in 'Perspectivas inversion extranjera' *Servicio Universal de Noticias,* 11 November 1998; Faya-Rodriguez 2005. This was also repeatedly the justification given for the treaties in public. See e.g. 'La inversion espanola se desfonda en México, con un 47% menos hasta junio', *Cindo Dias,* 12 September 1997; 'Mexico potencial exportador', *Servicio Universal de Noticias,* 17 July 1999 (Ese es un marco importante para que fluyan las inversiones a esta nación); and the German BIT; 'Firman proteccion reciproca a inversiones Mexico-Alemania', *Novedas,* 9 October 1997; and the investment protection chapter in the PTA with Chile; 'TLC Mexico Chile', *Servicio Universal de Noticias,* 2 August 1998.

[27] Mexican official I.   [28] Faya-Rodriguez 2005.   [29] Mexican official II.

[30] Faya-Rodriguez 2005.

120   A less than rational competition

strategy compared to many other developing countries, including the cases described in the previous chapter. Yet, the content of Mexico's investment treaty obligations was more than puzzling. Investment protection chapters in Mexico's PTAs with Colombia (1994), Nicaragua (1997), and Chile (1998) included a prohibition on performance requirements, and the Chile PTA also included national treatment for the establishment of investment – just as NAFTA. This was not the case for Mexican BITs signed during the same period, however, which instead were based on the simple European templates.[31] Not even the BIT with Argentina in 1996 followed the liberalizing NAFTA approach, even though Argentina had already agreed to similar provisions in its BIT with Washington five years before.

The reason for this peculiar outcome was not a sophisticated cost–benefit analysis of different treaty designs, but rather because different officials were in charge of investment provisions in PTAs and BITs. Up through the 1990s, the office involved with the NAFTA negotiations promoted NAFTA-type obligations in PTAs, whereas the Ministry of Economy adopted BITs based on European models.[32] Rather than carefully seeking to optimize the treaties' design the two negotiation teams simply stuck with the 'default rules' they were used to, which in turn resulted in an incoherent set of obligations.

In Ecuador, the process was somewhat similar. When Sixto Ballén was elected president of Ecuador in 1992 he continued, and deepened, a series of liberal economic reforms initiated a decade earlier. Ballén opened up practically all sectors of the economy to foreign investors and to underpin this policy, his administration began signing investment treaties.[33] The first was with the United States, where shifting American ambassadors in Quito convinced the Ecuadorian government that without additional legal protections foreign investors could not trust the Ecuadorian legal system.[34] Apart from including the US provision banning performance requirements, this was a remarkable agreement as Ecuador reserved only 'traditional fishing' and 'broadcast radio and television stations' from the pre-establishment obligations. This meant that Ecuador relinquished its right to limit and screen American foreign investment in *all* areas of the economy ranging from foreign investments in oil and mining, over banking and insurance, to manufacturing.

---

[31] An exception was the 1995 Mexico-Switzerland BIT, which prohibits performance requirements (Art. 5).
[32] Mexico official II.
[33] Ecuador had previously signed only three BITs with Germany (1965), Switzerland (1968), and Uruguay (1985).
[34] Hey and Klak 1999.

Bounded rational competition

After the agreement with Washington, Ecuador continued to sign investment treaties, primarily with Latin American partners and European states. But rather than cautiously considering the costs and benefits of different provisions, Ecuadorian officials negotiated based on European models primarily because they were easy and quick to adopt.[35] On some occasions, as in the case of Denmark, Ecuador sent a copy of its 'own' BIT model to initiate negotiations, yet it had simply been copied word for word from BIT models of European countries.[36] This meant Ecuador only included liberalization obligations in agreements with Washington and Canada. And again, even the 1994 BIT with Argentina reverted back to the European model. Had the two governments followed their BITs with Washington and included bans on performance requirements and comprehensive liberalization provisions it would have made their own agreement stand out in a Latin American context. But instead, policy-makers in Ecuador (and Argentina) anchored to the simple and easy agreements crafted by European governments. Satisficing rather than optimizing was again the preferred strategy.

The same was the case for the choice of BIT partners, where there was 'no real strategy'.[37] One official 'tried to know why we were choosing different countries. But there wasn't anything; we were signing with pretty much all types of countries'.[38] Whether Chile, Bolivia, Venezuela, and other 'competitor' states signed up to BITs was entirely irrelevant. Occasionally, BITs were pushed by embassies and foreign affairs officials as photo-ops for state visits.[39] Some Ecuadorian ambassadors, for instance, initiated the treaties at the end of their posting to 'finish with a bang'.[40] Overall, however, the treaties were seen by Ecuadorian policy-makers as useful during a transition to a market-based regime because 'we thought these treaties were very important to attract investments'.[41] Although the introduction of arbitration provisions was controversial, given Latin America's history with the Calvo doctrine, it was found necessary as 'all government stakeholders thought of BITs as very important drivers of investment'.[42] This meant Ecuador was ready to negotiate with practically every country. A former negotiator notes:

A lot of firms have invested in Ecuador in oil for instance and a few years ago a lot of mining firms have come, so it has been good for the country. You need to give investors these assurances. They attracted investments in some areas. I still believe that.[43]

---

[35] Ecuador official III.   [36] UM 400.E.13.Ecuador.12.   [37] Ecuador official I.
[38] Ecuador official IV.   [39] Ecuador official II.   [40] Ecuador official I.
[41] Ecuador official III.   [42] Ibid.   [43] Ibid.

122   A less than rational competition

But this was never actually investigated. Oil companies told the Ecuadorian government that international arbitration clauses were important in concession agreements, and officials took this to imply that BITs would be important to attract investment as well[44] – despite the fact that Ecuador already gave major oil companies recourse to international arbitration in their contracts. And not until Ecuador became subject to a major investment treaty claim in 2006 were any attempts made to assess the treaties' economic implications.[45] The Ecuadorian Central Bank conducted a simple analysis to see whether the treaties were in fact worth the costs or the main justification had been based on wishful thinking.[46] The results were more than discouraging and contributed to Ecuador's decision to denounce several BITs in recent years; something I'll return to in the coming chapter.

Finally, we find similar patterns in Chile. Since the days of Pinochet and the 'Chicago boys', Chile had been open to foreign investment and after the Pinochet regime the liberal economic reforms were further deepened during the 1990s.[47] To underpin this policy, Chile entered into a series of PTAs and would have joined NAFTA had it not been for the expiration of Clinton's fast-track authority.[48] Stand-alone investment treaties were also used, and just as UNCTAD and other organizations stressed that BITs were important for the provision of political risk insurance (PRI), this was also the case for Chile when it initiated its BIT programme in the early 1990s. In the *traveaux préparatoires* for the statute approving the ICSID Convention, the president of Chile noted lower insurance premiums as a primary reason not just to sign up to ICSID but also to BITs, as this would:

permit foreign investors to obtain lower insurance premiums than those actually obtained in the normal situation [without a BIT]. Therefore, the accession of Chile to this type of treaties would permit the country to keep an advantaged position in order to attract foreign investment.[49]

So although Chile had earlier been one of the leading opponents of international investor–state arbitration, as it conflicted with the Calvo

---

[44] Ibid.   [45] Ecuador official II. See next chapter.
[46] Schneiderman 2013, pp. 151–2.
[47] While the Chilean BIT programme took off in the 1990s, the Pinochet regime was open to signing agreements. Chile indicated to the German government in 1978 that it was ready to finalize a BIT with Germany for instance. A treaty had been signed in 1964, but was never ratified. Chile sent a proposal to the German government that was very similar to the German model, but Germany refused – on principle – to restart negotiations and the agreement didn't materialize; PA, AA, Zwischenarchiv, 121318.
[48] Manger 2008.   [49] Quoted in Montt 2009, p. 115.

doctrine,[50] this policy had to be reversed to attract foreign investment. The president of Chile's Council on Foreign Relations in the early 1990s, Francisco Orrego-Vicuna, later noted (after becoming an arbitrator) that 'if countries don't sign up to BITs they will have nothing to offer and will lose the investment'.[51] This was also the general attitude among Chilean officials at the time.[52] So although in some cases BITs were signed simply because of a presidential visit,[53] the overall aim of the programme was to attract investment. As noted by the Foreign Ministry when signing a BIT with Switzerland in 1991 for instance: 'the agreement will encourage Swiss investments and increase the presence of Swiss companies in Chile'.[54]

Yet, no analyses were ever made to investigate whether the treaties actually worked. 'Everybody thought they were good to attract foreign investment, but we did not make any economic analyses'.[55] And similar to the cases above, the inflated expectations about the economic benefits of the treaties meant the Chilean government did not have a particularly strategic approach about when to sign BITs and with which partners. Although the behaviour of Argentina, for instance, could be factored in when Chile considered its own investment treaty programme on occasion, this was an exception as 'the negotiation of these treaties was regardless of what other developing countries were doing'.[56] In the end, Chile managed to sign BITs with a great number of countries – more than 50 from 1991 to 2000 – whether they were strategic economic partners or not.

With respect to the design of the treaties, Chile's BITs again followed European templates. The 1994 Chilean model BIT looked exactly the same to European counterparts, though with an exception for Chile's capital transfer regulations. And although Chile's PTAs with Canada (1996) and Mexico (1998) included detailed NAFTA-type investment provisions, for instance on performance requirements, this was not the case in Chile's BITs signed at the same time. The BIT with Hungary, for instance, was signed just a few months after the PTA with Canada, but again reverted back to the much simpler and less comprehensive European template. As in Mexico, Chilean negotiators thereby negotiated otherwise similar provisions, but depending on the form of the treaty – PTA or BIT – they anchored to North American or

---

[50] See statement of Felix Ruiz, Governor for Chile, 9 September 1964, Tokyo in 2 *The History of the ICSID Convention*, p. 606.
[51] Quoted in Ross 2010.   [52] Montt 2009, p. 115.   [53] Chile official I.
[54] Daily Report, Latin America, FBIS-LAT-91–219, 13 November 1991, p. 60.
[55] Chile official I.   [56] Ibid.

124   A less than rational competition

European default rules for no logical reason other than a preference for satisfactory, rather than optimal, solutions.

Asia

Moving to Asia, Turkey was also first introduced to BITs in its negotiations with the United States, as had been the case in Mexico and Ecuador. After Turkey had gone through a deep economic crisis in the late 1970s, the military government liberalized the Turkish economy and began welcoming foreign investment.[57] Bretton Woods institutions provided structural adjustment lending and the reforms were overseen by Deputy Prime Minister Turkut Ozal – himself a former World Bank staff member – and his team of American-educated technocrats.[58] The structural adjustment programme began in 1980 and the same year a new Foreign Investment Directorate (FID) was established within the State Planning Organization. As FID was told by Ozal 'just to do everything you can' to lure investors to Turkey,[59] its small team looked around for useful instruments of investment promotion. During this process, a legal advisor within the FID stumbled upon the 1962 Turkish BIT with Germany and thought this type of agreement seemed to be a useful tool.[60] As it happened, the Asian-African Legal Consultative Organization (AALCO) also had a meeting in Istanbul in 1981, where the members 'recognized the need to promote bilateral umbrella agreements between the countries in the region to provide a basic framework under which wider flow of investments could be facilitated'.[61] So when the United States approached Turkey around the same time to sign a BIT, Ankara accepted the invitation.

The US treaty was initiated in connection with a major American investment in a plant producing parts for F16 fighter jets, and the legal advisor did most of the negotiations on behalf of Turkey. Two sessions ensued after which Turkey signed off on a treaty in 1985 closely following the US model. It was a very low-key event with hardly any

---

[57] During the first decades of the republic, Turkey was wary of foreign investors, in part due to Attaturk's concerns with Turkey's former quasi-colonial status after the capitulation treaties imposed on the Ottoman empire; Schneider and Bilgen 1992, p. 101.

[58] Aricanli and Rodrik 1990; Senses 1991.   [59] Turkey official I.   [60] Ibid.

[61] 'Asian-African legal consultative committee: models for bilateral agreements on promotion and protection of investments', 23 *ILM* (1984), p. 237. The meeting resulted in a series of model BITs with different levels of investment protection, but all closely followed those of European states.

press coverage.[62] No one in Turkey saw it as anything but a technical affair, and as long as it didn't contradict Turkish laws the Parliament had no issues ratifying it.[63] On this basis, Turkey initiated a BIT programme 'with a view to creating and maintaining favourable conditions for foreign investment to foster its economic growth'.[64] This was also how the treaties were justified in (rare) press reports as well as by the chief architect of the programme.[65]

Ankara's own model treaty ended up much simpler than the American template but nevertheless stood out slightly by having the MFN clause cover the establishment phase. Although Washington had not been able to get the Turkish negotiator to accept national treatment for establishment without the qualification that it had to be in accordance with Turkish laws and regulations, the MFN clause had no such qualification.[66] This was followed in later BITs as well, except if the other party refused.[67] Yet, this was not part of an effort to conclude ever more 'competitive' BITs by Turkey, but simply because the US BIT was the first Turkish negotiators were introduced to. Parts of it therefore came to serve as 'the default reference for other BITs'.[68] So although this mixing of European and American BIT practise was somewhat unique, it doesn't depart from the basic expectation of a bounded rational framework where governments copy-paste from pre-existing default rules that seem satisfactory. On the continuum between fully rational design and bounded rational anchoring to default rules, Turkey was still much closer to the latter.

---

[62] A very brief note was included in Turkish newspapers; '10 year investment agreement signed with U.S.,' FBIS-WEU-85-233, 4 December 1985. Similarly in US news; 'Briefing: treaty with Turkey', *New York Times*, 3 December 1985 (135 words); 'Turkey and US have agreed upon a joint investment protocol', *Middle East Economic Digest*, 7 December 1985 (57 words).

[63] Turkey official I.   [64] WT/WGTI/W/51, 18 September 1998.

[65] The treaties were regarded as 'vehicles to attract foreign direct investment'; Turkey official I. See also similar justifications in 'Agreement signed with Japan for investments', FBIS-WEU-92–030, 13 February 1992. See also 'Government signs two agreements with Austria', FBIS-WEU-88, 21 September 1988, 'Investment agreement signed with Kuwait', FBIS-WEU-88–209, 28 October 1988; 'Cooperation agreement signed', FBIS-WEU-90–242, 17 December 1990 (Soviet BIT); 'Investment protection agreement signed with UK', FBIS-WEU-91–055, 21 March 1991; 'Investment agreement with Turkey "initiated"', FBIS-MEA-87–043, 5 March 1987.

[66] See USTR's explanation of the treaty; 99TH Congress 1st Session Senate Treaty Doc. 99–19.

[67] Turkey's BITs with Bulgaria (1994), Moldova (1994), Ukraine (1996), Egypt (1996), Latvia (1997), Morocco (1997), Russia (1997), and Croatia (2009) thus also granted MFN treatment pre-establishment. As all those partners had granted national treatment in their BITs with the United States, this effectively means the BITs with Turkey do it as well via the operation of the MFN clause.

[68] Turkey official I.

126   A less than rational competition

Also, just as in the aforementioned cases, Turkish policy-makers were equally subject to motivational biases when assessing the benefits of the treaties. Although Western partners kept repeating the message that BITs could attract investment,[69] 'no research [was] made to see whether these BITs were instrumental or not'.[70] The first time this assumption was investigated was in 1998 when a Turkish submission to the WTO included a simple table comparing investment authorizations according to the country of origin with BIT coverage.[71] This was rather sophisticated compared to information-gathering strategies in most other developing countries at the time. But although it showed there was no apparent correlation, that didn't shake the causal belief that the treaties were somehow important to attract investment. The Turkish government was still of the view that 'these agreements are important as an imperative for including foreign firms at least to consider undertaking investments in a given country'.[72] The strong policy commitment to attract foreign capital meant Turkish policy-makers *wanted* to believe BITs were crucial to attract investment, which appear to have impacted their information processing. In any event, it is noteworthy that the analysis took place after Turkey had already signed more than 40 BITs over the course of a decade.

Although a radically different context, the case of Thailand is largely similar. Thailand concluded only five BITs during the Cold War. One was signed with Germany in 1963 in order to facilitate German investment guarantees.[73] And in the 1970s and 1980s Thailand signed BITs with the Netherlands (1972), the UK (1978), China (1985), and Korea (1989), while pursuing an export promotion strategy with foreign firms playing an increasingly important role.[74] In 1987, Thailand also signed on to the regional investment agreement in ASEAN which included BIT-like provisions, including recourse to investor–state arbitration. But it was in the 1990s that Thailand began to rapidly expand its network of investment treaties. Ten were signed between 1990 and 1995 alone. By complementing ongoing domestic reform efforts, 'the idea in the 1990s was that we would have more investment if we negotiated those bilateral instruments'.[75]

---

[69] When signing the Turkish BIT, the UK Trade Ministry, for instance, said 'These agreements are great for Britain which is the world's biggest overseas investor in proportion to its GDP. They are also good for the host countries – including many developing countries – who are increasingly reliant on foreign investment rather than borrowing or aid to finance their development'. Quoted in 'DTI – UK ratifies investment agreement with Turkey', *COI's HERMES-Government Press Releases*, 22 October 1996.
[70] Turkey official I.   [71] WT/WGTI/W/51, 18 September 1998.   [72] Ibid.
[73] PA, AA, B67, 74.   [74] Nikomborirak 2004.   [75] Thai official I.

The first agreements were with regional neighbours (such as Laos and Vietnam), but also a number of Eastern European countries and a treaty even was signed with Peru – not exactly core investment partners for Bangkok. Yet, whenever the prime minister went abroad embassies and foreign policy officials argued 'there was a need for a treaty', and BITs were easy and quick to adopt to 'intensify relations' with other countries.[76] The choice to sign BITs had nothing to do with 'competitor' states either: 'we rarely looked at other countries in terms of how many they had – whether they were competitors or not'.[77] Instead, invitations would simply be accepted if there was an expectation that the treaties could somehow promote economic integration – which there typically was – in which case BITs would be part of a sequence of treaties that also included double taxation treaties (DTTs) and, potentially, PTAs.

The content of Thailand's BITs entirely anchored to European templates. The agreements with other developing countries, for instance, looked practically similar to standard European BIT models and no attempts were made to pursue ever more 'competitive' treaty designs. As an example, article five of the BIT with the UK in 1978 travelled into treaties signed up through the 1990s (Table 5.4)

The investment promotion impact of the treaties was never investigated in Thailand either. 'We didn't make any surveys or anything like that', one official recalls.[78] Not until dozens of treaties had been signed over decades did economists in the Thai bureaucracy find a survey indicating BITs might not have lived up to the expectations during the 1990s.[79] Before then 'the perception ... was simply that this was a precondition for foreign investors making the decision to invest, so we thought there is nothing wrong with that'.[80] So although Thai officials were sceptical in the 1960s when Broches claimed that signing up to ICSID would promote investment (see Chapter 3), the strong policy commitment to pro-investment policies during the 1990s meant Thai officials now *wanted* to believe investment treaties worked.

We find similar strategies in the case of Pakistan, already introduced in the Preface. Here, the justification for the treaties was also that they could help Pakistan attract foreign investment.[81] After signing a few

---

[76] Thai official III.   [77] Ibid.   [78] Ibid.   [79] Thai official I.   [80] Thai official III.
[81] See comments on Germany-Pakistan BIT in Chapter 3. See also, e.g. 'Pakistan, Romania sign agreement', *Business Recorder*, 22 January 1978 (justified BIT as necessary to proceed with economic integration in the investment field); 'PAK-ROK investment accord to yield fruitful results', *Business Recorder*, 27 May 1988 (justified as critical instrument to 'inspire more confidence among investors'); 'PAK-Dutch accords on economic ties, investment signed', *Business Recorder*, 5 October 1988 (expected to

Table 5.4 *Anchoring of Thai BITs to UK treaty*

UK BIT, 1978, Art. 5	Hungary BIT, 1991, Art. 4	Czech BIT, 1994, Art. 4
1. (a) Investments of nationals or companies of one Contracting Party in the territory of the other Contracting Party, as also the returns therefrom, shall receive treatment which is fair and equitable and not less favourable than that accorded in respect of the investments and returns of the nationals and companies of the latter Contracting Party or of any third State. (b) Each Contracting Party shall in its territory accord to nationals or companies of the other Contracting Party as regards the management, use, enjoyment or disposal of their investments, treatment which is fair and equitable and not less favourable than that which it accords to its own nationals and companies or to nationals and companies of any third State. 2. Each Contracting Party shall observe any obligation, additional to those specified in this Agreement, into which it may have entered with regard to investments of nationals or companies of the other Contracting Party.	1. Investments and returns therefrom of nationals or companies of one Contracting Party in the territory of the other Contracting Party shall receive treatment which is fair and equitable and not less favourable than that accorded in respect of the investments and returns of the nationals and companies of the latter Contracting Party or of any third State. 2. Each Contracting Party shall in its territory accord to nationals or companies of the other Contracting Party as regards the management, use, enjoyment or disposal of their investments, treatment which is fair and equitable and not less favourable than that which it accords to its own nationals and companies or to nationals and companies of any third State. 3. Each Contracting Party shall observe any obligation, additional to those specified in this Agreement, into which it may have entered with regard to investments of nationals or companies of the other Contracting Party.	1. (a) Investments made by investors of one Contracting Party in the territory of the other Contracting Party, and the returns therefrom, shall receive treatment which is fair and equitable and not less favourable than that accorded in respect of the investments and returns of the investors of the latter Contracting Party or of any third State. (b) Each Contracting Party shall in its territory accord to the investors of the other Contracting Party as regards the management, use, enjoyment or disposal of their investments, treatment which is fair and equitable and not less favourable than that which it accords to its own investors or to the investors of any third State. 2. Each Contracting Party shall observe any obligation, additional to those specified in this Agreement, into which it may have entered with regard to investments of the investors of the other Contracting Party.

Bounded rational competition 129

treaties since 1959 onwards, the programme took off during the 1990s while Pakistan was liberalizing its investment regime and shifting prime ministers aimed to 'cater for all the needs of foreign investors'.[82] 'Pakistan was looking for FDI', one official notes, 'so there was a climate that since we are providing the protections and liberalizing everything, why not add some confidence to the investors with BITs?'.[83] As noted to the Danish government, 'Pakistan is fully committed to promote foreign investments and has recently taken many steps to facilitate foreign investors in the establishment of their projects. The Government of Pakistan is also concluding bilateral agreements with other states towards this end'.[84]

Treaties entered into by 'competitor states', such as India, Bangladesh, or Iran, didn't have any bearing on Pakistan's investment treaty strategy. The approach was much simpler. Whenever the Pakistani leadership went abroad or played hosts to world leaders in Islamabad, they would typically suggest a BIT. In some cases this could be to promote diplomatic links,[85] and in other cases it was for less kosher reasons: 'when there is ever a proposal for an international agreement to be negotiated everyone says yes, because you get a free trip out of it', as one Pakistani official notes.[86] Overall, however, the main driver of the programme was the expectation that BITs could help the country attract much needed capital. Yet at no point during the heyday of the Pakistani BIT movement was the causal link between investment flows and investment treaties assessed. This was despite the fact that investors hardly ever seemed interested in the treaties when meeting with Pakistani officials.[87] Not until 2009, after policy-makers realized the potency of the treaties as a result of the claims, did officials begin analyzing the role of BITs

'increase Dutch investment in Pakistan'); 'Pakistan, UK sign accord to promote investment', *Dawn*, 1 December 1994 (BIT is seen to 'reinforce the economic links' between UK and Pakistan); 'Pakistan, Italy sign investment promotion accord', *Business Recorder*, 20 July 1997 (BIT justified by the 'hope that the agreement would help bring more Italian investment in Pakistan').

[82] 'Pakistan now ready to cater for all needs of foreign investors: PM', *Business Recorder*, 8 March 1998. See also 'Markets have replaced missiles: Benazir', *Business Recorder*, 15 March 1995.

[83] Pakistan official VII.   [84] UM.400.E.11.Pakistan 12.

[85] This was the case with the central Asian republics, for instance, where 'there was a lot of enthusiasm to have some kind of contact with them. So any kind of proposals would prop up at inter-ministerial meetings; we can have this, and we can have that, and we can have a BIT'; Pakistan official VII; Pakistan I (noting that the Kazakh agreement 'was signed for purely ceremonial reasons. The Kazakh president was visiting and we had to sign certain treaties – cultural agreements, scientific cooperation agreements, bilateral investment treaties, things like that'). See also 'Pakistan, Kyrgyzstan sign pacts', *Business Recorder*, 27 August 1995 (BIT signed alongside many other agreements laying 'a foundation for further strengthening of our bilateral relations').

[86] Pakistan official VI.   [87] Pakistan official I.

130 A less than rational competition

for attracting investment with some basic economic data.[88] This was 50 years after Pakistan began its investment treaty programme.

The content of the treaties was approached with a similar attitude: despite Islamabad pleading for the United States to enter into a BIT during the 1990s,[89] Pakistan's investment treaties followed the much simpler – but less comprehensive – European templates. Rather than trying to optimize the content of the treaties, the inputs given by Pakistan officials in negotiations 'were solely proof-reading. Correcting punctuation, and correct English – but that was about it'.[90] Anchoring to simple European model treaties was again the preferred strategy.

Similar policies were pursued even in India, a country otherwise so careful to protect its sovereignty.[91] During Delhi's experiments with import substitution during the 1960s and 1970s foreign companies were discouraged except in high-priority sectors. ICSID was criticized by India for putting foreign investors at par with domestic investors and when Western states invited India to negotiate BITs, Delhi countered that foreign investors were 'adequately protected under the Constitution, and accordingly bilateral investment protection agreements are not required'.[92] This changed during the 1990s when a major balance of payments crisis made India open up its economy and allow greater foreign participation in an increasing number of sectors. To underpin these reforms, India signed a BIT with London in 1994 largely along the lines of the British model and thereafter proceeded to sign a considerable number of similar treaties with one primary aim: to facilitate investment inflows.[93] The 1995 BIT with Germany, for instance, was intended to 'make investment by German companies in [India] more attractive',[94] and when signing a BIT with Denmark the same year, then finance minister Manmohan Singh, noted that 'we are determined to promote investor friendly environment and the investment protection treaty with Denmark signed yesterday will be a milestone in bringing the business communities of the two countries closer together'.[95] This justification for Indian BITs persisted up through the 1990s.[96]

---

[88] Pakistan official V.   [89] See Chapter 1, ftn. 53.   [90] Pakistan official III.
[91] If not otherwise stated, the following paragraphs are based on Ranjan 2014.
[92] FCO 98/213.   [93] Ranjan 2014.
[94] *Daily Report: Near East & South Asia*, FBIS-NES-95–122, 26 June 1995.
[95] 'Denmark offers $5 m. soft credit to India', *The Times of India*, 8 September 1995.
[96] Ranjan 2014, pp. 9–10. In a few cases, Indian BITs were justified in more political terms. See e.g. Jandhyala, Henisz, and Mansfield 2011, p. 1056 (quoting joint statement after the BIT with Hungary mentioning that 'both sides expressed satisfaction over the progressive growth of the Indo-Hungarian relationship, which is marked by strong cultural affinity and understanding').

Bounded rational competition 131

Again, however, it was not until 2011 that the government began to seek information about the link between BITs and FDI. The analysis was prompted by a series of claims against India (see Chapter 6), and the conclusion was that the treaties had little impact on India's ability to attract foreign investment.[97] At this point, India had already signed more than 80 treaties – one of the largest BIT networks in the world. And as in the previous cases, the content of India's BITs had also anchored entirely to European templates by largely replicating the UK model in its subsequent agreements.[98] When talks with the United States were stalled over the intellectual property right provision, Delhi suggested that the two countries could just sign an agreement based on a European model instead because India 'was keen on securing American investment and would like to sign a treaty to promote investment prospects'.[99] Recall from Chapter 1 that India had a similar reaction when investment protection got on the WTO agenda in the early 2000s. Here, the Indian team did exactly as we would expect from a bounded rationality perspective: as existing solutions (BITs) seemed 'good enough', there was no need to engage in institutional innovation in a multilateral agreement. Continuing to participate in UNCTAD's signing sessions, for instance, was a far easier option.[100]

Africa

In Africa, the approach was similar. In the previous chapter we heard from policy-makers in Ghana and Zimbabwe, and they were no exceptions. Take the case of Ethiopia for instance. With the fall of the Soviet Union, the transitional Ethiopian government instead sought to embrace economic liberalism.[101] Ethiopia joined MIGA in August 1991, and the year after an investment proclamation was made to expand the areas available for foreign investment and offer a range of incentives for investors engaged in international trade. The aim was to gradually liberalize the investment regime, as suggested by the IMF and the World Bank during Ethiopia's structural adjustment programmes from the mid 1990s onwards.[102] Investment treaties were seen as a useful instrument to underpin the process, as they would 'give further confidence to investors

---

[97] Quoted in Ranjan 2014, p. 21.   [98] Ranjan 2014.
[99] 'Chidambaram firm on investment treaty with U.S.,' *India West,* 30 June 1995.
[100] WT/WGTI/M/14 (suggesting that UNCTAD, rather than WTO, should be responsible for international investment rules). See Table 4.4 for India's participation in UNCTAD's signing sessions.
[101] Naudé 1998.
[102] IMF and World Bank, *Ethiopia: Enhanced Structural Adjustment Facility; Medium-Term Economic and Financial Policy Framework Paper,* 1998.

132 A less than rational competition

from Europe and Asia'.[103] In 1994, one year into its structural adjustment programme, Ethiopia therefore entered into its first BIT with Italy (not counting the 1964 BIT with Germany). And over the coming years, Addis Ababa kept spreading its network of investment treaties, including at UNCTAD's signing sessions, in an effort to 'encourage investors to invest confidently' in Ethiopia.[104]

Yet, no analyses or surveys were ever made to find out whether the treaties actually helped.[105] And unlike the process suggested by EGS, the government 'didn't really follow other developing countries' programs. It was mostly done in isolation'.[106] The content of Ethiopia's investment treaties was thus also largely determined by the other side, and it is not until very recently – two decades after the BIT programme began – that Ethiopian officials attempted to analyze whether treaty designs alternative to the short and simple European templates would be more in line with the national interest.[107] Although the treaties were expected to attract investment, they were 'signed and ratified as a matter of routine practise without due deliberation on their merits'.[108]

The same was the case even in a country such as Nigeria, one of the largest economies on the continent. Except for the 1979 BIT with Germany, Nigeria refused to sign investment treaties during the 1970s, while General Gowon supported the 1974 UN Charter and expropriated Western assets as part of his indigenization policy.[109] But with persistent mismanagement of the economy and a fall in global oil prices, the Nigerian economy collapsed in the early 1980s. After a series of failed reform efforts the government accepted structural adjustment programmes by the IMF and the World Bank, which from 1989 included liberalization of the Nigerian foreign investment regime. Investment treaties were now seen as a useful tool to support that process and in the early 1990s Nigeria began to enter into BITs with major European capital exporters.

---

[103] Ethiopian official I.

[104] Director of Ethiopian Investment Agency, quoted in; 'Ethiopia, Finland sign investment promotion agreement', *BBC Monitoring Africa,* 23 February 2006. See also comments by Ethiopia's foreign minister in 'India, Ethiopia Sign Investment Promotion Pact', *The Press Trust of India Limited,* 5 July 2007. ('This will facilitate the Indian public and private sector companies to invest more in Ethiopia'.)

[105] Ethiopian official II.   [106] Ethiopian official I.   [107] Ethiopian officials I and II.

[108] Ethiopian official II.

[109] The BIT was initiated already in 1974, but Nigeria refused. Without the treaty, German companies paid a 10 per cent premium on guarantees there and the German government planned to withdraw the guarantees entirely if Gowon's policies weren't reversed; PA AA, Zwischenarchiv, 121343; PA AA, Zwischenarchiv, 422 41335 GRO 1978–80.

Bounded rational competition 133

The first was negotiated with France during a three-day visit in Paris by the Nigerian president in February 1990 and regarded by the *Financial Times* as 'evidence of a new mood' in Nigeria.[110] Nigerian policy-makers agreed with their European counterparts that the treaties would help promote investment.[111] 'Why do it for other reasons?', a senior official asks.[112] In some cases, such as the 1996 Turkey agreement, the treaties were the result of politicians using BITs as photo-ops when travelling abroad ('this was purely for personal and political reasons'[113]). And as part of the public posturing that took place during the MAI discussions, one Nigerian official noted at a 1997 UNCTAD meeting that investment treaties only played a 'minimal role' in attracting FDI.[114] But his colleagues didn't agree. Overall, the expectation was that although BITs would not guarantee inflows of foreign investment, they could assist with convincing foreign investors to come. 'At the end of the day, both parties go home smiling because you are sure that both economies will improve. We can attract investment that way'.[115] Prodded by UNCTAD,[116] Nigeria was therefore 'prepared to enter into such accord[s] with any other country that is wishing to do so',[117] and had there been more funds available for travelling to negotiations the treaty network would have been much wider.[118] Yet, no information was ever sought to assess the benefits of the treaties,[119] there was no real strategy of negotiations, ratifications were 'not well organized',[120] and officials hardly considered the treaty content. Liberalization obligations were not contemplated until very recently as Nigeria mainly just signed off on European BIT templates, which in turn were copy-pasted into a 'Nigerian' BIT model.[121] Policy makers were again satisfied with passively following simple and easy default rules.

---

[110] 'Africa may come second', *Financial Times*, 19 March 1990.

[111] See e.g. 'Investment promotion agreement signed with France and Britain', *BBC Monitoring Service: Africa*, 6 August 1991 (Air Vice-Marshal Yahaya noted that the agreement with London 'would go a long way in restoring investors' confidence in the Nigerian economy'); 'Pact guarantees investments', *The Guardian*, 13 December 1990 (conservative member of British Parliament stated that BIT was intended to 'boost the confidence of British investors in Nigeria's economy'); FBIS-WEU-92-038, 26 February 1992 (Helmuth Kohl said 'The shared interest in increased German investment in Nigeria can be promoted especially by the early conclusion of an investment promotion treaty').

[112] Nigeria official I. [113] Ibid. [114] Quoted in Raghavan 1997.

[115] Nigeria official II.

[116] UNCTAD 2006d, p. 27 (urging Nigeria to ratify more BITs and be more proactive in negotiating new ones).

[117] FBIS-AFR-95-056, 23 March 1995. [118] Nigeria official I.

[119] Nigeria officials I and II. [120] UNCTAD 2006d, p. 27. [121] Nigeria official II.

Conclusion

It is no surprise that the quantitative evidence in favour of the rational competition model is precarious. Because instead of carefully weighing the costs and benefits of investment treaties, as assumed in standard rationalist models, developing countries were primarily attracted to BITs because they were salient and easy instruments to adopt. Although they may not have been optimal to attract investment, they seemed good enough. Even this expectation was not based on any meticulous processing of information, however, but was instead driven by policy-makers *wanting* to believe the treaties worked. And rather than cautiously considering the behaviour of 'competitor states' due to fears of investment diversion, most developing countries pursued much simpler adoption strategies by signing BITs whenever they could identify easy negotiation partners. Similarly, instead of trying to optimize the content of the treaties in the competition to attract investment, policy-makers had a strong preference for easy and satisfactory solutions, which meant the European templates were perfect as simple default rules. As also found by Jupille, Snidal, and Mattli in the context of the trade regime, decision-makers stopped 'searching when they reach[ed] a satisfactory institutional solution, rather than continue searching for a perfect one'.[122] All of this is what we would expect if policy-makers were bounded, rather than perfectly, rational.

But before throwing out models based on comprehensive rationality, we need to look at the risks of BITs as well. Because if there was no information about the potency of the treaties at the time they spread rapidly, it would not necessarily have been unreasonable to avoid spending time and scarce resources to find out whether they had an impact on investment flows. Nor would it be inherently irrational to sign as many as possible and stick with easy and quick templates. If available information gave the impression that the risk of treaties was close to zero, then even the most negligible impact on investors' decision-making would have made them appear as prudent instruments to adopt. Yet the following chapter will show that relevant information about the risks of BITs *was* available, but developing country governments rarely sought and processed it in ways we would expect from standard rationalist models.

---

[122] Jupille, Mattli, and Snidal 2013, p. 38.

6 Narcissistic learning

Before the explosion of investment treaty claims from the late 1990s and early 2000s, even specialized international lawyers had only limited information about the practical implications of the treaties. That said, this chapter will show there was plenty of information available up through the 1990s that obligations enshrined in BITs were binding and potentially costly. So while the relatively few claims could have made rational governments underestimate the possible liabilities of BITs, they should not have entirely ignored them. Nevertheless, that is what most developing country governments did. While some were fortunate to have expert negotiators carefully considering the potential implications in consenting to investment treaty arbitration based on vaguely drafted provisions, they were the exception. And because negotiators and stakeholders typically failed to learn from the experiences of other countries becoming subject to claims, they only appreciated the risks of BITs when hit by claims themselves. This is precisely what we would expect if policy-makers were bounded rational when learning about the low-probability but potentially high-impact risks of investment treaty arbitration.

Information about risks

Although the adjudication of treaty-based investment disputes has developed into a sui generis combination of international public and commercial law,[1] the substantive protections enshrined in BITs have a long history and have been discussed and applied in a developing country context time and again. Clauses on full protection and security as well as transfer of funds can be traced back to FCN treaties from the 18th and 19th centuries. Expropriation clauses were also enshrined in many FCN treaties and the specific compensation standard included in the majority of BITs goes back Hull's letter to the Mexican government after the 1938

---

[1] Bjorklund 2008, p. 1270.

136   Narcissistic learning

expropriations. With respect to indirect expropriation, the Iran-United States Claims Tribunal rendered numerous awards on this issue since its establishment in 1981.[2] Similarly, while the fair and equitable treatment standard has been inflated significantly in investment arbitration compared to its use in previous international disputes,[3] the international minimum standard has been a constant source of tension between developing and developed countries since the 19th century. Finally, most-favored-nation clauses have been around for centuries in international trade relations and the very idea goes back almost a millennium.[4]

There is nothing inherently new in the substantive protections enshrined in BITs, and if this was not clear to developing countries in the early years of the BIT movement, the United Nations went to great lengths to inform them with detailed reports about their scope and potential implications. UNCTC not only reminded developing countries about the potential scope of clauses covering indirect expropriation, for instance, but also the treaties' broad definitions of investments were discussed, the meaning of umbrella clauses, and so forth.[5] Fair and equitable treatment was presented as 'a classical international law standard', which could be subject to a wide range of interpretations, some of which could be far-reaching.[6] These reports clearly reflected the view that BITs should not be considered merely as 'toothless' tokens of goodwill, but rather as serious legal obligations.

What was (somewhat) new, however, was the adjudication mechanism. Non-state actors occasionally used international law to pursue compensation claims against host governments since the inter-war period,[7] and the drafters of the Abs-Shawcross convention didn't see it as 'a departure from legal tradition' to allow investors to file international disputes directly against host states.[8] This was a bit of a stretch, as even the German government considered the right of private investors to pursue international claims against sovereign governments to be rather 'unknown territory in international law'.[9] But the intent was clear and 'arbitration without privity'[10] was not artificially created by arbitrators themselves, as suggested by some commentators. Sornarajah is incorrect, for instance, when stating that Broches, the 'founding father' of ICSID, was 'cautious' about the effect of BITs' arbitration clauses.[11] This is what Broches wrote in 1982:

---

[2] Brunetti 2001.   [3] Paparinskis 2013.   [4] Hornbeck 1909.
[5] See e.g. UNCTC 1986, E/C.10/1986/7; UNCTC 1988.
[6] UNCTC 1988, pp. 30–3.   [7] See generally Parlett 2011, ch. 2.
[8] Comment on the Draft Abs-Shawcross Convention by its authors 1960, sec. VI.
[9] PA, AA, B56, 61.   [10] Paulsson 1995.
[11] Sornarajah 1994, pp. 268–9. See also, Pauwelyn 2014, p. 30.

Information about risks   137

[A] large and increasing number of investment protection treaties contain provisions which clearly establish host State consent to conciliation and/or arbitration before the Centre... Provisions of this kind ... will enable the investor to institute proceedings against the host State before the Centre ... [BITs may] lay the foundation for the jurisdiction of the Centre in such a manner as to enable an investor to invoke it without requiring further consent of the host State.[12]

A decade earlier, in 1971, Broches similarly told British officials that:

while consent by the parties was a prerequisite for arbitration by ICSID, once that consent had been given it could not be withdrawn. Inclusion therefore of a clause providing for reference to ICSID in a bilateral treaty (as was intended in the UK's draft model treaty) would give teeth to ICSID as it would constitute the consent of the host government.[13]

The architects of European and North American BIT programmes also clearly intended modern arbitration provisions to provide an irrevocable consent to investor–state arbitration.[14] This was how academics at the time interpreted such provisions as well,[15] and UNCTC told developing countries time and again that investor–state arbitration provisions in BITs were binding and enforceable. In a 1984 report, for instance, UNCTC wrote that the gradual inclusion of wide-ranging investor–state arbitration clauses in BITs was important for developing countries to consider. It meant that if investment disputes:

are not resolved by the two parties themselves of through local remedies within a certain period, then either party may submit the dispute for conciliation or arbitration ... the standard provision is that such disputes shall be submitted to an *ad hoc* arbitration tribunal, if they cannot be resolved by diplomatic means ... The award of the tribunal is binding upon both parties.[16]

But while there was plenty of information that the treaties were enforceable and wide-reaching in theory, another question is of course whether BITs were seen to be effective in practice. Some thought they were. One view promoted in the 1970s and 1980s by the International Chamber of Commerce (ICC), ICSID, and the OECD was that the treaties had deterred investment disputes and this explained the lack of treaty-based arbitration claims.[17] But while the German government, for instance, had referred to the treaties when resolving a couple of investment

---

[12] Broches 1995, pp. 450–1, 457.   [13] FCO 59/633.
[14] On the UK, Denza and Brooks 1987, p. 911. On the US, see Vandevelde 2009.
[15] For example, Gallins 1984, pp. 91–4; Peters, Schrijver, and de Waart 1984, pp. 118–19; Robin 1983–1984, pp. 953–6.
[16] UNCTC 1984, p. 7. See also UNCTC 1988, pp. 66–70, 74.
[17] Broches 1995, p. 263; ICC 1977; OECD 1985, par. 79. See also Peters 1991, p. 95.

138   Narcissistic learning

disputes,[18] this did not necessarily mean that investors themselves could rely on arbitration provisions to invoke the treaties. The UNCTC noted to developing countries in the mid 1980s that whereas BITs included 'increasingly rigid' arbitration clauses it was unclear whether they had much bite in practice, as they were not being relied on in actual investment disputes.[19] A former legal advisor to the US State Department similarly referred to doubts at the time, whether the brief and simple European BIT texts did in fact provide sufficient guidance to be useful in the enforcement context.[20] What was needed to resolve these questions was an actual investment treaty claim.

The rise of investment treaty arbitration

This happened in 1987. The claimant was a Hong Kong firm – Asian Agricultural Products (AAPL) – which brought a case to ICSID arguing that Sri Lankan security forces had failed to protect their farm against Tamil rebels.[21] The stakes were high – and not only for the parties involved. For instance, what should be the applicable law of such a dispute: national law, customary international law, the BIT itself, or some combination of the three? Did it matter, for instance, that the Sri Lankan constitution stated that international investment treaties were binding *except* if administrative or executive actions were taken in the interest of national security? Also, could a tribunal constituted to deal with investment matters have competence to decide on the legality of force during times of war? These were not minor questions of interest only to a limited circle of international lawyers. On the contrary, they addressed fundamental issues of state sovereignty, and they were to be decided by a tribunal consisting of three arbitrators, none of which had a background in public international law.[22] The tribunal decided largely in favour of the investor. Without hesitation, the tribunal agreed with the claimant that by entering into the BIT, Sri Lanka had allowed AAPL to initiate international arbitration without a specific arbitration agreement or first having exhausted local remedies. Secondly, the majority of the tribunal held that as both the parties had relied heavily on the BIT during the course of the proceedings, an implicit 'mutual agreement' could be inferred that the parties agreed the BIT should have prominence over national law (such as the Sri Lankan constitution). On this basis, the

---

[18] See Chapter 5.
[19] Asante 1988, 607; UNCTC 1986, pp. 24–5; UNCTC 1988, pp. 73–5.
[20] Gudgeon 1986, pp. 110, 130. See also Grewlich 1980, p. 56.
[21] ICSID Case No. ARB/87/3, Award, 27 June 1990.   [22] Amerasinghe 1992, p. 155.

Information about risks 139

tribunal proceeded to the merits of the case, where it also found in favour of AAPL and awarded compensation of $460,000 plus interest. The small damages awarded combined with the fact that the tribunal denied a key argument concerning liability made Sri Lankan officials see the award as a great success.[23] Nevertheless, given that the provision on which jurisdiction had been established was included in many BITs, it was reported by both international organizations[24] as well as in legal scholarship.[25] One commentator rightly noted that the AAPL decision 'appears to mark the beginning of a trend that will have to be carefully watched'.[26]

Whether developing countries followed that advice will be discussed below, but let me first review subsequent developments so as to establish what additional information was actually available to developing country governments about the scope of BITs in practice. Several BIT claims were pursued up through the early 1990s, but this took place outside the ICSID system, and they were thus kept secret to anyone but the parties themselves.[27] So we jump to 1997 when the second investment treaty award was made public. The dispute was brought by a US company that wanted Zaire to pay compensation for property that had been looted during riots in Kinshasa.[28] The ICSID tribunal found in favour of the investor and awarded AMT $9 million plus interest. That was a considerable sum for one of the poorest countries in the world. The government in Zaire probably regretted sending a defense team consisting only of one government lawyer and Zaire's ambassador to France.

In 1998 another claim was resolved based on a dispute concerning promissory notes from the Venezuelan government, which had been transferred to a Dutch firm by a Venezuelan company. The tribunal argued that because the applicable treaty – as most BITs – referred to 'investment' as 'every kind of asset' and the ICSID Convention didn't itself provide a definition, it didn't matter that assets had only been transferred on paper and no actual capital had flowed from the

---

[23] Sri Lankan officials I and II. [24] Zaidé 1991, p. 514.

[25] Amerasinghe 1992; Asiedu-Akrofi 1992; Vasciannie 1992. Note that ICSID offered free subscriptions to governments wanting to follow legal commentary on international investment law, see e.g. the offer to Lithuania in CEELI 1993c, pp. 452–3.

[26] Asiedu-Akrofi 1992, p. 376.

[27] We know of cases against Poland, Russia, Kazakhstan, as well as an unnamed Latin American country. But although some claims touched on sensitive areas of regulation, such as environmental protection, and one claim involved half a billion US dollars, we still know little of their nature or outcomes. See Peterson 2004; *Biederman* v. *Kazakhstan*, SCC rules, 1996; *Sedelmayer* v. *Russia*, SCC rules, 1996.

[28] ICSID Case No. ARB/93/1.

140   Narcissistic learning

Netherlands to Venezuela.[29] The decision showed how BITs allow investors to 'become foreign by a paper transfer of assets among companies without any commitment of new money to the host economy'.[30]

An even more notable dispute came the same year. It involved a dispute under Chapter 11 of NAFTA brought by the American firm Ethyl Corporation, which asked Canada for more than $250 million in compensation.[31] The Canadian health ministry had introduced an act prohibiting inter-provincial trade of a specific fuel additive; one reason being the fear of health risks when its by-products were released into the atmosphere. For Ethyl this constituted indirect expropriation. And after the tribunal decided in July 1998 that it had jurisdiction to hear the claim, Canada settled by reversing the ban, paying $13 million to Ethyl, as well as issuing a statement that available scientific information did not show that the substance had any harmful effects on the environment. This outcome became highly politicized in Canada, and Western NGOs began using the claim in their campaign against the ongoing MAI negotiations.[32]

Not long after the Ethyl decision, the number of investment treaty claims increased exponentially.[33] In the context of NAFTA, several disputes were pending or partly completed, some of which were equally controversial. When the denial of a permit to operate a hazardous waste site in Mexico was construed as a treaty violation in *Metalclad*, for instance, it again raised questions of how to balance environmental and public health concerns with the rights of foreign investors. And outside of the NAFTA context, the cases against Argentina in the wake of its 2001 financial crisis were particularly notable. Here, foreign utility firms sued the country after the government withdrew from a promise that their tariffs would be pegged to inflation-adjusted US dollars. This guarantee had been enshrined in investor–state contracts during the heydays of Argentina's liberalization in the early 1990s, yet the financial crisis meant that the government had to restructure its finances rapidly to prevent a complete economic meltdown. Investors such as Enron and Vivendi considered these measures a breach of Argentina's investment treaties and filed a surge of claims, which by 2002 amounted to more than $4 billion.

---

[29] ICSID Case No. ARB/96/3, Award, 9 March 1998.   [30] Van Harten 2007, p. 116.

[31] *Ethyl Corporation* v. *Canada*, UNCITRAL Rules, Decision on Jurisdiction, 24 June 1998.

[32] See generally Graham 2000, ch. 2; Walter 2001, pp. 62–3.

[33] In 1999, yet another investor was awarded almost $10 million in compensation under a BIT claim against Kazhakstan, yet this was pursued under SCC rules and thus under public radars; *Biederman* v. *Kazakhstan*, SCC, Award, August 1999.

Also in 2002, news had come out about a peculiar set of events the year before concerning a dispute involving the American cosmetics billionaire Ronald Lauder against the Czech Republic. The dispute was already alluded to in Chapter 4. Lauder had filed two claims, one as an American national based on the US-Czech BIT and one based on the Dutch-Czech BIT through his holding company in the Netherlands. But despite being based on the same set of facts and two similarly worded BITs, the tribunals came to completely opposite conclusions within 10 days of each other.[34] The decision of the second tribunal resulted in a compensation requirement of $350 million, which provoked the dissenting arbitrator to note that:

> Even States which have been held responsible for wars of aggression and crimes against humanity are not subjected to economic ruin ... It would be strange indeed, if the outcome of acceptance of a bilateral investment treaty took the form of liabilities 'likely to entail catastrophic repercussions for the livelihood and economic well-being of the population' of the Czech Republic.[35]

Bounded rational learning

By the early 1990s investor–state arbitration clauses in BITs had been shown to be binding and enforceable not just in theory but also in practice. And at the end of the decade the potency of the regime should have been crystal clear for anyone caring to seek relevant information. So how did developing country governments respond to the claims? Did they gradually update their 'risk assessments' based on a meticulous consideration of other countries' experiences, as expected in rationalist frameworks? Or did policy-makers ignore the claims unless they were particularly salient, as expected in a bounded rational framework? We already heard from policy-makers in otherwise widely different countries such as the Czech Republic, Zimbabwe, and Pakistan that they entirely failed to seek information from other countries' experiences. Recall the feedback from Zimbabwe: '[W]e didn't follow the disputes during the 1990s. We only started getting interested when we were taken to court ... We were negotiating treaties to promote investment without paying much attention to the cases and not necessarily knowing the implications'.[36] And from the Czech Republic: 'Negotiators really didn't

---

[34] *Lauder (Ronald S.)* v. *The Czech Republic*, UNCITRAL Rules, Award on Merits, 3 September 2001; *CME Czech Republic B.V. (The Netherlands)* v. *The Czech Republic*, UNCITRAL Rules, award on merits, 13 September 2001.
[35] *CME* v. *Czech Republic*, UNCITRAL, Separate Opinion, 14 March 2003, par. 77–78.
[36] Zimbabwe official I.

142   Narcissistic learning

know that the treaties had any bite in practice ... They were neither aware of the costs or the fact that it could lead to arbitration'.[37] Were these cases exceptions or did they reflect a broader pattern? Did other policy-makers also ignore the risks of BITs until hit by claims themselves?

The slowdown in investment treaty adoption

As a first cut, one way to assess this is to look at the speed with which developing countries signed BITs. Whereas an average of four treaties was signed every week during the mid 1990s, it would be surprising if this mad rush continued as the costs of the treaties revealed themselves with the rise of claims. When observing claims against other countries, rational stakeholders with an interest in more cautious investment treaty policies should have been careful to prevent diplomats and investment promotion officials to simply sign BITs whenever possible. And at first sight, this appears to be what happened. Figure 6.1 below shows that the adoption of BITs clearly slowed down after investment treaty arbitration took off. The slowdown is clear also if one considers that some countries today prefer to include investment protection chapters in preferential trade agreements (PTAs). Although this is an important development, particularly if trans-Pacific and trans-Atlantic negotiations are concluded (both were still on-going by 2015), it had yet to become truly significant at the time of writing: in 2008, for instance, only seven investment protection treaties other than BITs were signed, bringing the total number of treaties with BIT-like protections up to 77 that year – which is still less than half of what was signed just 10 years before.[38]

The exception to the slowdown was in 2001, and from Chapter 4 we know why: that was when UNCTAD had a particularly productive year managing to facilitate more than 70 BITs at its negotiation rounds. This is notable. Because at this point several claims had already been filed, including the controversial *Ethyl* dispute, yet developing countries still seemed to rush into the treaties at the UNCTAD sessions with no real negotiations. This is far from the considered and careful approach to binding treaty negotiations expected in rationalist models and also

---

[37] Czech official I.
[38] See UNCTAD 2009d, annex 2. Apart from the PTA between Singapore and the Gulf Cooperation Council, all were bilateral trade and investment deals. Note also that the development holds for BITs, which do not involve EU countries. This is important as EU member states put their BIT negotiations almost entirely on hold in the early 2000s, when it became clear that the competence to enter into investment protection agreements might be delegated to the European Union.

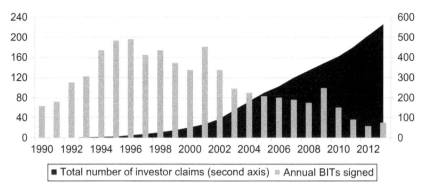

Figure 6.1 The rise of investment treaty arbitration and the slowdown in BIT adoption
Note: The vast majority of investment treaty claims are based on BITs.

provides a first hint that developing countries may not have been particularly concerned with other countries' claims.

And indeed, when we look more closely at the patterns, Figure 6.2 below indicates that rather than developing countries slowing down their BIT adoption after gradually updating their risk assessments from other countries' claims, the rapid adoption of treaties only slowed down considerably once countries themselves became subject to their first dispute. While average signing rates were already going down prior to the time of first claim, probably due to saturation (see below), this trend intensified considerably after their first claim. Particularly noteworthy is that the upward trend in ratified BITs reverses in the year of the first claim.

Note that the figure is a conservative assessment of the importance of a country's own experiences with BIT claims. This is for several reasons. Firstly, I refrain from distinguishing between claims that have been 'won', 'lost', or settled by respondent states, as this is more than difficult in an aggregate setting.[39] Secondly, the secrecy of some disputes adjudicated under non-ICSID rules means that although it is reasonable to assume that the vast majority of investment treaty awards have in fact

---

[39] For instance, did Sri Lanka really 'lose' the AAPL claim when AAPL was only awarded a tenth of what it claimed, and the tribunal found entirely in favour of Sri Lanka on the key question on merits? Legal officials in Sri Lanka didn't think so; Pererra 2000; Sri Lankan official I. The key question was whether the obligation to provide 'full protection and security' entailed a 'strict liability standard' (it didn't). See also above. Similarly, did Pakistan really 'lose' $110 million to Imbregilo in their settlement, given that the ruling on jurisdiction was so favourable for Pakistan that Imbregilo agreed to settle for less than a fourth of its claim rather than proceeding to the merits? That, at least, is not the perception among key legal officials in Pakistan. Pakistan official VI.

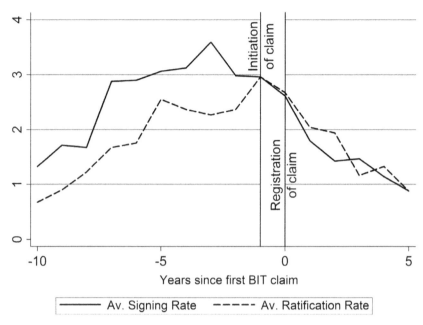

Figure 6.2 Slowdown in BIT adoption after first claim
Note: The *y*-axis shows the average annual number of BITs signed or ratified by developing countries, which had at least one BIT-based claim brought to arbitration by 2013. The *x*-axis shows time relative to the year of registration of the first BIT claim against the country.

found their way to the public domain,[40] we actually do not know for sure when a country found itself on the respondent end of a BIT claim for the first time. To the extent that first claims for certain countries are missing, it would again bias against finding an effect of the first treaty claim in the data. Finally, the year a country was subject to its first BIT claim is not necessarily the year it was first threatened with a claim.[41] This information is typically not in the public domain.[42] So although threats of arbitrations also have potential to 'reveal' the potency of BITs to the respondent government, only actual BIT claims are included in the

---

[40] Van Harten 2007, p. viii.
[41] See generally Schneiderman 2008, pp. 120–9; Tienhaara 2009, ch. 8.
[42] We know today, for instance, that Panama was notified as early as 1992 about a potential breach of its BIT with the United States, and changed its practice to avoid a dispute; Vandevelde 1993, p. 11. Similarly, although Cambodia is reported as having its first investment treaty claim in 2009, reports indicate that a French investor threatened it with a dispute five years earlier; Peterson 2005; Vis-Dunbar 2006.

Bounded rational learning

Table 6.1 *When the claim hits*

	(1)	(2)	(3)	(4)	(5)
First BIT claim	−0.433***		−0.423***	−0.418***	−0.409***
	(0.099)		(0.101)	(0.102)	(0.102)
Cumulative BIT		−0.020	−0.007	−0.007	−0.000
claims		(0.016)	(0.014)	(0.014)	(0.014)
First BIT claim in				−0.032	−0.019
region				(0.097)	(0.096)
Region cum. BIT					−0.005***
claims					(0.003)
Year dummies	Yes	Yes	Yes	Yes	Yes
Country fixed effects	Yes	Yes	Yes	Yes	Yes
Observations	2002	2002	2002	2002	2002

Note: Standard errors in parentheses.

* $p < 0.10$, ** $p < 0.05$, *** $p < 0.01$.

Dependent variable is the annual number of BITs signed. Table reports coefficients from negative binomial estimation based on updated dataset of Poulsen and Aisbett (2013) ending in 2012. The model includes a full set of year dummies to control for time-specific shocks shared by all countries – such as the end of the Cold War or changing global norms towards foreign investment. To control for time-invariant effects specific to individual countries – such as geography or legal culture – the model also includes country fixed effects. Coefficients not reported for year dummies, inward and outward FDI, GDP, lagged cubic function of total number of BITs signed (to control for saturation), lags of total number of ratified BITs, the Political Risk Services Group index of investment protection, as well as a constant. Except for year dummies, all controls are lagged one year to avoid simultaneity. To include only 'modern' BITs allowing for investor-state arbitration the sample begins in 1990. See further robustness tests in Poulsen and Aisbett (2013).

calculations, which again implies that only a particularly systematic and strong response to countries' first claims would show up in the data.

Yet, the 'narcissistic' learning implied from Figure 6.2. holds also after controlling for a range of factors, including global developments (e.g. the rise and fall of the Washington Consensus, total number of BIT claims, etc.), national or regional characteristics (e.g. changing investment policies or levels of development), as well as saturation (i.e. governments had less significant BIT partners left to sign with). Using data from 1990 to 2012, Table 6.1 shows that as a conservative estimate the experience of the first BIT claim reduced signing by 35 per cent[43] after

---

[43] For example, 1-exp(-0.433)=0.35.

146 Narcissistic learning

controlling for the total number of claims against all countries (column one). Subsequent claims, on the other hand, were only slightly negatively correlated with the adoption of the treaties and not statistically significant (columns two and three). Whereas a rational learning framework would expect that governments responded to the information revealed by each additional claims this is not what we see. Also, even if we assume that information from claims close by is easier to come by than information from claims far away, there is no evidence that governments responded to the first claim within the region (column four). And while the cumulative average number of claims per country in the region has significant effect it is substantively very small (column five).[44] The general pattern is clear: it is not until countries themselves became subject to a claim that they begin slowing down their rush to conclude the treaties.

Although the calculations control for a wide range of covariates, there could of course be several reasons for this finding. So in order to understand if it is due to salience bias or some other factors we need to go back to the cases. And the following section will show that the narcissistic learning implied by the broad patterns of adoption is because hardly any developing country governments carefully sought and processed information about the treaties. Instead, most assumed that because they had not been subject to a claim themselves, the risks of BITs were essentially zero. This explains the haphazard policies described in previous chapters and corresponds with our expectations if policy-makers were bounded rational. We begin by returning to Latin America.

Latin America

In the case of Mexico, recall that policy-makers signed a large number of investment treaties after the NAFTA agreement, but negotiators pursued one set of obligations in BITs based on European templates and another in PTAs based on the NAFTA template. According to a previous negotiator, stakeholders didn't take much notice because 'during the 1990s, BITs were a very different animal than FTAs, the WTO, and other globalization instruments'.[45] In contrast to negotiations of PTAs, where the risks were more salient, 'there was no legal review, control, or

---

[44] In other robustness tests not reported here, controls were included for political institutions and partisanship, home country characteristics, different 'types' of BITs and investment treaty claims along with other tests – yet the results were still robust. The effect holds also when using ratified BITs as the dependent variable as well as the number of BITs signed by a developing country in a given year, which came into force within three years thereafter. See Poulsen and Aisbett 2013.

[45] Mexican official II.

Bounded rational learning 147

scrutiny to the content ... Often BIT negotiations have been done by a couple of guys; they sent it to parliament with no real discussion... Apart from a copy of the BIT in the negotiator's office no one was even aware how many BITs the country had in the 1990s'.[46] This is surprising. For while there may not have been many claims up through the 1990s, Mexico had adhered to the Calvo doctrine for most of its modern history and even enshrined it in its Constitution. March 18 is still 'Oil Expropriation Day' in Mexico, a national holiday celebrating the 1938 oil expropriations, so one would perhaps have expected some discussion about a growing network of treaties based on a radically different set of principles for investment protection and with the potential to expose the government to expensive arbitration claims. But instead of carefully considering the potential costs of the treaties, government stakeholders ignored them entirely.

The learning process that resulted from the disputes against Mexico, such as the *Metalclad* case, remained within a small circle of technical staff. For even though the legal interpretations taken by arbitrators were surprisingly broad, the claims never received a great deal of attention by stakeholders at large. A key official notes, 'I would have expected reactions against BITs after the ICSID cases, but there has never been such discussion here, unlike with FTAs. No doubts or inquiries by the Senate ... Also, no regulatory agencies are aware of the treaties at all'.[47]

The absence of political demand for significant reforms meant Mexican negotiators decided to pursue only incremental changes after the claims. Apart from slowing down the adoption of BITs, the main modification was to start using North American templates as the basis for the agreements – as in the Mexican PTAs – because they were more clearly specified than the European models.[48] The response has mainly been to write slightly more 'complete contracts' based on templates already existing in the status quo, and more fundamental changes to the treaty design have thus far remained off the agenda in Mexico. I'll return to this in Chapter 8. For now, the key point is that the risks of treaties providing protections over and beyond the Mexican constitution were entirely ignored until they were invoked by investors

---

[46] Ibid. [47] Mexican official I.

[48] In the 2008 BIT with the United Kingdom, for instance, London had to depart from its model on the insistence of Mexico. The dispute settlement provisions have thus been adjusted in accordance with 'NAFTA-style' provisions allowing for a consolidation of claims (Art. 14), for instance, and include a 'fork-in-the-road' requirement to preclude investors from pursuing claims both in domestic courts and under international arbitration (annex to Art. 11).

148   Narcissistic learning

against Mexico. And Mexican officials saw this in other parts of Latin America as well:

> Many here in Latin America thought it was harmless to sign these treaties; no-one had an idea what they meant. Many who negotiated were not lawyers, so they just signed them off within a few days, hours, or even over email because travels are too expensive ... Governments want to display co-operation, and one way to do that is to sign promotion treaties that sounds nice ... No discussion, analysis, goes into it ... And even if it gets a legal review, the lawyers don't have the experience what to check for ... No one cares until the dispute comes.[49]

This impression exactly fits the experiences of Ecuador. While Ecuador signed a large number of BITs up through the 1990s, the treaties were never politicized in Quito either, as the risks were not understood.[50] According to an official involved, the programme continued 'without understanding the responsibilities and obligations. We didn't start to worry about it before we ourselves were sued'.[51] That is why stakeholders allowed embassies and investment promotion officials to initiate BIT negotiations, even when there were hardly any commercial links with partner countries. As late as August 2001, for instance, the Danish foreign ministry told the Ecuadorian embassy in Copenhagen that it didn't find any real justification for the Ecuadorian initiative to negotiate a treaty.[52]

The haphazard policy ended in 2004, when Ecuador lost more than $75 million to Occidental Petroleum Corporation ('Oxy') in a claim based on the US BIT. The claim by Oxy prompted the Ecuadorian government to begin analyzing the commercial and legal implications of its existing BITs.[53] This was the first time since beginning the BIT programme more than a decade earlier. A few years later the review process was intensified due to a second, and even more notable, claim by Oxy. The Ecuadorian government had by then come under increasing public pressure to evict the American oil giant due to concerns about its operations in the Amazon. The opportunity arose in 2006 when Oxy broke both Ecuadorian law as well as its contract with the government by selling 40 per cent of its operations to a Canadian firm without first getting ministerial approval. Two days after the contract was terminated and Oxy's operations were seized, Oxy took the billion-dollar dispute to ICSID. This resulted in even greater outrage in Quito. The president-elect, Rafael Correa, objected fiercely to the idea of having ICSID determine the dispute, and after taking office

---

[49] Mexican official II.   [50] Ecuador official III.   [51] Ecuador official IV.
[52] UM 400.E.13.Ecuador.12.   [53] Ibid.

he notified ICSID that Ecuador would no longer consent to arbitration of disputes involving natural resources.

As more high-profile claims were filed against Ecuador during Correa's tenure, the treaties were ultimately seen as so dysfunctional that the government decided they had to be terminated. The Central Bank had concluded in 2007 that Ecuador's BITs had been ineffective in attracting investment to the country,[54] and as Correa was already seeking to distance himself from Washington and neoliberalism, the ICSID claims became a lightning rod for the administration. Starting in 2008, Ecuador therefore began to terminate several of its BITs and suspend new negotiations until a policy had been defined. This was done the year after, when the Foreign Trade Council directed the government to renegotiate BITs that could not be immediately terminated, and in July of the same year Ecuador withdrew from ICSID entirely. That was necessary, Correra said, as ICSID 'signifies colonialism, slavery with respect to transnationals, with respect to Washington, with respect to the World Bank and we cannot tolerate this'.[55] To make the exit credible, the administration and parliament had even had Article 422 of the 2008 Constitution state that Ecuador could not enter into treaties with investor–state arbitration provisions. Only national or Latin American bodies should be allowed to resolve such disputes, which made the constitutional court declare all existing BITs unconstitutional. Instead, Ecuador proposed that a Latin American investment court should take the place of ad hoc ICSID arbitration and initiated a new high-profile review of its past and future investment treaty policy.[56]

In short, whereas the treaties were still perceived to be 'good enough' for Mexico despite their unanticipated costs, Ecuador decided an incremental response was not enough. The different reaction is what we would expect from a bounded rationality framework: first Ecuadorian officials entirely ignored the (low-probability) risks of investment treaties, as in Mexico, but then reacted very strongly as controversial and high-profile claims made the costs become particularly salient for a left-wing government opposing what it perceived as American capitalist hegemony.

Few countries have followed Ecuador's example. For while most governments also entered into BITs not appreciating the implications, they have by and large followed the example of Mexico by proceeding

---

[54] Wikileaks 09Quito973, 17 November 2009. See also Chapter 5.
[55] Quoted in Diaz 2009.
[56] 'Ecuador to establish commission to audit bilateral investment treaties', Herbert Smith Freehills Arbitration note, 14 October 2013.

150   Narcissistic learning

with only minor reforms after the claims, for instance by slowing down their adoption. One such case is Chile. Here, one official notes that, 'like most countries in the 1990s, we signed a lot of treaties not knowing sometimes what we were committing ourselves to'.[57] This resulted in easy negotiations, not least when Chile adopted treaties with other developing countries, where counterparts had a similar laissez-faire attitude. Chile signed a BIT with the Dominican Republic in 2000, for instance, where no one took much notice of the treaties either. For just as in Chile, officials in the Dominican Republic 'never thought about disputes that may arise from the treaty'.[58]

Chilean officials did, however, learn from other countries' experiences: 'We didn't know the scope of the treaties, and the arbitrations got started and the awards and interpretations came, we began to rethink our view'.[59] Yet, the defining moment for the Chilean BIT programme was not when other countries became subject to disputes, but when Chile itself was subject to a claim. 'It is when we started to be sued, we understood the implications'.[60] As a result, Chile is today reviewing its approach. As in Mexico, this has involved moving away from the European template agreements to the more specified NAFTA model as well as enshrining investment protections into broader regional pacts, as the expectation is that this will have a greater impact on investment flows than stand-alone BITs.[61] But because no claims against Chile have resulted in particularly costly or controversial outcomes, policy-makers still find the investment treaty regime 'good enough' and have therefore decided to stick with it for now.

Asia

Moving to Asia, risk neglect also explains much of the past behaviour of Thailand. Here, the bureaucracy failed to appreciate the potency of private recourse to arbitration, which resulted in a severe misperception of the treaties' practical implications up through the 1990s.[62] This persisted to as late as 2005 when Thailand became subject to its first investment treaty claim over a toll way concession awarded to a German investor.[63] While numerous countries had been subject to claims in the late 1990s and early 2000s, 'the shift in attitude came with the German claim'.[64] Before then, 'few took BITs very seriously. We had very complex obligations on paper, but no one used them so

---

[57] Chilean official I.   [58] Dominican Republic official I.   [59] Chilean official I.
[60] Ibid.   [61] Ibid.   [62] Mangklatanakul 2012, p. 82.
[63] The claim was *Walter Bau* v. *Thailand*, 2005, UNCITRAL.   [64] Thai official I.

that was fine'.[65] Based on the understanding that the treaties entailed no real risks, the level of expertise going into negotiations was minimal: 'Most of the time we put the best people on the agreements with high priority such as FTAs rather than BITs. That has implications for the legal expertise going into BIT negotiations'.[66] When PTA negotiations covered investment the liberalization provisions were carefully considered, as their implications were clear.[67] BITs, on the other hand, 'were not scrutinized',[68] and it was not until Thailand itself got hit by the claim that 'officials suddenly learned these things mattered in practice. ... Before, they didn't pay much attention, but now they look at the agreement very carefully'.[69] So although the Thai Board of Investment was still very much in favour of BITs at the time of writing ('their mandate is to promote investments, so they want BITs')[70] other agencies had become more careful.

Looking back at Thailand's investment treaty programme, a Thai official notes that this learning experience is important for other countries to consider: 'they must be careful, lest they inadvertently find themselves to be victims of their own creation'.[71] By 2014, however, there was no indications that the Thai government were seeking to significantly reanchor its investment treaty policies. The German claim resulted in a loss of 29 million euros, which was a significant but not a catastrophic sum. And because there has yet to be a significant political backlash against the treaties, as in Ecuador, the changes in policy have remained limited. Although policy-makers may have entered into the agreements significantly overestimating their benefits and ignoring the risks, the reaction has primarily been a slowdown in adoption as well as the development of a slightly revised Thai BIT model. All in all, a highly incremental response – just as we should expect from a country where the claims have yet to result in particularly salient costs.

A similar process transpired in India. Delhi occasionally involved well-trained legal officials who made difficult negotiation partners,[72] but this was the exception as BIT negotiators often failed to appreciate the scope of the treaties up through the 1990s and early 2000s. Despite the growing number of claims, the absence of expertise among relevant officials and the absence of claims against India itself meant that 'the Indian government hardly considered that BITs could impact

---

[65] Ibid.   [66] Ibid.   [67] Thai official III.   [68] Ibid.   [69] Ibid.   [70] Thai official I.
[71] Mangklatanakul 2012, p. 84.
[72] See e.g. Rao 2000. The 1995 German BIT took more than three rounds of negotiations for instance; German official I.

152   Narcissistic learning

the exercise of India's regulatory power'.[73] This meant no stakeholders took much interest in BITs – unlike trade agreements, where the implications were far more salient.[74] And the failure to seek relevant information about the potency of the treaties is an additional reason India refused to include investment obligations into the WTO in the early 2000s.[75] According to an official involved, the perception was that because BITs did not include liberalization provisions they *had* to be flexible – thereby overlooking the most important feature of modern BITs, the investor–state arbitration clause.[76]

It was not until recently that more than a few Indian officials realized that the treaties offered wide and rigid protections. The change in attitude came not from the NAFTA arbitrations or claims against other developing countries, but when India itself came on the respondent end of arbitration claims related to the Dabhol power project, which in 2005 resulted in a settlement of as much as $1 billion dollars according to some estimates.[77] Based on this experience the government decided to review available evidence as to whether the treaties helped attract investment and revise its model investment treaty. But because of the lack of coordination between the ministry of finance, which negotiated BITs, and the ministry of commerce, in charge of trade treaties with investment provisions, India pursued different obligations depending on who was in charge of negotiations.[78] BITs continued to anchor to European template language, while trade policy officials simultaneously negotiated investment provisions in PTAs with Singapore, Korea, Japan, and Malaysia, which included more narrow and specified provisions. Exactly as we saw in the cases of Mexico and Chile in Chapter 5, officials stuck with the default rules they were used to, which resulted in an entirely incoherent approach to otherwise similar treaty obligations.

The final blow to this disorganized BIT policy was two more recent arbitration claims. The first was an adverse award against India in the *White Industries* case, which also 'took the Indian government by surprise'.[79] This time, Indian officials – and even the attorney general – had

---

[73] Ranjan 2014, p. 20.   [74] Ibid., pp. 18–19.

[75] WT/WGTI/W/86. (BITs were preferred over a multilateral investment treaty as they give 'flexibility to a lot of countries enabling them to channel FDI into areas of priority determined by them'.). See also WT/WGTI/M/12; WT/WGTI/M/14; WT/WGTI/W/71, par. 6.

[76] Costa Rican official I.   [77] Ranjan and Raju, 2014.

[78] Ibid. On overlapping investment treaty obligations in BITs and PTAs, see generally Alschner 2014.

[79] Ranjan and Raju 2014.

Bounded rational learning 153

failed to appreciate that their BITs covered decisions taken by Indian courts.[80] The second claim was filed by Vodafone in 2012 through its Dutch subsidiary. This dispute had also been adjudicated in Indian courts – including the Supreme Court – and involved a tax bill of more than $2 billion. Combined with other claims being filed against India at the time, this became too much for the Indian government, and the finance minister decided in 2013 to put a hold to all negotiations and revisit previous treaties. The (relatively) strong reaction was mainly due to the shock of Indian policy-makers that even the Indian judiciary could be second-guessed by investment tribunals. The finance minister said: 'We cannot allow the highest court of the land to be subjected to any foreign courts or tribunals'.[81]

Had the Indian government sought and processed information about the implications of the treaties in ways predicted by rationalist models this could not have come as a major surprise: acts of the judiciary are generally attributable to the state under international law and tribunals had already allowed similar investment treaties to question judicial acts in other countries at the time.[82] This information had been ignored, as it was not sufficiently salient.

Africa

In Africa, as well, the main reason investment treaty adoption was so haphazard up through the 1990s and early 2000s was a complete failure to appreciate the nature of the agreements. We heard this from officials in Zimbabwe and Ghana in Chapter 4, and elsewhere in Africa the Ghanaian officials found even less understanding of the treaties:

> We came across many countries that handled this in a very superficial level ... We did not find capacity to negotiate in most places in Africa. It has to with an understanding and appreciation of what is involved. It is not just another cooperation agreement without teeth, yet most negotiators on the other side of the table didn't actually negotiate.[83]

This was the case in both Ethiopia and Nigeria, for instance. In fact, at the time of writing neither country had become subject to investment treaty claims, which meant that by 2014, after more than 500 investment treaty claims had been filed, officials had still not undertaken

---

[80] See discussion in Ranjan and Raju 2014.
[81] 'Invest pacts can't be subject to foreign jurisdiction', *India Post*, 17 April 2013.
[82] See discussion in Ranjan and Raju 2014.   [83] Ibid.

154   Narcissistic learning

any risk assessments. In Ethiopia, a former negotiator had learned from particularly salient disputes against other countries, but the bureaucracy was still not 'aware of the potential risk these treaties entail'.[84] In Nigeria, the situation was even more critical. Here, the official in charge of the BIT programme had heard of only a couple of particularly salient disputes but:

> [t]here has been no claim against Nigeria that I know of ... There are no considerable risks involved, as it is worth it signing them. There are a lot of claims against Argentina I think. Yukos has also used the treaties I think. This is relevant because of the weakness of our institutions, but if the condition for investors going into Nigeria is the treaties then why not sign them ... No one [is] objecting to signing them. No one really cares within the bureaucracy ...[85]

Another Nigerian official similarly notes that no efforts had been done to assess the potential liabilities entailed by the agreements: 'We have not made any comprehensive analyses on this I think'.[86] It is therefore not without irony that a previous Nigerian investment official noted in the mid 1990s that governments should 'be assisted to prevent them from entering into defective treaties whose implications they had not considered before signing'.[87]

Similar attitudes are found in other African countries yet to be subject to disputes. In Kenya, for instance, relevant officials in the country are not oblivious to the fact that the treaties are binding and could result in liabilities, but have heard only of the most egregious cases – just as counterparts in Nigeria:

> I have not heard of any countries being sued under investment treaties. I vaguely remember some investor who went to COMESA court of justice, but I don't know if it was under a bilateral investment treaty or some other legal instrument. As far as I know, investment treaties are not used very often to settle investment disputes around the world.[88]

The costs of investment treaties are still considered miniscule as the risks have yet to be sufficiently salient. This has meant that Kenya has been happy to continue negotiating investment treaties. Although few have been ratified, eight BITs were signed between 2006 and 2013, which was more than half of the country's total treaty network.

A similar example is Libya, which signed 26 BITs from 2001 to its civil war in 2011. This is a report on the BIT signed with Spain during Qadhafi's visit there in 2007:

---

[84] Ethiopia official II.   [85] Nigeria official I.   [86] Nigeria official II.
[87] Quoted in Raghavan 1997.   [88] Ibid.

Bounded rational learning 155

[T]he Government of Libya (GOL) indicated ... that it wished to quickly finalize language for an education and culture agreement, a defense cooperation agreement, a bilateral legal cooperation and extradition treaty, an investment security agreement and a double taxation-exemption agreement ... [A Spanish official] lamented that the rush to finalize agreements for signature in time for Qadhafi's visit had precluded meaningful bilateral discussions of what the two sides' understanding of those accords would mean and how they would be implemented.[89]

At the time, Libya had not been respondent in an investment treaty claim, and it still rushed through the treaties alongside all sorts of diplomatic tokens of goodwill without 'meaningful bilateral discussions'. Unlike the early days of the Qadhafi regime, when he had yet to embrace foreign investment and therefore declined invitations to sign BITs,[90] there was a rush to adopt the treaties in the early 2000s. And as the Spanish official remarked, 'The form is more important to the GOL than the substance'.[91] This was in 2007, after about 300 claims had already been filed.

These country experiences present a radically different picture of the way developing countries contemplated and negotiated BITs compared to standard accounts of the BIT movement. Key stakeholders did not just slightly underestimate the risks of disputes or learn from claims abroad if they were relevant for their own BIT programme. Instead, they often ignored the risks entirely and did not even consider other countries' experiences before they themselves were hit by a claim. They were 'prisoners of their own experience'. Even negotiators often failed to appreciate that the treaties entailed binding and enforceable obligations until their own government was subject to a claim, as only then did the risks become salient for non-experts.

This is confirmed by developed country negotiations as well. As an experienced Dutch negotiator recalls, '[D]uring the 1990s, developing countries often asked what even basic provisions meant'.[92] Similarly, a Canadian official notes that, 'in the past we actually had to drop some negotiations simply because the level of understanding was lacking'.[93] And a former German official also confirms that during the 1990s some developing countries were very well prepared, but often:

---

[89] 'Qadhafi's travel to Spain', Report by American Embassy in Tripoli, 12 December 2007; Wikileaks 07Tripoli1033.

[90] Germany, for instance, was told that the Libyan domestic law provided sufficient protection for investments; PA, AA, B36, 295.

[91] 'Qadhafi's travel to Spain', Report by American Embassy in Tripoli, 12 December 2007; Wikileaks 07Tripoli1033.

[92] Dutch official I.   [93] Canadian official I.

156   Narcissistic learning

we had the impression that they had very little knowledge about BITs. But that didn't make negotiations easy, because then we had to explain everything. And then there were countries who just wanted to sign – whatever the text, but these are extreme examples. In most cases, we were bombarded with questions. What does non-discrimination mean? What does free transfer mean? And in each negotiation we had to explain not just one, but many times.[94]

Hardly, the type of sophisticated engagement with binding international legal obligations one would expect from rationalist accounts of economic diplomacy.

The role of expertise and experience

There have – naturally – been exceptions, as some governments were considerably more careful when negotiating BITs. Let me mention a couple of cases as illustrations. The first is Costa Rica, which ratified the ICSID Convention in 1993 to stop the pressure from the US government in an investment dispute. A few years before a multilateral loan from the Inter-American Development Bank was delayed until an (unrelated) investment dispute involving an American investor in Costa Rica was referred to arbitration.[95] Senator Helms had pushed for this move against Costa Rica, and one his advisors noted that it would 'scare the living daylights out of them'.[96] Helms was right. Costa Rica ratified ICSID that year and subsequently consented to the arbitration to stop American pressure.[97] Yet Costa Rica's BIT programme had begun already in the early 1980s and was based not so much on the need to de-politicize investment disputes, but rather the need to attract foreign capital. By the early 1990s, the Costa Rican Central Bank and Treasury Department found that because the country had already liberalized its capital account and generally provided strong protections to foreign investors, it would be logical to also have a BIT programme to complement those reforms.[98] Before the liberalization of the capital

---

[94] German official I.   [95] ICSID Case No. ARB/96/1.

[96] Quoted in Brower and Wong 2005, p. 5. Note that IADB is the only multilateral organization where the United States can veto an individual loan – and that, too, only if it is provided through its Fund for Special Operations. When in 2012, the United States was joined by Germany and Spain wanting to block a 'hard' IADB loan to Argentina – partly due to its refusal to comply with ICSID awards – the loan went ahead anyway.

[97] Costa Rican official II.

[98] Costa Rican official I. Note that although Costa Rica signed a few BITs during the 1980s, this was done on an ad hoc basis with no real strategy – unlike Sri Lanka for instance.

Bounded rational learning 157

account, the treasury had been sceptical of the treaties' transfer clauses, which was the reason an agreement was not reached with Germany in the late 1970s or early 1980s, for instance.[99] But now scepticism was replaced with a full-fledged embrace as 'we thought they would be very important tools to attract investment'.[100] And although not always rejecting invitations that made little economic sense, such as a BIT with the Czech Republic, there was an actual strategy in Costa Rica: '[W]e didn't just want a BIT, whenever a president was visiting'.[101] What makes Costa Rica stand out even more, however, is that the task to negotiate investment treaties was given to a small but highly skilled team within the ministry of trade. Most of the staff had graduate degrees in international economic law from Western universities, and all coordination pertaining to both trade and investment agreements happened within that unit. The result was that Costa Rica pursued a coherent strategy pushing for investment treaty obligations not just bilaterally but also in the context of the WTO[102] as well as the MAI, where Costa Rica was an invited observer. The staff occasionally rotated to stations abroad, such as the WTO, yet always returned to the same unit, such that the legal expertise and experience remained.[103]

This meant that although not all obligations were well understood due to the lack of disputes,[104] Costa Rica's negotiations were based on a sound understanding of the legal questions involved. So even though the CAFTA negotiations with the United States led to considerable debate in Costa Rica over the implications of investor–state arbitration, it did not lead to major changes in strategy apart from putting in place an appropriate defense team.[105] Neither did the arbitration cases against Costa Rica that started a few years after.[106] Instead, it was the many cases against Argentina that led Costa Rica to make certain restrictive changes in the content of its treaties.[107] This follows the expectations of the rational decision making model outlined in Chapter 2: the government realized the treaties involved enforceable protections all along, but made adjustments in treaty practice after learning from other countries' experiences.

---

[99] PA, AA, Zwischenarchiv, 121318.

[100] Costa Rica official I; Costa Rica official II. Daily Report. Latin America, FBIS-LAT-96–137, 16 July 1996 (Chilean BIT justified by President Figueres as a useful way to attract investments). See also comments by former negotiator in Echandi 2011, pp. 11, 13.

[101] Costa Rica official I.   [102] See e.g. WT/WGTI/M/14.   [103] Costa Rican official I.

[104] Ibid.   [105] Costa Rican official II.

[106] For example, ICSID Case No. ARB(AF)/07/3.   [107] Costa Rican official II.

158   Narcissistic learning

Another example is China, which began signing BITs with European countries from 1982.[108] Whereas international economic law had earlier been rejected by China as a tool 'used by the imperialists and hegemonists . . . to carry out aggression, oppression and exploitation',[109] investment treaties were now seen as useful to show that the recent opening up of the Chinese economy was serious so as to win 'the trust and confidence of foreign investors'.[110] Yet, Beijing carefully construed its investor–state arbitration regime as it moved from being a capital importer only to also an important home country to outward investment. At first, international tribunals were allowed to determine only whether sufficient compensation had been paid in expropriation disputes. Whether expropriation had occurred in the first place – and thus questions of liability – were up to the Chinese courts to decide,[111] and disputes about other matters could not be subject to treaty-based arbitration (including disputes involving indirect expropriation). When European negotiators tried to include broad arbitration provisions, China insisted that because 'a foreign investor – individual or company – does not have the same status as a state, the investor's recourse to arbitration should remain much more limited'.[112] This was a conscious decision on the part of Beijing to strike a balance between investor rights and the preservation of state sovereignty,[113] so when China acceded to the ICSID Convention in 1993 it thus also notified the Centre that 'the Chinese government would only consider submitting to the jurisdiction of ICSID disputes over compensation resulting from expropriation or nationalization'. Only in the late 1990s, when China needed BITs to protect its growing stock of outward investment, did Chinese officials 'upgrade' China's model BIT to include a comprehensive consent to investor–state arbitration.[114] And even in its most recent model, arbitration can be initiated only after an initial administrative review – an innovation seemingly intended to alert Beijing about local protectionist practices.[115] In short, Western BIT models have at least in part been

---

[108] On negotiations with the UK, see Denza and Brooks 1987. Germany approached China with a BIT in 1979 so as to facilitate investment guarantees, though it took four years before the agreement was finalized; PA, AA, Zwischenarchiv, 121316.

[109] Former diplomat and chairman of the Chinese Society of International Law, Huan Xiang, quoted in Kong 2003, p. 108.

[110] Shishi 1988, p. 165. On China's expropriation of foreign capital after the revolution, see Kong 1998–9. On China and international arbitration, see Hale 2015.

[111] Some arbitral decisions have questioned this view, compare e.g. *Berschader* v. *The Russian Federation*, SCC Case No. 080/2004, Award, 21 April 2006, par. 153; with ICSID Case No. ARB/07/6, Award on Jurisdiction, 19 June 2009, par. 188.

[112] Denza and Brooks 1987.   [113] Shishi 1988, p. 166.   [114] Berger 2011.

[115] Gallagher and Shan 2009, pp. 371–6.

Bounded rational learning 159

tailored to Chinese perceptions of the national interest – as indeed one would expect from a rationalist model of treaty adoption.

There have been other exceptions. In the Middle East, for instance, both Turkey and Lebanon were fortunate to have skilled lawyers in place to negotiate their BITs. In the case of Turkey, we saw in Chapter 5 that officials based their expectations about the economic benefits of the treaties on little more than a hunch. But at least when it came to the risks of the treaties Turkey did not enter into the regime blindfolded. The lead negotiator was startled about the lack of understanding among most negotiating partners. In one major negotiation, 'I found out their delegation had no clue. So in [the] middle of the negotiation, I had to sit and explain what the provisions meant'. In other contexts, 'some didn't even know what ICSID was', and occasionally the official had to negotiate with bureaucrats sent just because they knew how to speak English.[116] And indeed, just as we should expect from a country where policymakers had the experience and expertise necessary to engage carefully with negotiations, the couple of claims filed against Turkey did not lead to major surprises about the very nature of the treaties.

Also in Lebanon, the negotiator had a legal background with a focus on international arbitration and was hired on a UN contract, thereby avoiding being part of diplomatic rotation schemes. So while stakeholders in Lebanon thought the dozens of treaties adopted by Lebanon were just 'ink on paper' until hit by the first claim, the negotiator did realize the potential scope of the treaties and negotiated them more carefully than many of Lebanon's treaty partners.[117]

Finally, a country such as Argentina has had a long legal history with international arbitration.[118] So although no real negotiation records exist in Argentina of the almost 60 BITs signed from 1991 to 2001, negotiators were aware of the potential for claims even if they were surprised about some of the interpretations after the 2001 crisis.[119] And indeed, the Argentinean government noted in negotiations with Denmark in 1992:

The acceptance of arbitration by the Republic of Argentina as a dispute settlement mechanism between a private investor and the host State has implied an almost revolutionary change in our juridical traditions. This issue was the object of long and difficult internal discussions before we were able to achieve a consensus on this matter. This provision is, therefore, the result of a compromise between many governmental areas and we cannot change it without going through long consultations again.[120]

---

[116] Turkey official I.   [117] Lebanon official I.   [118] See Hale 2015.
[119] Argentina official I.   [120] UM.400.E.13.Argentina.12. Own translation.

160   Narcissistic learning

This is the type of 'normal' politics expected in most accounts of the international investment regime. It corresponds more closely to standard political economy models, where actors fight for their own interests rather than passively relying on default rules while ignoring important information. But both quantitative and qualitative evidence suggests that cases such as Argentina are the exception rather than the rule. As expertise and experience were typically absent in developing countries, the bounds of rationality were narrowed, and information processing constrains led to mistaken inferences about the potency of the treaties time and again.

Conclusion

Looking back at the 1990s, a former Swiss investment treaty negotiator notes that 'the big question is whether developing countries actually knew what they signed'.[121] By now it should be clear that for most countries the answer is no. While it may have been perfectly reasonable for (some) developing countries to sign (some) BITs, the *process* with which many did so was predictably irrational. Rationalist accounts of the BIT movement are therefore incorrect when arguing that the sovereignty costs of BITs were known by governments deciding to consent to investment treaty arbitration.[122] Most governments did not just vastly overestimate the economic benefits of BITs, but also ignoredtheir risks until hit by a claim themselves and that explains why so many were content to simply sign off on European models.

The chapter also alluded to the largely incremental changes, which have taken place after the rise of investment treaty arbitration. Despite signing up to BITs without appreciating the potential liabilities, it is only in countries where the treaties have been considered outright dysfunctional that governments have begun reanchoring their policies. I'll return to this observation in the final chapter. Before then, the following chapter will provide further flesh to the bone to understand the underlying causal mechanism for the bounded rational BIT diffusion by providing a fine-grained analysis at the micro level of how officials in one country learned about the implications of investment

---

[121] Swiss official I.
[122] Montt 2009, p. 128. See also Büthe and Milner 2009, p. 214; Elkins, Guzman, and Simmons 2006, p. 825; Rose-Ackerman 2009, p. 313. For examples in legal scholarship, see Paulsson 2010, p. 344; Vicuña 2002, p. 31. For exceptions, see Pauwelyn 2014; Van Harten 2010, pp. 42–6.

treaties both within and between government bureaucracies. The focus will be on the 'deviant' case of South Africa, which recently decided that the costs of the regime were too high to justify only incremental reforms. But unlike Ecuador, Bolivia, and Venezuela, where the costs of the treaties were particularly salient for governments which pursued socialist and anti-American policies, the changing attitude in South Africa was not preceded by a markedly different investment protection policy. The case of South Africa is also particularly useful as it allows us to more clearly distinguish between the roles of imperfect information and imperfect processing of information than in many other countries. For among all the governments adopting BITs during the 1990s, the one in Pretoria had a particularly strong incentive to seek information about the scope of what they were signing. Yet it didn't.

7   Letting down the guard: a case study

When the African National Congress (ANC) won the elections in 1994 it marked a new beginning for South Africa. Not only could the country begin rectifying deeply entrenched racial inequalities, it could also begin to reverse the disastrous economic management under apartheid. To do this, the ANC's economic platform aimed at providing basic welfare provision to South Africa's poor. But rather than populist redistributive policies, wide-scale nationalizations, and booming rates of inflation and public debt, the ANC pursued borderline conservative macroeconomic reforms, including liberalization of commodity trade and the investment regime.

Due to the combination of international sanctions and tight capital controls, South Africa received next to no FDI inflows during apartheid – a mere $300 million from 1980 to 1993. This had to be reversed. 'The rates of economic growth cannot be achieved without important inflows of foreign capital', Nelson Mandela told an audience of American business leaders in 1991.[1] 'We are determined to create the necessary climate, which the foreign investor will find attractive'.[2] The new government therefore welcomed foreign investment in the 1994 white paper on the Reconstruction and Development Programme and aimed to provide foreign investors national treatment.[3] Nelson Mandela assured investors that 'not a single reference to things like nationalisation' was present in his government's economic policies and that his platform had been cleansed of 'any Marxist ideology'.[4]

South Africa liberalized its investment regime in practically all sectors, allowing foreign investors 100 per cent ownership, dismantling earlier discriminatory taxes towards non-residents, losing restrictions on capital

---

[1] Quoted in Marais 1998, p. 123.   [2] Marais 1998, p. 123.
[3] Parliament of the Republic of South Africa, 'White Paper on Reconstruction and Development', *Government Gazette*, 23 November 1994, p. 23.
[4] Quoted in Marais 1998, p. 95.

162

An unquantifiable liability 163

repatriation, provided cash incentives to invest in manufacturing, avoiding performance requirements, signing double-taxation treaties, ratifying the MIGA Convention, and established an investment promotion agency. In short, the government followed the international trend at the time by replacing 'red tape with red carpet treatment of foreign investors'.[5] Yet, with sluggish economic growth and one of the highest unemployment rates in the world, the reforms had disappointing outcomes[6] and South Africa also failed to attract much FDI through the 1990s. The limited interest of foreign investors in the early years of the post-apartheid regime has been attributed to a range of factors,[7] but one thing is clear: it was not due to a lack of investment protection treaties. South Africa entered into almost 50 BITs from 1994 onwards (Table 7.1). Although not realized at the time, this later proved to be perhaps the most controversial aspect of ANC's economic diplomacy. To understand why, let me begin by briefly outlining South Africa's experiences with investment arbitration, which culminated in a compensation claim of more than a quarter of a billion US dollars concerning a constitutionally enshrined policy to redistribute wealth to the black population.

An unquantifiable liability

The first investment treaty claim against South Africa happened in 2001.[8] After a Swiss-owned farm had been looted and destroyed, the owner used the 1997 BIT to ask for compensation.[9] As the claim was pursued under UNCITRAL rules it was kept entirely under the radar until 2006.[10] The Swiss investor made two key arguments: first of all, the investment was subject to 'creeping' expropriation due to the subsequent land-claims process by local black and other historically disadvantaged South Africans (HDSA) seeking restitution for land takings during apartheid. This process was part of South Africa's Black Economic Empowerment (BEE) regime, which, based on the Constitution, mandates

---

[5] Sauvant 2009, p. 222.   [6] See Lundahl and Petersson 2009; Rodrik 2006
[7] See e.g. Akinboade, Siebrits and Roussot 2006; Arvanitis 2005.
[8] Note that previously the same year the British government objected to a proposed ban on private security firms arguing that it would breach the 1994 UK-South Africa BIT. Eventually, the foreign-owned companies won the argument: kicking out firms who brought in close to 2 billion South African rand a year turned out to be too costly an endeavour – even without a BIT claim – and the government withdrew its plans; 'An industry hijacked', *The Economist*, 6 October 2001; Peterson 2006, pp. 15–16.
[9] Trade Law Centre for Southern Africa 2004, p. 14.
[10] All information on this case referred to below is from Peterson 2006; Peterson 2008.

Table 7.1 *South Africa's BITs*

Partner	Signed	Ratified	Partner	Signed	Ratified
United Kingdom	20 September '94	27 May '98	Czech Republic	14 December '98	17 September 99
Netherlands	9 May '95	1 May '99	Uganda	8 May '00	.
Switzerland	27 June '95	29 November '97	Nigeria	29 April '00	.
Korea, Rep.	7 July '95	6 June '97	Turkey	23 June '00	.
Germany	11 September '95	10 April '98	Algeria	24 September '00	.
France	11 October '95	22 June '97	Rwanda	19 October '00	.
Canada	27 November '95	.	Brunei	14 November '00	.
Cuba	8 December '95	7 April '97	Benin★	2 February '01	.
Denmark	22 February '96	23 April '97	Burkina Faso★	2 February '01	.
Austria	28 November '96	1 January '98	Chad★	2 February '01	.
Mozambique	6 May '97	28 July '98	Mauritania★	2 February '01	.
Italy	9 June '97	16 March '99	Tunisia	28 February '02	.
Iran	3 November '97	5 March '02	Libya	14 June '02	.
China	30 December '97	1 April '98	Yemen	1 August '02	.
Mauritius	17 February '98	7 October '98	Qatar	20 October '03	.
Sweden	25 May '98	1 January '99	Eq. Guinea	17 February '04	.
Senegal	5 June '98	.	DR Congo	31 August '04	.
Ghana	9 July '98	.	Israel	21 October '04	.
Argentina	23 July '98	1 January '01	Angola	17 February '05	.
BLEU	14 August '98	14 March '03	Tanzania	22 September '05	.
Finland	14 September '98	3 October '99	Congo	1 December '05	.
Spain	30 September '98	23 December '99	Madagascar	13 December '06	.
Egypt	28 October '98	.	Sudan	7 November '07	.
Chile	12 November '98	.	Ethiopia	18 March '08	.
Greece	19 November '98	5 September '01	Zimbabwe	27 November '09	.
Russia	23 November '98	12 April '00			

★Neither UNCTAD nor the South African Department of Foreign Affairs have a full list of the treaties signed, and while these four treaties do not appear in official lists, their signature is confirmed by both South African officials as well as in UNCTAD 2002. On the 1974 agreement with Paraguay listed in UNCTAD's database see note 28.

Sources: UNCTAD and South Africa's Department of Foreign Affairs

An unquantifiable liability 165

redistributive efforts to mend the vast economic inequalities as a result of apartheid. These vital social policies were now argued to conflict with South Africa's investment treaty obligations. Secondly, the investor argued that a lack of effective policing of the investor's property – or the lack of prosecution of apprehended looters – was a breach of the BIT's provision on 'full protection and security'. The expropriation claim was dismissed by the tribunal even though the land-claims process was still ongoing and the outcome uncertain at the time – including the possibility of compensation under domestic South African law. However, by not having effectively protected the Swiss-owned property, the tribunal found South Africa in breach of its obligation to provide full protection and security. In 2004, the tribunal therefore awarded the investor approximately $1 million in compensation, which the South African government paid the year after.

Also in 2004, a letter was sent to the South African government from the Italian embassy. It indicated in not-so-subtle terms that a second BIT claim was underway.[11] This time it concerned recently enacted legislation for the mining industry in South Africa. The legislation had been many years in the making. Up through the 1990s and early 2000s, various sticks and carrots in the BEE programme had led multinationals such as Deutche Bank, Merrill Lynch, and de Beers to sell off equity stakes to black-owned enterprises or black employees, appoint black managers and enter into joint ventures with black operators.[12] After a long consultative process[13] the time had come to extend the programme to the mining industry – the largest in Africa, and one of the largest in the world. To rectify the unequal access to South Africa's natural resources as a result of the apartheid regime, mining legislation was enacted in 2002 to replace the old Mining Act of 1991. Along with the 'Mining Charter', the new Mineral and Petroleum Resources Development Act vested all mineral rights with the South African state and only allowed holders of 'old order rights' to obtain new licenses ('new order rights') if they divested a considerable percentage of their shareholdings to HDSA. This gave effect to the South African Constitution, where Section 25(4) (a) encourages 'reforms to bring about equitable access to all South Africa's natural resources'.[14] The act moreover obliged companies to provide special programs for HDSA employees – such as housing, training, and medical care – as well as reach 40 per cent HDSA

---

[11] Peterson 2006, p. 28; Peterson and Garland 2010, p. 7.
[12] See references in Schneiderman 2008, pp. 152–4.
[13] Leon 2009, p. 599; South Africa's Department of Minerals and Energy 1998.
[14] Constitution of the Republic of South Africa, Act 108 of 1996.

166   Letting down the guard: a case study

participation in management by 2009. Finally, 'new order rights' would be for a limited time period, they *had* to be exercised, and holders would be subject to a thorough review of their social and environmental obligations.

During discussions with the industry, both foreign firms and South African law firms made the government aware that the new regulatory regime was likely to conflict with South Africa's BIT obligations.[15] And although there is no publicly available evidence that it was due to potential conflicts with investment treaty obligations, the fierce opposition from the industry led the South African government to reduce the target HDSA ownership in the mining sector from 51 per cent to 26 per cent to be achieved by 2014. This was still considered too high by the industry, which argued BEE groups did not have the billions of rand necessary to pay 'fair market value' for the rights.[16] Italian investors, in particular, continued to object strongly to the commercial losses they were bound to suffer and tried to use their BIT to push the South African government to further water down the legislation. They were backed up by their government, which in 2004 sent the letter referred to above to the South African Minister for Minerals and Energy arguing that the 'social upliftment objectives' of the act 'might produce a breach' of the 1997 BIT between Italy and South Africa by favouring South African investors as a group.[17]

If true, this was not to be taken lightly. Even if compensation was required for the mining act according to South African law – as a judge in a High Court case alluded to[18] – the 1997 BIT with Italy gave the investors a right to 'immediate, *full* and effective compensation', rather than the 'less than market value' standard proscribed by South African law when compelling social objectives are involved.[19] The following year the threat materialized: along with a group of Belgian investors, the Italian miners initiated a BIT claim arguing that the mining legislation

---

[15] Peterson 2003; Peterson 2006, p. 17.   [16] Sergeant 2010.

[17] Quoted in Peterson 2006, p. 28; Peterson and Garland, p. 7. Similarly, in 2004, British Foreign Minister Jack Straw was asked in the British Parliament about the 'expropriation of privately-owned common law mineral rights under the 2002 Act', upon which he replied that 'under the provisions of the UK/South Africa Investment Promotion and Protection Agreement any dispute between a UK investor and the South African government may be submitted to international arbitration'. British firms – such as AngloAmerican – chose not to file a claim due to the political ramifications that would have for its future relationship with the South African government. See Peterson 2006, p. 17.

[18] *Agri South Africa and Annis Mohr Van Rooyen* v. *The Minister of Minerals and Energy* (Case No 558896/2007), Judgment of 6 March 2009 in the High Court of South Africa (North and South Gauteng High Court, Pretoria).

[19] Peterson 2009.

An unquantifiable liability 167

was tantamount to discrimination and expropriation and asked for $350 million in compensation.[20] This was a sizeable claim for the South African government: it translated into more than $7 per capita and corresponded to 70 per cent of its entire Strategic Health Programme for preventing and treating HIV/AIDS that year for instance. More importantly, it touched upon fundamental issues of concern to the South African polity. If successful, it had potential to open the floodgates for similar claims questioning the redistributive efforts of the post-apartheid regime,[21] which could result in 'a significant – and potentially unquantifiable – liability for the South African government', as one South African lawyer put it.[22]

Unlike the Swiss investor a few years earlier, the mining investors pursued their claim under ICSID's Additional Facility Rules, which meant that its existence had to be made public. The immediate result was predictable: after ICSID had approved the claim in 2007, NGOs in South Africa and abroad were quick to pick up on the politically charged case, and both the International Commission of Jurists, a Geneva-based NGO, and four additional NGOs led by the Centre for Applied Legal Studies in South Africa sought amicus curia status in the arbitration proceedings.[23] Apart from the question of compensation to the claimants in question, the NGOs argued that the case touched upon 'a wide range of issues of concern to the citizens of all countries'.[24] In 2010, however, the investors eventually withdrew the case as they managed to negotiate favourable terms with South African mining regulators: instead of having to sell off more than a fourth of their investment to obtain their licenses again, they were now allowed to sell only 5 per cent – and that too as part of a share-ownership scheme to their own employees.[25] Out of the almost $8 million spent by the South African government on legal fees and costs, the tribunal made the investors reimburse only a little more than half a million US dollars.[26]

These claims, and particularly the controversial *Foresti* dispute, raise a set of pertinent questions: why did South Africa enter into treaties that allowed foreign investors the right to claim millions of dollars in damages

---

[20] While arguments were not specified in the award (see below), investors further argued that the act was a breach of provisions on 'fair and equitable treatment' as well as 'national treatment'; Case No. ARB(AF)/07/1, Decision on Jurisdiction, par. 78.

[21] Centre for Applied Legal Studies 2009, pars. 54.2.3–54.2.4.

[22] Peter Leon, quoted in Ryan 2005.   [23] CELS, in ICSID ARB(AF)/07/01.

[24] ICSID ARB(AF)/07/01, par. 41.   [25] Ibid., 21.

[26] Note that a few months before the Foresti claim was discontinued, South Africa was threatened by yet another BIT claim of approximately $20 million. See submission by Michael Duerr in front the South African Parliamentary Select Committee of Finance, 25 August 2010.

168   Letting down the guard: a case study

over issues as sensitive as its affirmative action policies? Also, why would South Africa offer protections to foreign investors that went over and beyond the South African Constitution, when the stated policy goal was merely to provide foreign investors national treatment? Even if we relax the unitary actor assumption and see the BIT programme from a public choice perspective, the questions still stand: although it would be understandable if negotiators pushed for the treaties for individual gains, why did politicians and other stakeholders agree? If embassies and politicians wanted 'photo-ops', why not instead use some inconsequential agreements that didn't contradict South Africa's own Constitution and expose the government to liabilities? The major South African newspapers from when the BITs were signed show that except for the first BIT with the UK, very little attention was paid to the treaties.[27] So although BITs may have provided some benefits in terms of diplomatic measures of goodwill, many other bilateral instruments could easily have been used for this purpose instead. Similarly, why would legal officers or regulatory agencies agree to treaties, which contradicted sensitive domestic social policies? Not being directly involved in the negotiations, the BITs entailed no individual benefits for these actors (e.g. foreign travels or larger budgets). Yet, if they did not make sure the treaties were carefully drafted, they exposed themselves to considerable criticism for neglect of their professional duties in case any disputes arose. The answer to these questions relies, as we shall see, on a BIT-adoption strategy that was bounded rational from the very beginning.

The crucial first treaty

The first BIT South Africa ever signed was with the UK. As the apartheid regime was crumbling and South Africa was about to end decades of isolation from the international community, John Major's government had approached the South African government to enter into a BIT in 1992.[28]

---

[27] Selected dates of *Mail and Guardian* and *Cape Times*, 1994–2010. A typical example was when the Dutch BIT was signed: 'SA, Dutch sign investment pact', *Cape Times*, 10 May 1995 (the full article reads: 'Agreements to protect investments and promote small business in South Africa were signed by Trade Minister Mr. Trevor Manuel and Dutch Foreign Trade Minister Ms Anneke Dok van Weele in Cape Town yesterday. The investment guarantee agreement is designed to strengthen economic ties and stimulate capital and technology flow between SA and the Netherlands').

[28] South African official I. According to UNCTAD's online database, the apartheid regime entered into a BIT with Paraguay in 1974. However, the treaty signed when President Stroessner visited South Africa cannot be characterized as a BIT, but is rather an economic cooperation agreement with mostly aspirational obligations and no means of dispute settlement.

The crucial first treaty 169

Accounting for a third of South Africa's inward FDI stock, British firms were the largest investors in South Africa,[29] and the administration feared that the new ANC government – which partly relied on communist backing – would begin expropriating British assets. The proposed text was the English template BIT, based on a six-page 'standard' OECD model. In very brief terms it stipulated that foreign investors and their investments had to be treated fairly and equitably, there should be no discrimination or expropriation, contracts should be upheld, and there should be no capital restrictions.

Despite sounding harmless at the time, it was serious indeed for South Africa. It granted a wide range of protections, which touched upon all government agencies administering the regulatory framework affecting foreign (British) investors at the national and subnational levels. These protections were backed up by a general consent that allowed private investors recourse to international arbitration – which would be a first for South Africa. The draft also included a number of provisions that potentially conflicted with South Africa's broader economic policies.[30] For when the BIT was being proposed, the expropriation policy had taken centre stage in the heated constitutional negotiations between the ANC, which wanted to redress economic inequalities, and the former ruling regime, concerned about redistribution of land. A series of careful compromises was reached. The 1993 interim Constitution expressly encouraged affirmative action measures in order to advance the black population's ownership and participation in the economy, yet the national treatment provision in the BIT did not reserve to South Africa a right to give preferential treatment to South Africa's historically oppressed people groups. So to the extent British companies and nationals would be structurally handicapped when competing with predominantly black-owned or managed local companies over licenses or acquisitions of state-owned enterprises, this could violate the national treatment provision as enshrined in the UK model.

Similarly, the interim Constitution made a clear distinction between expropriation and mere deprivation. No compensation was due for the latter if the measures were pursuant to law and not arbitrary. This distinction was nowhere to be found in the British BIT, which covered both direct expropriation and measures having equivalent effect to expropriation (indirect expropriation), and the British draft

---

[29] South Africa Reserve Bank, *Quarterly Bulletin*, September 1997.
[30] If not otherwise stated, the following section is based on Peterson 2006, 22–36; and Schneiderman 2009, pp. 16–29.

170   Letting down the guard: a case study

therefore left up to private arbitrators whether British investors could be granted expropriation protections greater than those in the South African Constitution. Finally, after lengthy negotiations, the Constitution provided for compensation for expropriation, though not always based on fair market value.[31] By contrast, the British draft did not allow deviations from 'prompt, adequate, and effective compensation' amounting to the 'genuine value of the investment'. If property was redistributed to the black population, for instance, the BIT could be construed as setting a stricter compensation standard than the South African Constitution.

So although the regulatory agenda in the early post-apartheid regime was obviously packed and only few claims had been filed at this stage, this was clearly not a treaty to be taken lightly. A binding document which, under international law, could override the perhaps most sensitive constitutional compromise surely required careful consideration. But this never happened, as no one realized the scope of what the British proposed. The treaty was sent to the investment promotion agency, which was later to become the lead agency in South Africa's BIT programme. There, a key official did not find the BIT to be in any sort of conflict with South African laws, and he therefore saw it as 'a win-win situation without any risks or legal problems ... BITs just established basic principles and we found nothing in there contrary to good common sense'.[32] The only difference between the BIT and South African national laws, he continued, 'was the international arbitration clause. That's it ... It was very simple and straightforward. Europe had used these agreements for some time and had standard texts. When Britain came to us they presented the text and we did not have a problem with it'.[33] So although the arbitration clause was discussed superficially,[34] the risk of investment disputes was not only considered low, it was thought to be practically zero. As the officials did not have a salient treaty claim on their radars, they completely disregarded the risks of such claims. 'The risk of claims was not present ... No departments raised such concerns at all'.[35]

The bureaucrats charged with negotiating the treaties were not government lawyers. Rather than having detailed legal and technical expertise in international law, their job was investment promotion. Yet, when they forwarded the draft for legal vetting, the responsible officials did not find any critical issues with the proposed British text either. It was sent to the small team of six lawyers in the Ministry of Foreign Affairs, who dealt

---

[31] Chaskalson 1994.   [32] South African official I.   [33] Ibid.
[34] 1994 DTI file on UK BIT.   [35] South African official IV.

The crucial first treaty

with everything from law of the seas, legal issues pertaining to Antarctica, customs unions, double taxation agreements, and now also BITs.[36] The official who was eventually charged with vetting it was very junior in the department, and found the British treaty to be 'clear and well drafted' not breaching the country's international obligations, and the state law advisor could not see 'any' problems pertaining to South Africa's national law either.[37] Also, this was the first treaty for South Africa to provide a general consent to investor–state arbitration over a wide range of regulatory issues, but the novelty of the arbitration provision in the British model was not realized at the time:

> Obviously we did not consider it [the arbitration provision] as an issue. From the legal position we did not have a problem because under our domestic legislation the state can be sued and under our Constitution discrimination based on ethnicity and nationality is also outlawed. So it would merely place a foreign investor in the same position that he in any case had ... So why should we have a problem with it?[38]

Clearly, this was – and is – a faulty analysis: by consenting to investor–state arbitration, South Africa gave foreign investors access to a dispute settlement forum and enforcement mechanisms not available to South African investors. Legal literature as well as UNCTC and UNCTAD reports were published at the time alerting officials that apart from the arbitration provisions, key protection standards – such as those on expropriation – often went over and beyond national laws. But these were not consulted. Rather than rationally seeking and processing information about BITs, important information was ignored as it was not salient, and key officials involved with the proposed British BIT systematically neglected the fact that they were dealing with a set of very serious and far-reaching legal obligations. According to a veteran BIT negotiator, one reason the officials so willingly accepted the British draft was evidently 'due to ignorance or a failure to appreciate the significance of the provisions they ... accepted'.[39]

This was also the reason practically no relevant government stakeholders got involved in the process. The impression that the treaty did not have any implications and its provisions corresponded completely to South African law meant there was no reason for key stakeholders to spend precious time and resources on learning about these new and somewhat exotic legal instruments. 'The only other department with a slight interest was the department of foreign affairs and they firmly endorsed what we were doing. They were the ones who had to get the

---

[36] South African official III.   [37] Ibid.   [38] Ibid.   [39] Robinson 1993, p. 9.

172   Letting down the guard: a case study

thing legally ready, so they were firmly on board', one official recalls.[40] The departments responsible for resource exploitation, for instance, were not pushing to make sure the treaty would not undermine their right to regulatory takings otherwise legal under the Constitution; the Chief Law Advisor's office did not alert decision-makers of the legal significance of the treaty, and so on. 'For the British treaty I invited all government departments, mining, labor – everything around the table. And they all gave us the mandate, said they were fine with these treaties and that they did not have to be present'.[41] Apart from the reserve bank – which made sure South Africa's foreign exchange policy was not undermined by the BIT (see below) – key interests of government stakeholders were evidently not realized.

But what about political stakeholders? Although bureaucrats may not have been too concerned about the proposed BIT, surely the political parties would want to thoroughly consider and insist on rigorous negotiations of a wide-ranging treaty with their former colonial power. Following much of the literature on why developing countries have entered into the BIT regime, one would expect that the economic rationale for entering into the treaty would be held up against its potentially serious legal implications. This is not least the case because the ANC government had a firm hold on political power and could safely assume to lead the country for considerable time to come – as indeed it did. This made the South African government less likely to constrain its long-term regulatory flexibility for (perceived) short-term benefits than governments with shorter time-horizons.[42]

Yet, no critical questions were asked from politicians about the scale of the legal guarantees granted to foreign investors – not even from the communist factions – as the negotiator presented the treaty based on what was clearly a faulty analysis: 'the agreement did not place British investors in SA in a better position than local residents because the agreement stated that SA law would apply'.[43] Moreover, no analyses were considered to understand its potential economic implications. Without any scrutiny or examination, the discussion with the British government led to the perception that the treaty was 'an important value-added enhancement that could add to the peace of mind for foreign investors' and 'prove to foreign investors ... that South Africa

---

[40] South African official IV.   [41] Ibid.

[42] Abbott and Snidal 2000. For a rationalist take on time horizons and investment treaty commitments, see Blake 2013.

[43] 'Parliamentary Committee approves investment agreement with UK', *BBC Monitoring Service: Africa*, 3 March 1998.

The crucial first treaty 173

was an investor friendly country'.[44] Remarkably, the protection of South African investors was also considered crucial as the BIT: 'reduced their capital risks and hence their insurance costs when doing business in Britain'.[45]

Information about the risks of the treaty was thereby not just short in supply (due to few investment treaty claims) and somewhat costly to obtain (due to an already crowded political agenda) but also processed in a way few rational choice scholars would be able to explain. Organizations such as UNCTC and UNCTAD had been telling countries like South Africa for years that while entering into investment treaties would be in their national interest, they had to carefully consider the legal implications. But this was ignored completely and hardly any stakeholders took much notice of the treaty making as it was completely depoliticized in the national policy-making process. As Weyland also found in his study of bounded rationality in bureaucratic decision-making,[46] imperfect processing of information biased officials' risk assessments and shaped who thought of themselves as a stakeholder in the process, and who did not. In this case, the risks and scope of the BIT were not understood, which meant hardly any departments realized the relevance of the treaty.

The two-day negotiations over the British BIT were therefore amicable to say the least. In fact, 'negotiations' is hardly a representative term. When comparing the British model BIT from the early 1990s[47] with what became the South Africa-UK BIT, it confirms that the treaty passed through both the bureaucracy and political system without any critical engagement from either. As an experienced negotiator has observed:

A drafting formulation in the midst of negotiations, especially when it is in written form, takes on a life of its own, and more importantly, a kind of permanence; it becomes fixed in the minds of the other negotiating States and can give the author a clear psychological advantage as the negotiations then begin to centre around his proposal.[48]

The British model text was not just the centre around the negotiations, however, it was agreed to with hardly any changes: the only provision which seems to have been discussed was the transfer clause,[49] where a

---

[44] South African official I. See also Chapter 6.
[45] Quote by South African official in 'Parliamentary committee approves investment agreement with UK', *Business Day*, 26 February 1998.
[46] Weyland 2006, p. 62.   [47] For the model, see Dolzer and Stevens 1995.
[48] Robinson 1993, p. 9.
[49] 'Reciprocal Bilateral Agreements on the Promotion and Protection of Investments with the British Government', 1994, South African file on UK BIT; 'Agreement for the Promotion and Reciprocal Protection of Investment (IPPA) – United Kingdom',

174 Letting down the guard: a case study

protocol devised by the Reserve Bank on South Africa's foreign exchange restrictions was included. Otherwise, the two texts were almost identical and the treaty was subsequently signed by Nelson Mandela and John Major, when the latter made his first visit to South Africa in 1994.

At the same visit, Major spoke of the need for liberalizing the South African economy and brought along pledges for 530 million rand in development aid.[50] Yet, there is no indication that the aid package was specifically tied to the treaty: although officials at the time did find there was considerable political pressure to finalize the treaty,[51] there are no signs of coercion from the British government, international organizations, or others. South African officials and politicians welcomed the British offer and no one within the government or political institutions raised any critical voices at any point. Although British investors themselves didn't find investment treaties important at the time,[52] the expectation in South Africa was that the treaty with London could 'prove to foreign investors ... that South Africa was an investor friendly country'.[53]

The BIT programme begins

Based on this experience, an administrative decision was made by the new South African government to begin an actual BIT programme. The government was adamant about opening the country up to trade and foreign investments to help rebuild an economy suffering from past populist economic mismanagement, and the type of treaty the British had brought to their attention seemed to be a useful legal tool to attract investment.[54] A few other treaties by major capital exporters were consulted,[55] but the standard OECD model enshrined in the British BIT was used as a de facto model for future negotiations. This was not because officials had carefully considered its provisions, but rather

---

1996, South African file on UK BIT; Letter from British High Commission Cape Town to Mr Alec Ervin, Minister for Trade and Industry, Republic of South Africa, 11 June 1996.

[50] 'Major tells of a new age for South Africa', *Cape Times*, 21 September, 1994; 'UK prime minister addresses national assembly', *Johannesburg Radio South Africa Network*, 20 November 1994. Reprinted in *Daily Report: Sub-Saharan Africa*, FBIS-AFR-94–183, 21 November 1994.

[51] 'Reciprocal bilateral agreements on the promotion and protection of investments with the British government', 1994, South African file on UK BIT.

[52] MIGA 1991b: 89, 91.   [53] South African official I.

[54] South African officials I, III, and V; South African government file on Italian BIT.

[55] South African official III; South African official V.

The BIT programme begins 175

because it was the first that had come to their attention. 'When Britain came to us they presented the text and we did not have a problem with it, so it was accepted by and large as the standard text to use'.[56] Another official remarks, 'obviously the US and Canada have their own models, which we were confronted with at a later stage, and there were some South-South agreements, but the first treaty was with a European country so we gravitated to those types of treaties'.[57]

Several of South Africa's negotiation partners saw the treaties in a similar light and negotiations were straightforward. Recall from Chapter 2, for instance, how Korean officials also failed to appreciate the implications of BITs and therefore anchored to 'the same simple provisions as in previous investment agreements'.[58] Apart from Korea, the first five BITs were with other European countries, and South African negotiators had no problem in signing off on their models, as they did not depart significantly from the British text.[59] The BIT with the Netherlands, for instance, nearly followed the Dutch model BIT of 1993 word for word.[60] Just as in the British BIT, no carve-outs were made for South Africa's affirmative action policies, and future tribunals were given no hints in the preambles as to the country's aspirations to promote social and economic equality.

The treaties were seen as crucial to 'stimulate capital and technology flow',[61] but had officials looked towards the surveys available at the time they would have found that investors hardly ever regarded the BITs as important to establishment decisions.[62] According to the negotiators involved, the process was 'very much learning by doing',[63] and often negotiations took only a day or two. At no point did anyone object to the process. 'We were trying to have as many agreements finalized as possible', one legal official notes, 'and because we used the European model we were quite effective with the European model, so there was a certain momentum'.[64] 'This allowed us to finalize a lot of agreements in a short span of time. From the lawyers' department, think of the amount of texts we finalized in so few months, just two people with many other responsibilities at the same time'.[65] The understanding that BITs could promote investment but entailed no real risks meant that a criteria of success became to sign as many, as quickly as possible.

---

[56] South African official I; Communication from DTI to South African Embassy in Rome, 3 November, 1994.
[57] South African official III.　　[58] Kim 2011, p. 68.　　[59] South African official III.
[60] Model is available in Dolzer and Stevens 1995.　　[61] *Cape Times*, 10 May 1995.
[62] On Dutch investors, see MIGA PAS 1991, p. 170.　　[63] South African official IV.
[64] South African official III.　　[65] Ibid.

176 Letting down the guard: a case study

This was despite the fact that the expropriation issue had become politicized once again. Land restitution and reforms had begun in South Africa, which led to calls to reopen the delicate 1993 compromise over the property clause in the Constitution.[66] A new Bill of Rights was drafted stating that the amount of compensation had to reflect a balance of interests between those affected and the public, including 'the nation's commitment to land reform, and to reforms to bring about equitable access to all South Africa's natural resources'.[67] No such carve-outs were included in BITs signed at the time.

Anchoring to the OECD model

Then along came Canada. As Schneiderman has observed, the Canadian model BIT was no different from earlier BITs in being 'discordant with the stated goals of the South African property rights regime'.[68] In fact, it was in some ways more far-reaching than the European models. Based on NAFTA's Chapter 11, it included extensive protections on intellectual property rights, for instance, legally binding establishment provisions and obligations on performance requirements. Unlike the US model, however, its liberalization provisions were not subject to investor–state arbitration, and even though some of the carve-outs included in Canada's latter model were not included until Canada later was sued under NAFTA, it was still a somewhat more flexible text than those which South Africa had already signed. Unlike the European models, it included carve-outs for measures taken to protect the environment for instance. Yet, Canadian negotiators have had a very difficult time concluding BITs:

> Even if we find interested developing countries, it is always a challenge to explain why our model actually provides more flexibility than European models. It takes a long time to explain to them why our model is better than what they've done in the past. The liberalization provisions are not that difficult, but it is a big challenge to convince developing countries that they are not being tricked by the detail of the post-establishment and dispute settlement provisions, but that our model is actually more balanced in terms of preserving regulatory flexibility.[69]

Accordingly, when Canada initiated talks with South Africa over a BIT it was not so much the scope of the agreement that intimidated the South African negotiating team as it was its lengthy and 'legalistic' appearance as compared to the briefer and more vaguely worded European models.

---

[66] Klug 2000. [67] 25(4)(a). [68] Schneiderman 2008, p. 146.
[69] South African official VII.

Anchoring to the OECD model 177

The Canadians were a nightmare. I think it was mostly an ego thing, but they took a very difficult stance. These were people who took BITs as real and serious legal instruments with teeth, rather than what they really are, namely pure signals ... why be so pedantic and difficult in worrying so much about the legal details? It was very difficult.[70]

But despite the 'difficult' and 'pedantic' approach taken by the Canadians, the South African negotiation team nevertheless agreed to the text. The result was curious. For instance, the treaty expressly specified that the treatment and protection provisions did not apply to preferential rights and measures provided to *Canadian* aboriginal peoples, but the South African negotiation team did not make sure this carve-out also covered their constitutionally enshrined affirmative action policies. South Africa therefore ended up agreeing to *more* stringent standards than the Canadians did, because South African officials considered such differences in BITs to be 'mostly about cosmetics'.[71]

Apart from the fact that the Canadian treaty departed significantly from the 'standard' OECD model, it also stood out among the early treaties because it was not eventually ratified. The failing ratification was a result of domestic 'veto players' blocking the treaty, but hardly the way rationalistic accounts would have expected.[72] For instance, although the treaty would arguably have allowed major Canadian mining companies to bring claims based on South Africa's redistributive policies in the natural resource sector, there was no opposition from the responsible regulatory agencies, as they remained oblivious to the implications of the treaty.[73] Instead, it came down to a single legal officer, to whom I will return below.

It was not only with Canada that the South African negotiating team had difficulties accepting treaty texts, which in some ways were more flexible than European models. South Africa and Malaysia, for instance, had agreed to enter into a BIT,[74] and during the negotiations South Africa was asked to exclude a national treatment clause from the agreement due to Malaysia's infant industry protection policies and preferential treatment of its indigenous peoples (the bumiputra).[75] Although this would have made sense given South Africa's own affirmative action

---

[70] South African official II.   [71] Ibid.
[72] For a rationalistic account of why some BITs are ratified and some are not, see Haftel and Thomson 2013.
[73] South African official II; South African official IV.
[74] 'Memorandum of understanding between the government of the Republic of South Africa and the government of Malaysia on concluding agreements that enhance trade and investments between the two countries,' 8 August 1994.
[75] South African official II.

178   Letting down the guard: a case study

measures – at least compared to national treatment clauses where such measures were not excluded – the South African negotiators did not want to depart from their initial OECD-based model. A more careful consideration of the legal implications would almost undoubtedly have appreciated the Malaysian approach, particularly as there were no South African investors to protect in Malaysia. But the treaty never materialized, as South African officials were committed to their OECD-based approach.[76] This may appear irrational, but the status-quo bias reminds us it was not unpredictable.

Multilateral versus bilateral investment obligations

South Africa's investment obligations were not just negotiated in BITs, and during discussions over the MAI a number of South African BIT negotiators occasionally went as observers. As many others, they were dismissive of the project. This was not so much because of the substance of the agreement, but rather because of the approach. 'The MAI was take-it-or-leave-it with the whole agenda set by the OECD without any sense of negotiating or hearing the views of developing countries. This annoyed us and many others out of principle'.[77] The continued reliance on bilateral deals rather than support for a comprehensive multilateral investment treaty was not based on ingenious cost–benefit analyses, as expected by rationalist models.[78] In the case of the MAI, it was more simple: 'BITs at least give us a feeling that we are listened to. We are craving to be treated as equal partners with respect, and BITs do that; the MAI did not'.[79] However, when in 1996 it was suggested that the WTO – a more inclusive forum – should include investment protection rules, South Africa was also sceptical. Although never at the forefront of multilateral investment discussions,[80] including those in the WTO,[81]

---

[76] Ibid.   [77] South African official IV.

[78] See Guzman 1998, as well as the more refined argument in Bubb and Rose-Ackerman 2007.

[79] South African official IV.

[80] In UNCTAD, for instance, South Africa hardly ever made any submissions in the Commission on 'Investment, Technology and related financial issues' concerning international investment rules. See reports at www.unctad.org.

[81] Hardly any submissions were made by South Africa in the WTO's working group on the Relationship between Trade and Investment, and South Africa was not a major player in the subsequent investment discussions during the Doha Round either. For an overview, see Sauvé 2006.

an advisor to South Africa's trade minister commented in the press about the possibility of investment protection rules in the WTO that:

it is '*absolutely clear*' that some of the proposed new measures '*would be destructive to weaker economies*' whose domestic firms cannot compete with transnational corporations. It would be unfair to impose such new rules before these countries have had a chance to engage in full economic reforms.[82]

Any new investment rules, he said, would 'remove the last vestiges of national planning and pose a threat to national sovereignty'.[83] This was a puzzling statement. While willingly entering into BITs, which included broadly drafted protections that went over and beyond South Africa's new Constitution, a multilateral agreement negotiated in a forum where developing countries could act as a bloc was rejected as being a 'threat to national sovereignty'. But again, although the exact explanation remains somewhat uncertain, even for officials present at the time, the contradictory policies were not a result of sophisticated considerations about negotiating at bilateral versus multilateral levels. Rather it happened for more mundane reasons, among which ignorance was a deciding factor. A key official in a senior position at the time was of the view that:

BITs did not go over and above WTO commitments ... you shouldn't make commitments at the bilateral level in BITs that you haven't made at the multilateral level in WTO. So until we had found a multilateral compromise we did not want to push BITs above WTO obligations. We did not want to further add to the WTO agenda, but were content with signing BITs *as they did not have any risks*. That was our position.[84]

In other words, the understanding was that BITs did not go over and beyond existing investment obligations in the WTO after the conclusion of the Uruguay round.[85] This view was mistaken.

Another reason for the paradoxical position was a lack of coordination. Within the Department of Trade and Industry (DTI), officials working on BITs were vaguely aware that they went above WTO obligations, but those officials had nothing to do with WTO negotiations even if they touched upon investment. In fact, the multilateral and bilateral cells of the DTI's international trade division had little, if any, contact. 'People work almost entirely in silos', a senior official notes, 'which at times lead to such contradictory policies. We had a WTO unit and a bilateral unit, and we never communicated so there was no coordination what-so-

---

[82] Quoted in Wall 1996.   [83] Wall 1996.   [84] South African official V. Italics added.
[85] South African official XIII.

180   Letting down the guard: a case study

ever'.[86] So whereas the WTO officials 'wanted to push WTO into a direction more in line with developing country interests ... we had nothing to do with the officials negotiating BITs'.[87]

This meant that despite the critical stance at the multilateral level, the bilateral trade relations unit of DTI continued the BIT programme unabated. And the systematic failure to appreciate the implications of investment treaties initially led to a strange choice of BIT partners. Cuba was an early example. The two countries had embarked on a number of cooperation projects in the area of health, for instance, where Cuban doctors were assigned to South African hospitals and South African medical students sent to Cuba.[88] Cooperation was also initiated in the education field, where Cuban teachers were invited to teach in South African rural schools.[89] So although the two countries had hardly any economic links in terms of trade or investments, Cuba asked South Africa to also enter into a BIT to further seal their diplomatic relationship and stimulate investment flows. This was part of a broader move by Castro to sign BITs in order to complement his 1995 Foreign Investment Law intended to attract foreign investment after Soviet assistance disappeared.[90] The South African team couldn't see any reason to decline the invitation, so on the way home from their negotiations in Canada, they stopped in Havana to quickly finalize an agreement.[91]

Cuba was no exception. After South Africa produced its own template BIT – primarily based on the British model[92] – officials asked the foreign office to pass it out to all its embassies to see who would be interested in signing a BIT.[93] The embassies were highly supportive of this new instrument. 'The ambassadors used them as a possible achievement during their tenure, so we had requests from embassies all the time to sign these agreements'.[94] Politicians were equally thrilled and began

---

[86] South African official VIII.   [87] South African official XIII.   [88] Ibid.

[89] See e.g. 'The Cuban option for SA schools', *Cape Times*, 29 November 1995.

[90] Hansard, 27 June 1994, vol. 556 cc521–3 ('It was quite difficult to get Cuba to look at Investment Protection Promotion Agreements until fairly recently ... In fact, Cuba ... only expressed interest in an IPPA last year when we [the British government, ed.] proposed a draft text to them.'). See 'Investment agreement signed with Cuba', Madrid RNE International, 28 May 1994. Republished in *Daily Report: West Europe*, FBIS-WEI-94–104, 31 May 1994 (BIT justified as an agreement to 'stimulate the flow of more Spanish capital into the island, capital that hitherto has been concentrated in the tourist industry'). 'German investment accord with Cuba', *Financial Times*, 1 May 1995 (BIT justified as a tool to integrate the two markets).

[91] South African official II; South African official IV.

[92] Compare the two in UNCTAD 1996.   [93] South African official II.

[94] South African official VIII.

Multilateral versus bilateral investment obligations 181

using the treaties as photo-opportunities when going abroad or receiving international guests:

A lot of South African politicians went all over Africa, and because politicians want to be seen doing something constructive, they would often suggest a BIT even if no investments were flowing between the countries ... So when an inward or outward visit would happen, politicians looked for something to put on their agenda and they suggested the BIT.[95]

The fact that embassies and politicians acted upon their individual incentive to push for BITs should come as no surprise for public choice students of bureaucratic politics. It does not, in and by itself, signify limited rationality on the part of policy-makers. For without proper control and oversight mechanisms, domestic stakeholders can successfully pursue their own interests at the expense of broader national welfare concerns. Yet, the lack of information about the implications of the treaties, and the imperfect processing of whatever information was available, meant that government agencies with an incentive to *oppose* the treaties did not. This was not because they lacked oversight or other factors principal–agent models point to when 'shirking' occurs, but rather because they remained oblivious of their own interests. The treaties remained:

very under-politicized. Apart from a few technical things in the reserve bank pertaining to exchange control, which were usually the hardest issues, there were no problems at all. One or two times we explained it all to the parliamentary committee, but even there it was acknowledged as a technical agreement ... The parliament never discussed it, the Justice department was fine, and so were other stakeholders. No one thought it was a bad idea to sign these treaties.[96]

As no one told politicians and embassy officials that BITs were in fact serious agreements, South Africa's web of BITs spread quickly. The policy of finalizing investment treaties whenever there was a state visit somewhere meant the guiding principles of South Africa's BIT policy was left almost entirely to chance. A bizarre example of this was Mali. During a formal visit there, the South African foreign minister convinced his counterpart to sign a BIT. The process went so fast, however, that the document sent back to the foreign office in Pretoria was just a copy of the South African model: it did not even have the two countries' names on it, which made it impossible to submit for ratification.[97]

---

[95] South African official II.   [96] South African official II.   [97] Ibid.

182   Letting down the guard: a case study

With a few exceptions – such as one treaty signed as a precondition for an investment project[98] – BITs were thereby being (mis-)used based on a mistaken understanding of their basic implications. This 'shot-gun approach'[99] of embassies and politicians signing BITs as 'merely pieces of paper'[100] led to even further capacity constraints as only one South African official was present during several of the negotiations during this period. Initially, he was satisfied with this situation as it gave him the freedom to finalize a great number of agreements. Negotiations were easy as the expertise and experience in many other developing countries was even less than in South Africa.[101] But eventually, the time pressure became tremendous. 'I actually had to sit down and calculate: it took fifteen minutes to walk to the department to get their opinion on it; it took fifteen minutes to walk back and put it all together – and I worked out how much time it took on average. It became too much in the end'.[102] When telling this to his superiors, they realized that even though no one actually objected to the content of the agreements, this approach was too haphazard and chaotic.

An intended rational approach

A targeted two-track approach was agreed upon instead: South Africa should continue to accept invitations to sign with capital-exporting states that were major trading or investment partners, but they should also actively pursue South-South BITs in countries where South African companies had conducted, or were planning to conduct, investments – particularly on the African continent. Rather than merely signing BITs whenever possible there was an objective of pursuing a strategic and reasoned BIT strategy, an 'intended rational behavior' as Herbert Simon would put it.[103] Also, it is notable that the official who suggested a more careful approach was the same official who had most to benefit from promoting BITs, as it allowed him extensive travel, perhaps larger budgets, or career promotion. Yet, by contrast with the predictions of a public choice framework, he was the one who slowed down the process.

Officials also began thinking through the relationship between the Constitution and investment treaties and decided it might be prudent

---

[98] Ibid. It concerned a French investment into Mozambique channeled through South Africa, where a precondition for the investment was a BIT between South Africa and Mozambique. See 'SA and Mozambique sign up for the next great trek', *Cape Times*, business section, front page, 7 May 1997.
[99] South African official II.   [100] Ibid.   [101] Ibid.   [102] Ibid.
[103] Simon 1957, p. 199.

An intended rational approach 183

to make certain exceptions to safeguard South Africa's affirmative action policies. The treaties with Iran, China, Mauritius, Ghana, Russia, and the Czech Republic explicitly stated that provisions on national and MFN treatment as well as fair and equitable treatment would not apply to measures taken to promote equality or protection or advancing natural or legal persons disadvantaged by unfair discrimination. As the legal officer vetting many of the early agreements noted, 'we were clear that we should not provide more rights than our Constitution, and created some wording to take that into account'.[104] After having signed 12 BITs already, the South African BIT negotiators had clearly become aware of the potential legal implications of an investment treaty programme out of sync with their country's constitutional priorities.

Or had they? As was so often the case in developing countries' BIT programs the adaption to the treaties remained entirely inconsistent. Although exceptions to promote equality were included in the treatment provisions, the expropriation standards remained the same and had no such carve-outs.[105] And in the Swedish and Finish BITs, for instance, no exceptions were included even in the treatment provisions, despite being signed during exactly the same period. The same was the case for the Belgium/Luxembourg BIT, which, along with the Italian BIT, was later to be used in the major investment treaty claim on this very issue. So although there might have been a better understanding that such exceptions could be important than during the first wave of treaties, it remained superficial. The key South African negotiators looked at it this way:

> Some people were like, my goodness; we can't give them these provisions as others are going to invoke them through the MFN clause. As negotiators, we were much more pragmatic in our approach, understanding that it did not really matter whether we included various reservations as it would never become an issue in practise.[106]

And as the expectation was still that 'the moment a BIT was signed with a country, capital would start flowing from there',[107] the treaties were seen to entail only benefits, and no risks. Although investment treaty claims were beginning to pop up against other countries, these remained outside the officials' radar screen. When asked whether they followed the ongoing claims against other developing countries, it became apparent that by 2009 some former officials still did not know such claims existed: 'We did not follow those arbitrations you are referring to. Personally, I do

---

[104] South African official III. [105] See e.g. South Africa – Czech Republic BIT.
[106] South African official II.   [107] South African official I.

184   Letting down the guard: a case study

not know of any international arbitrations under BITs. Perhaps rogue regimes like Burma and North Korea have been hit'.[108] Another official, now retired, was more well-informed, yet he never sought information about the disputes as this was 'the last thing people would think about'.[109] So although the negotiators would participate in UNCTAD seminars, where nuances in various models would be discussed,[110] there was not much reason to update the South African model as it seemed 'good enough'. With a biased assessment of the implications of what they were negotiating, South African officials therefore continued to enter into BITs which, if they were to be honoured, could prevent measures to pursue South Africa's developmental agenda, and if they were not, would subject the country to potentially costly and far-reaching investment treaty disputes.

The targeted approach did not last long either. After South Africa's sole negotiator was posted overseas in 1999, the responsibility to negotiate BITs was delegated to regional desk officers within the foreign office. This augmented the lack of expertise and experience that went into the actual negotiations even further. 'All the negotiation skills, experience, and so forth were lost, which was unfortunate but I think the decision was made simply because the treaties were low on the priority list'.[111] Accordingly, regional desk officers were allowed to negotiate treaties they, until then, had hardly heard of. They were delighted about this opportunity: 'the BITs really gave the regional desk officers something to do. Do ten agreements and you have been successful during that year. It also gave them an opportunity to travel'.[112] The regional officers confirmed this view. 'We used to call them apple-pie agreements intended to give comfort to politicians: it was really nice for a politician to say they had signed a BIT, and the officers from foreign affairs also really liked to see the treaties signed under their tenure'.[113] When embassies would request a BIT ('they like photo-sessions and smiles, so they love to have a minister to come and sign an agreement, no matter how small the country')[114] the regional desks proceeded assuming 'the treaties as a mere piece of paper with no real implications, and they did not go through any channels'.[115] As one senior official recalled: 'No one had any legal qualifications ... BITs became used as perks because no one informed them what the consequences of these agreements were about'.[116] So based on the understanding that there was 'absolutely no

---

[108] South African official IV.   [109] South African official II.   [110] Ibid.   [111] Ibid.
[112] South African official VIII.   [113] South African official IX.   [114] Ibid.
[115] South African official II.   [116] South African official VIII.

A new approach 185

risk in signing BITs for South Africa as they were entirely consistent with the constitution and national legislation',[117] the South African web of BITs proliferated, particularly in 2000.

South Africa also gladly accepted the invitation from UNCTAD in 2001 to join one of their BIT-signing sessions. Due to a last-minute cancellation, a legal officer from the multilateral trade negotiations unit within the DTI went along.[118] This officer had specialized degrees in international trade and commercial law and a background as a practicing lawyer. So although the fact that he was more of a legal expert than his colleagues did not make him less prone to inferential biases, he was able to have a much more informed understanding of the treaties' legal importance. But although puzzled about the rapid adoption of treaties in Geneva,[119] he could not object at the time and South Africa signed four BITs at this one UNCTAD session alone (with Benin, Burkina Faso, Chad, and Mauritania).[120]

A new approach

Later that year, however, the same officer was put in charge of South Africa's investment negotiations. After he began investigating just what South Africa had signed up to over the last six years, he urged the government to take a much more conservative approach. As no one bothered much about the agreements he had his way, and a decision was taken not to enter into any more BITs until a proper strategy was in place and under no circumstance should South Africa participate in UNCTAD 'signing sessions' again.

This new, and more hesitant, approach had major implications for South Africa's external investment policy. First of all, the officer blocked the ratification of numerous BITs – including the one with Canada – and renegotiated others, such as the treaty with Cuba. Secondly, PTA negotiations between the Southern African Customs Union (South Africa, Botswana, Lesotho, Namibia, and Swaziland) and the United States began in 2003,[121] but talks had stalled already the year after and

---

[117] South African official IX.   [118] South African official VIII   [119] Ibid.
[120] See also UNCTAD 2002b,
[121] Note that according to the former South African negotiators, the United States also approached South Africa for a BIT around 1996. According to press reports, the Clinton administration 'promised to work out a bilateral investment treaty with South Africa' ('South Africa wooing U.S. businesses', Associated Press, 1 June 1994), but no records exist of these negotiations, and when asked, top officials in both the US Trade Representative and State Department at the time did not recall such negotiations having taken place. Also, they are not mentioned in any of the extensive works on the American BIT program by veteran BIT negotiator Kenneth Vandevelde. According to the South

186   Letting down the guard: a case study

negotiations collapsed in 2006. Among the reasons was the American refusal to exclude comprehensive investment disciplines from the agreement, which South Africa thought conflicted with their BEE programme.[122] Particularly the establishment provisions in the US model were problematic. '[T]he South African government is unwilling', Karan Bhatia, Deputy United States Trade Representative (USTR), complained, 'to provide equitable access [to government procurement] for foreign firms as this could negatively impact on its black economic empowerment initiatives'.[123] Eventually, the investment obligations in the PTA turned out to be a 'major obstacle'[124] and combined with other conflicts over intellectual property rights and trade in services, for instance, the negotiations collapsed. Third, South Africa refused to include investment obligations as part of an economic partnership agreement (EPA) with the EU. Starting in 2006, South Africa had joined the negotiations but was, along with Namibia, the only African country that did not give in to European pressure to include investment and services in the negotiating process.[125]

Finally, and crucially, South Africa is one of the only countries in Africa that is not a member of ICSID.[126] When in 1998 the South African Law Commission made its recommendations concerning South Africa's outdated arbitration law,[127] joining ICSID was one of them. After having obtained inputs from a number of experts, including Antonio Parra from ICSID[128] as well as prominent arbitrators Karl-Heinz Böckstiegel and Jan Paulsson[129] (who was later to become counsel to South Africa in the Foresti claim), the commission recommended that:

African team, however, the (alleged) negotiations collapsed partly due to the conflicts over intellectual property disputes with South Africa (South African official IV), but also because, 'When we met with the USTR, they rolled out 15 or 16 lawyers sitting in 2 rows. On the other side of the table we were 3 people. Each of the lawyers explained us the articles in details ... We did not have the capacity to work with that.' (South African official III). Another recalls, 'Talks were held, but the parties were quite far apart concerning the scope of the envisaged agreement – the USA wanted a very broad agreement including issues such as services, patent rights, and a host of other matters over and above the normal matters covered in the BITs previously concluded by South Africa with other countries. ... My understanding was that South Africa was not yet comfortable with extending the scope of BITs to include the aspects requested by the USA' (South African official I).

[122] South African official VIII.   [123] Quoted in Schneiderman 2010, pp. 32–3.

[124] 'Administration, business pressure SACU for comprehensive FTA', *Inside US Trade*, 10 December 2004.

[125] Carim 2010.

[126] During its pariah status before 1994, the country was generally on the outside of the international legal order, which explains its non-participation in ICSID at the time. See Butler and Finsen 1996, p. 198, ftn. 37. See also Agyemang 1988.

[127] South African Law Commission 1998. See generally Agyemang 1989; Butler 1994; Christie 1993.

[128] South African Law Commission 1998, ftn 48.

A new approach 187

Ratification of the Convention would ... be another positive signal which South Africa could send out to indicate that the new government is eager to create the necessary legal framework to encourage foreign investment. ... On the other hand, South African companies are eagerly looking for investment opportunities in other African countries, virtually all of which are members of ICSID. Ratification of the Convention by South Africa would facilitate such investment and further the economic development of the region.[130]

It further noted the need to join ICSID now that South African BIT negotiators had included ICSID arbitration clauses in their BITs, which 'created the expectation among potential investors in those countries that South Africa intends acceding to the Washington Convention'.[131] But a few years into the hearing process after the bill had been submitted to Parliament in 2001, the DTI officer put in charge of investment negotiations objected. Although not taking issue with the broader arbitration bill, the experience with the Swiss and Italian/Belgium BIT claims led DTI to conclude that it was not in South Africa's interest to join ICSID.[132] DTI was adamant on this point and eventually ICSID membership was removed from the bill.[133]

Yet at the same time as South Africa objected to investment obligations in the EU EPA, the US PTA, and in the context of ICSID, the South African stock of BITs continued to grow as regional desks continued their negotiations despite the imposition of the moratorium. One of the regional desk officers saw it like this,

Taking a legalistic perspective on these treaties is a bit problematic because then they become very difficult to negotiate. When legal people meet, they have all their jargon, which is a bit boring. So since the other side was typically not very legalistic either, we did not always involve the South African lawyers.[134]

---

[129] South African Law Commission 1998, Annex C1. Note that a major conference was held in 1997 with participation from a considerable amount of prominent figures in the international arbitration community, including from the London Court of International Arbitration (LCIA), the International Chamber of Commerce (ICC), ICSID, and others. Not surprisingly, the discussion paper by South Africa's Law Commission recommended joining ICSID was well received (South African Law Commission 1998, p. 11).

[130] South African Law Commission 1998, pp. 144–5.   [131] Ibid., p. 145

[132] A key argument was that joining ICSID would remove the option of having domestic courts in the state of arbitration review and set aside arbitral awards, for instance, based on public policy grounds.

[133] In a ruling at the Pretoria High Court, briefly mentioned above, the judge relied heavily on the Law Commission's arbitration report and strongly encouraged the Cabinet to enter ICSID; *Crawford Lindsay Von Abo* v. *The Government of the Republic of South Africa, et al.*, High Court of South Africa (Transvaal Provincial Division), Case No. 3106/2007, Judgment of Prinsloo J., 24 July 2008 (pars. 26–399) (hereafter '*Von Abo v. South Africa*').

[134] South African official X.

188   Letting down the guard: a case study

The leadership of the DTI therefore had to block the ratification of a number of agreements with North African countries, for instance, which took place behind their backs. Similarly, when reading in the newspaper that a minister had travelled to Israel to sign a BIT in 2004, the leading official involved in the new BIT policy raised a red flag realizing that because Israeli diamond cutters considered the South African export duty on rough diamonds to constitute expropriation, the BIT could have been used to initiate a claim.[135] In short, the South African BIT programme was chaotic much to the frustration of officials trying, for the first time, to analyze the complexities and potential liabilities involved.

South Africa's BIT programme after Foresti

This all ended after the Foresti claim, which turned into a major affair. For although the first Swiss claim was not unimportant, its modest size meant the risks of the treaties were not particularly vivid. By contrast, Foresti's $350 million claim made clear to all stakeholders that the treaties were more than just soft law. In one of the hearings South Africa not only sent its considerable legal team from Freshfields, but also one ambassador, two senior officials from the state attorney of Pretoria (including the state attorney of Pretoria herself), the directors general of the DTI and the Department of Minerals and Resources, the head of legal services at the Treasury, as well as senior officials from the president's office.[136] Until the Foresti claim, few of these had ever taken BITs seriously. As stated by one senior official: 'it was not until we got sued, we truly realized that we should have had red flags up when signing these treaties'.[137] Upon DTI's suggestion, the government therefore started a thorough review of its investment treaties – the first in the country's history. In the words of the appointed task team, the review 'was partly necessitated by various arbitral proceedings initiated against the Republic of South Africa ... and the need to conduct a comprehensive risk assessment'.[138]

As was the experience in many other developing countries it was thereby not until South Africa came on the receiving end of a salient

---

[135] Ibid.

[136] See *Piero Foresti, Laura de Carli & Others* v. *The Republic of South Africa*, ICSID Case No. ARB(AF)/07/01, Award, 3 August 2010, pp. 10–11.

[137] South African official XI. Another official notes: 'It was the Foresti claim that made Cabinet realise that we really had to review what these treaties were all about'. (South African official XIII).

[138] DTI 2009, p. 5. Freshfields offered to assist in this process, yet the offer was declined by the South African official in charge; South African official X.

investment treaty claim that reforms ensued. Yet by contrast with most other governments, who apart from slowing down their BIT adoption have pursued more incremental changes – something I shall return to in the following chapter – the controversial claim made the treaties appear so dysfunctional for South African policy-makers that the government decided to significantly depart from the status quo. As the policy review was finalized, DTI made its concluding recommendations to the cabinet in late 2010: South Africa should not sign any more investment treaties with investor–state arbitration clauses.[139] Existing BITs should be renegotiated on these terms, or allowed to expire. Although South Africa should continue to provide necessary legal guarantees to attract FDI at home and protecting South African investors abroad, investment treaties in their most potent form should be a thing of the past.[140] As this book went to press, South Africa had therefore begun to denounce its investment treaties and allowed others to expire. Their replacement was a new Promotion and Protection of Investment Bill, which included standards more closely following the Constitution and without recourse to international investor–state arbitration (Figure 7.1).

Although accompanied by a predictable outrage from some corners of the arbitration community[141] and complaints by a number of governments, the South African government remained steadfast. 'If there are investors who stay away because they feel that we don't have old-style, dated, antiquated bilateral investment treaties in place', the trade minister told European officials and business group leaders, 'I can assure you there are plenty of other investors from other parts of the world who are happy to come and don't insist on this'.[142] And although it is too soon to tell the implications of this reform, European investors themselves still seemed 'unfazed' about the decision at the time of writing.[143]

---

[139] South African official VIII.
[140] South Africa nevertheless proceeded to enter into a BIT with Zimbabwe, yet this had a specific background in the expropriations of South African property there; see DTI 2010. Note also, that the Investment Protocol in the South African Development Community still remained in place at the time of writing, which – remarkably – didn't require an investor to be a national of a SADC member state to file a claim.
[141] See e.g. Brower and Blanchard 2014.
[142] 'South Africa, European Union lock horns', *Business Day Live*, 24 September 2013.
[143] 'Dutch unfazed by SA's cancelled trade treaty', *Business Day Live*, 17 July 2014.

Figure 7.1 Bounded rationality in South Africa's investment treaty programme
Note: Misperception about implications of BITs meant South Africa willingly accepted the UK BIT model (SA$_1$), which provided investment protections over and beyond those in its Constitution as well as the stated policy objective of national treatment. Anchoring led to only minor adjustments in subsequent treaties (SA$_2$), and major adjustment did not take place until a controversial and major claim South Africa made the risks particularly salient (SA$_3$).

Conclusion

Whatever the future that South Africa's investment protection policy may hold, the architects of its early investment treaty programme behaved in ways difficult to account for without insights on bounded rationality. As mentioned in a draft of the DTI report: 'the impact of BITs on future policies were not critically evaluated', and 'the inexperience of negotiators at that time and the lack of knowledge about investment law in general resulted in agreements that were not in the long term interest of [South Africa]'.[144] These were the harsh conclusions drawn in an official report about the now retired South African officials, not least because hardly any written policy documentation was available and no interviews were made with the BIT negotiators from the mid 1990s, as the authors of the report were unable to trace them.[145] But I did, and my review suggests that the report's conclusions are a fair characterization of the time when South Africa spread out its web of investment treaties.

This illustrates – once again – how expectations in much of the literature about the sophistication and rigour with which developing countries negotiated BITs are in stark contrast with realities on the ground. Instead, the international investment regime is one of those cases where 'bounded rationality, like elephants in a living room, [is] sometimes just too much to ignore'.[146] For although careful cost–benefit

---

[144] DTI 2009. With respect to the lack of coordination between – and within – departments, the report similarly mentioned that, 'the formal legal basis for FDI policy is scattered across various line function departments that do not always coordinate policy interventions' and 'there does not appear to be a consistent approach to bilateral policy-making and strategic planning'; DTI 2009, pp. 6, 15.
[145] South African official VIII.   [146] Conlisk 1996, p. 691.

considerations drove some developing countries to adopt investment treaties, this was rare. By overestimating the economic benefits of investment treaties and ignoring their risks, South Africa was but one of many developing countries failing to carefully consider the implications of some of the most powerful legal protections offered under international economic law. This could have important implications for the arbitration community as well as policy-makers themselves, as I shall turn to in the next and final chapter.

8 Expanding the bounds of rationality in the investment regime

One of the reasons practitioners rarely find the international political economy (IPE) discipline relevant is that mainstream studies tend to be based on entirely unreasonable assumptions of decision-making.[1] More than a decade ago, John Odell urged scholars of IPE to depart from this trend. Instead of sticking with the perfect and optimizing actor, they should root their models in how people make decision in the real world. He argued that if the discipline continues to ignore imperfections and biases when 'monetary and economic policy decisions [go] awry', it will remain detached from the decision-making processes resulting in international economic rules and principles.[2]

This study took up the challenge from Odell by documenting how decisions often went 'awry' in the international investment regime due to bounded rationality. By merely relaxing the assumption of perfect information processing but otherwise sticking with standard rationalist frameworks, the book showed how a few simple insights from behavioural psychology and economics can have considerable payoffs for studies of economic diplomacy. So what are some of the practical lessons? Might the architects of the international investment regime be more likely to improve their decisions in the future once they understand mistakes of the past? Given the increasingly contentious nature of the regime, this question seems more pertinent than ever.

Negligence and law

As a starting point, we may ask whether bounded rational BIT adoption has any relevance for arbitration practitioners charged with adjudicating investment treaty disputes. Intuitively, the answer would be no. Although many developing countries may have misjudged the character of investment treaties and rushed to sign them without appreciating the potential

[1] Odell 2002. See also Katzenstein, Keohane, and Krasner 1998, p. 684.
[2] Odell 2002, pp. 192–3.

Negligence and law 193

implications, this could be irrelevant as a matter of law. The intent of a treaty is almost only important for interpretation insofar as it is expressed in the treaty text.[3] When adjudicating disputes in the investment regime or elsewhere, international dispute resolution bodies will have to assume that governments knew the implications of their actions when signing up to international obligations. In the absence of outright imposition, ratified treaties are binding upon states whether they like it or not. Loewenfeld notes, for instance, that although the reason so many developing countries suddenly rushed to sign BITs is not irrelevant from a legal perspective, it 'is not dispositive' either.[4] After all, a fundamental premise of international law is that by granting its consent in a treaty the state binds itself to certain obligations 'even if it subsequently changes its mind about that behavior'.[5] The presumption must be that ignorance of the law is no excuse for breaking the law, as in most national legal systems. So although many treaty drafters did not appreciate BITs' far-reaching repercussions and overestimated their benefits, arbitrators could argue this is irrelevant for the adjudication of investment disputes. For whether the contracting parties were bounded rational or not, they still have to adhere to the principle of *pacta sunt servanda* – promises shall be kept.

But whereas ignorance may not be a legitimate defense, it could be relevant for the interpretation of certain treaty design decisions. This is particularly the case given the vague nature of several core investment treaty provisions.[6] Even if we disregard interpretive inconsistency among tribunals, it was far from clear during the 1990s which promises should be kept when agreeing to a standard such as fair and equitable treatment. So if there are strong reasons to believe a party quickly signed off on a 'default rule' based on a superficial set of negotiations, then arbitrators should perhaps be less forceful in their assumptions about the specific intent behind the scope of a vague provision. Often-heard arguments that 'if party X wanted to restrict provision Y it would explicitly and unequivocally have stated so in the treaty text' could be difficult to sustain.

So perhaps it is time for arbitrators to pay attention to, rather than ignore, the political realities of the treaty-making process. For although the burden of proof should arguably be on the responding state, negligence could be a legitimate factor in some investment disputes – also without rendering the treaties entirely ineffective for investors and home states.

---

[3] The Vienna Convention of the Law of Treaties, arts. 31 and 32. See a discussion in the context of BITs in Vandevelde 1988.
[4] Loewenfeld 2003–2004, p. 126.   [5] Beyers 1997, p. 202.
[6] I am grateful to Federico Ortino and Wolfgang Alschner for discussions about this point.

194   Expanding the bounds of rationality in the investment regime

Improving adoption and design choices

Apart from arbitrators, might the findings of the book also have lessons for policy-makers in the developing world? If we are all subject to systematic biases and erroneous beliefs, can developing country governments do anything but to give up and let their investment protection policies continue to be piecemeal and inefficient? Not necessarily. For accepting that flaws in judgment are a fact of life, in politics or elsewhere, does not imply that the bounds of rationality cannot be extended.

The emerging consensus that decision-makers are often predictably irrational has resulted in a plethora of policy initiatives by Western governments, trying to 'nudge' their citizens into more efficient decisions by manipulating their choice environment.[7] Even the World Bank has embraced this new form of soft paternalism as a way to improve the welfare of the developing world.[8] Along the same lines, this final section will argue that the findings on the role of bounded rationality in the investment regime could have important policy lessons as well. Rather than proposing that developing country governments should be manipulated (nudged), however, I'll focus on policy implications with less thorny ethical implications.[9]

Expertise and experience

Some implications are straightforward. The first is to increase the problem-solving capabilities of officials in charge of negotiating investment treaties. As mentioned, spending time and effort on 'learning how to think' is essentially a coping strategy to minimize cognitive limitations and thus bounded rationality. Yet, many countries still lack sufficient legal capacity to engage carefully with investment treaties and investor–state arbitration. The most skilled legal bureaucrats have often been put in charge of trade negotiations – particularly in countries that have not been hit by a high-impact investment claim.[10]

So for governments that have the resources, a key long-term strategy to pursue more rational BIT policies would be to invest in at least a couple of 'in-house' experts. And those that do not have the resources to attract highly skilled legal expertise could call upon developed countries, or groups of developing countries, to fund one or more independent

---

[7] Advocates and activists include Thaler and Sunstein 2008.   [8] World Bank 2015.
[9] For a critical discussion of nudging, see Hausman and Welch 2010.
[10] See also Khayat 2012.

advisory centres on investment law, as recently initiated in Latin America.[11] Unlike the Advisory Centre on WTO Law, these would not just assist developing countries in case of disputes, but would also assist with negotiations and implementation.

Expertise can also be facilitated through experience. And although there may be good reasons why many developing countries promote generalist bureaucrats it hampers specialized learning. This narrows the bounds of rational decision-making for individual officials and thereby also for their organizations as a whole. Observers of the trade regime have noted that diplomatic career rotations undermine the establishment of experienced trade negotiators,[12] and the same was seen in this study in the context of investment negotiations in South Africa, for instance. Similarly, when Kenneth Vandevelde visited Lithuania in the early 1990s he was concerned whether his efforts would have any long-lasting impact and asked the lead negotiator whether she would continue to be involved with BITs in the future. 'She smiled grimly and said, "In six months, nobody knows what ministries or what ministers will be involved."'[13] This may be an extreme case, but frequent rotation of developing country bureaucrats is common, and it undermines their ability to gain sufficient knowledge of the intricacies and complexities of investment treaty arbitration. Developing countries should therefore consider facilitating experience with investment treaties by establishing specialized units in charge of negotiations, dispute settlement, and inter-agency coordination. This would also decrease the chances that individual bureaucrats promote investment treaties purely for private gain knowing they will not be around when the claims hit.

These recommendations may appear mundane in and by themselves. Yet, when reading existing studies on the international investment regime, the impression has thus far been that practically all developing countries *naturally* had the necessary institutional capacity when participating in the investment treaty movement. Unfortunately, such assumptions have been misguided and even today these problems continue to hamper developing countries' engagement in the regime.

The renegotiation of the German-Pakistan BIT is a case in point. The treaty was signed on 1 December 2009 at a large event commemorating the 50-year anniversary of the first BIT between Pakistan and West

---

[11] Leathley 2011. See also Gottwald 2007; Memorandum from Karl Sauvant, Executive Director, Vale Columbia Center on Sustainable International Investment, and other colleagues at Columbia University, to the Office of the President, Secretary of State, Secretary of the Treasury, Director of the National Economic Council, and US Trade Representative, 29 January 2009.

[12] Busch, Reinhardt, and Shaffer 2009.   [13] CEELI 1993c, p. 15.

196 Expanding the bounds of rationality in the investment regime

Germany. Arbitrators, academics, and policy-makers from around the world travelled to Frankfurt to celebrate and reflect on the history and future of the international investment regime. The venue was carefully chosen, the Herman Josef Abs Saal in the Deutche Bank, named after one of the 'founding fathers' of the investment treaty regime. The backdrop to the treaty, however, shows a less rosy picture than implied by the festivities in Frankfurt. The SGS claim mentioned in the preface resulted in a far more hesitant attitude towards investment treaties in Pakistan. Yet, staff rotations meant the changes were short-lived as investment promotion officials and embassies began to push for BITs yet again. So although the upgraded treaty had initially been blocked by Pakistani officials involved during the SGS case, new officials decided to rush it through without carefully considering the implications.[14] As noted by their more experienced colleagues in the law ministry: 'A decision to sign the treaty should certainly not have been taken in this manner ... No explanation has been provided for the haste'.[15] The reprimand reminds us that although there may be greater awareness of investment treaties today than in the past, bureaucratic constraints make some governments continue to expand their treaty networks without carefully considering the implications. In the absence of administrative reforms, this is bound to continue.

Beyond incrementalism

Another lesson from this study is that governments should be careful of the status quo bias. The majority of developing countries entered into investment treaties expecting they would be important to attract foreign investment. Many now realize those hopes have been largely unfulfilled, and have learned the hard way just how costly the treaties can be. Yet, similar to the lack of consideration that often went into joining the BIT movement in the first place, it appears that most governments have been equally haphazard in availing themselves of alternatives after the rise of investment treaty arbitration – at least thus far.

With respect to the adoption of investment treaties there has been a significant slowdown, but when looking at the treaties signed and negotiated in recent years the changes have mostly been incremental. Several countries have begun enshrining very similar provisions into trade agreements, for instance. This is often done based on the assumption that broader integration agreements will be more useful to attract

[14] Pakistan officials III and VI.
[15] Letter from Azhar Amin Chaudhary, Ministry of Law and Justice, to Pakistan's Board of Investment, 24 November 2009. On file with author.

Improving adoption and design choices 197

investment than stand-alone BITs. But although this may turn out to be true,[16] hardly any government officials interviewed for this book indicated that they had sought evidence to sustain this assumption. The motivated optimism that resulted in a rush to sign BITs during the 1990s seems to be repeating itself with investment chapters in PTAs.

As for the design of investment protection provisions, a number of countries have begun clarifying and restricting key standards – often with the assistance of UNCTAD and NGOs. 'The level of legal focus is incomparable compared to 15 years ago', according to a Canadian negotiator.[17] In the case of Malaysia, for instance, the claims have led the government to be more careful when drafting investment treaties than in the past:

We learned our lesson with the arbitration cases, the treaties have to be balanced ... So we are also tightening up our provisions, just like the Americans ... And we are limiting the role of arbitrators making sure they don't run wild favoring investors.[18]

This is but one example of how the rise of investment treaty arbitration has:

led numerous countries to realize that the specific wording of IIA provisions does matter, and that it can make a significant difference to the outcome of an investment dispute ... the increase in investment disputes has tested the wisdom of negotiating IIAs with extremely broad and imprecise provisions.[19]

This is undoubtedly important. Yet, not only have these efforts mainly been pursued by relatively wealthy developing countries with greater legal capacity,[20] the nature of the changes has often been remarkably limited and almost entirely copy-pasted from those pursued by the United States and Canada after the NAFTA claims. As in Mexico, Thailand, and Chile, discussed in Chapter 6, focus has been on creating slightly more 'complete contracts' anchored around existing templates rather than significant departures from the status quo.[21] A couple of examples should suffice as illustration, so let's focus on the core question of dispute settlement.

Firstly, investment treaty practice has not changed to allow for counterclaims. The drafters of the ICSID Convention explicitly noted the convention should be used for proceedings initiated by *both* investors

---

[16] Some preliminary, positive findings are included in Büthe and Milner 2014.
[17] Canadian official I.   [18] Malaysian official II.   [19] UNCTAD 2007d, pp. 91–2.
[20] Manger and Peinhardt 2013.
[21] An exception is the recent South African Development Community, SADC, Model BIT, see comments in Johnson and Sachs 2014.

198   Expanding the bounds of rationality in the investment regime

and states,[22] and early criticisms of BITs focused on their unbalanced nature by not imposing any substantive obligations on investors.[23] Yet, investment protection treaties negotiated today remain premised on the idea that foreign investors should be able to file international claims against host state governments, but not the other way around. As noted by one arbitration practitioner, policy-makers seem to have an 'uncritical adherence to this belief' in ways that 'blind host States' from seeing alternatives to overly path-dependent design choices.[24]

Another dispute settlement option curiously absent is the reintroduction of exhaustion of local remedies as a condition to initiate international arbitration. If one of the aims of investment treaty arbitration is to promote the rule of law, as has been occasionally suggested, why allow foreign investors to sidetrack domestic courts of host states and thereby remove their incentive to advocate for stronger judicial institutions?[25] A requirement to exhaust reasonably available and effective local remedies should be uncontroversial – it is included in the European Court of Human Rights for instance – yet at the time of writing only few governments have begun to rethink the prudence in allowing foreign investors to entirely avoid domestic courts.

Thirdly, hardly any governments have included provisions giving the contracting parties a greater role in coming up with joint interpretations binding upon the tribunal, or allowing the home state to block certain disputes it does not wish 'its' investors to bring forward.[26] Even in the absence of such provisions governments can make use of interpretive statements on the nature of their obligations as a low-cost, and potentially effective, option to limit the scope of arbitral tribunals.[27] Yet UNCTAD notes that apart from the NAFTA parties '[s]tates have largely neglected their role in interpreting IIAs'.[28]

Fourthly, the turn towards regionalism and broader economic integration agreements could be used as an opportunity to pursue institutional innovations. A country such as Ecuador has been promoting an alternative to ICSID in the context of the Union of South American Nations (UNASUR). At the time of writing, the European Union was also considering establishing a transatlantic investment court. But these are again exceptions. Given the unpredictable nature of ad hoc investment

---

[22] Report of the Executive Directors on the Convention on the Settlement of Investment Disputes between States and Nationals of Other States, 1964, par. 13.

[23] See e.g. UNCTC, E.C.10/1984/8.

[24] Laborde 2010, pp. 102–3. See also Bjorklund 2013.   [25] Ginsburg 2005.

[26] Alschner 2014.   [27] Roberts 2010.

[28] UNCTAD 2011c, p. 3. See Note of Interpretation of the NAFTA Free Trade Commission, 31 July 2001.

arbitration as well as concerns about private lawyers resolving public law disputes, one might have expected more initiatives for regional investment courts with tenured judges and real opportunities for appeal. A plethora of regional courts responsible for economic disputes already exist in the developing world, including the Andean Tribunal of Justice, the Economic Court of the Commonwealth of Independent States, the Central American Court of Justice, the Court of West African Economic and Monetary Union, the Court of Justice for the Common Market of Eastern and Southern Africa, the Caribbean Court of Justice, and others.[29] Many of these are defunct but could be invigorated if given authority over investment disputes as well.

Finally, one can go yet a step further and query why developing countries have not insisted on including only state-to-state dispute resolution clauses in their treaties. Although increasingly dissatisfied with investor–state arbitration as a governing institution, few countries have sought inspiration in the trade regime by having disputes resolved through inter-state adjudication instead. Brazil is an exception. Although Brazil signed a number of investment treaties in the 1990s, a small anti-globalization coalition in Congress blocked their ratification as the treaties 'were not really a priority' for the Brazilian executive.[30] In recent years, however, Brazilian investors have asked for treaty protections when going abroad, but having seen the unanticipated consequences of investment treaty arbitration the response of the Brazilian government has been a model treaty without an investor–state arbitration clause. Instead, disputes should be settled through inter-state mechanisms, domestic procedures, or negotiations.[31] Whether this model will get off the ground is unclear at the time of writing, but given the growing backlash against investment treaty arbitration it is intuitively surprising that hardly any developing countries have followed suit.

One reason could be fears that inter-state dispute resolution would 'repoliticize' the investment regime. But this would be surprising as home state involvement in investment disputes was rarely a driving factor for developing countries to sign the treaties in the first place.[32] Also, depoliticization is an often-heard justification for investor–state arbitration, but it is unclear whether it has actually happened in

---

[29] See Alter 2014.   [30] Quote by Brazilian official Lemos and Campello 2013, p. 25.
[31] Presentation by Erivaldo Gomes, Ministry of Finance, Brazil, Annual Forum of Developing Country Investment Negotiators, Jakarta, November 2013.
[32] An exception was Costa Rica; see Chapter 6.

200   Expanding the bounds of rationality in the investment regime

practice.[33] In fact, the recent controversy over the international investment regime has at least in part confirmed the fears of the German government in the late 1950s: once private investors have the ability to file treaty claims at will, it can turn almost every investment dispute 'into an international litigation with political relevance'.[34] Keeping this in mind, it is not obvious why developing countries should not insist on a dispute settlement system similar to that in the trade regime, where exporting firms have to convince their home government to file a claim at the WTO.

To be clear, the suggestion here is not that it is *necessarily* more 'rational' for developing countries to initiate any of these reforms. Nor is the suggestion that all of this path dependency is due to cognitive constraints. Particularly the (relatively few) developing countries who joined and stayed in the BIT movement based on clear and informed decisions may have already considered some of the aforementioned options and decided not to pursue them.[35] And in some cases, such as China, there is a renewed interest in securing as potent protections for their own investors abroad as possible. But countries that regret not being careful when negotiating investment treaties in the past should consider whether a status quo bias might be at least partly responsible for their incremental response to the rise of investment treaty arbitration. For even if a multilateral investment treaty or a World Investment Court may be unfeasible, numerous other options exist to reanchor the international investment regime.

A significant challenge, of course, will be resistance from developed countries and particularly those yet to experience the costs of investment arbitration. The few renegotiations that have taken place in recent years have primarily been among governments who *themselves* have been subject to a dispute.[36] At the time of writing, this excludes most of Western Europe.[37] Further resistance can be expected from investors

---

[33] For the US case, see Jandhyala, Gertz, and Poulsen 2015.

[34] See Chapter 3. See also Robert 2014, p. 26. Roberts includes a useful discussion of the value of state-to-state dispute resolution in the investment regime, for host states, home states, and occasionally even investors.

[35] On some of the minor reforms pursued, such as allowing for more transparency, fork-in-the-road provisions, or allowing for consolidation of claims, see UNCTAD 2014b.

[36] Haftel and Thompson 2014.

[37] As noted by an experienced European negotiator: 'Sometimes I'm astonished how little attention there is in Europe to arbitral decisions. NAFTA countries are incorporating tribunals' decisions into their treaty texts. But in Europe some countries completely neglect that and instead emphasize the integrity of their earlier text ... The reason is that there have not been cases against several European countries; some countries have just been lucky so they don't see themselves as exposed'. European negotiator, interview November 2012. Note the following perception in this regard by the Dutch negotiator:

and the arbitration community, which have increased lobbying efforts in recent years to block significant change after appreciating the potency of the regime.[38]

In that case, however, developing countries should not underestimate their 'voice' to assert pressure. They can join coalitions with each other as well as domestic stakeholders in developed countries, including NGOs. Also, if rationality is limited, the power of the mass media and the use of framing symbols make powerful allies. Developing countries could consider exploiting the salience bias by mounting campaigns in international media: the more headlines in Western newspapers about environmental and health regulations being questioned under BITs, the greater the pressure on developed country negotiators to compromise. NGOs used the *Ethyl* claim to help bring down the Multilateral Agreement on Investment, and as this book went to press the *Phillip Morris* claim contributed to growing European resistance towards including investor–state arbitration clauses into agreements with Canada and the United States. Whether these are outcomes to be praised is subject to dispute, but they show that particularly salient events have a remarkable impact on public opinion, whether they are representative of the regime or not.

Another overlooked strategy to promote reform is for developing countries to withdraw from their existing treaties. Again, this can be considered in isolation – as in South Africa – or with like-minded countries. The practical implications of cancelling treaties may be limited over the medium term as 'survival clauses' bind the parties with respect to investments made before the termination, sometimes for up to 20 years.[39] Still, if a significant number of developing countries threatened,

---

'We need to follow the gold-standard of maximum protection in our treaties ... We don't need policy space. The lack of claims against the Netherlands shows just how good our approach is'. Dutch negotiator II. On the failure of European countries to adjust their approach due to a lack of claims, see also Van Aaken 2009, p. 538; Peterson and Vis-Dunbar 2006.

[38] See generally Pauwelyn 2014, p. 43. When Australia recently decided to abstain from including investor–state arbitration clauses in its economic integration agreements, prominent investment lawyers referred to it as 'not worldly', 'naïve', and conveying 'a hint of pomposity'. Submission to the OGEMID listserv, 16 April 2011. See also Paulsson 2005, pp. 231–2 (referring to critics of NAFTA's Chapter 11 as 'neo-nationalist', 'attracted by sensationalist allegations of conspiracies against the public interest', 'disinclined to make an effort to grasp the more complex themes of international rules', and 'shrill voices'); Wälde 2006, p. 460 (describing criticisms of investment treaties by NGOs and others as 'autistic moralism').

[39] Most BITs are in effect for 10 or 15 years. At the end of that period each party can decide not to prolong it, usually with one year's notice. Most modern BITs have thereby gone past their first 'tenure', so in order to threaten to exit investment treaties, developing

202   Expanding the bounds of rationality in the investment regime

or actually began, to terminate their BITs, it could force developed countries to initiate significant reforms. As noted by Helfer, states can exit treaties:

> to challenge or revise disfavoured legal norms or institutions ... Withdrawing from an agreement (or threatening to withdraw) can give a denouncing state additional voice, either by increasing its leverage to reshape the treaty to more accurately reflect its interests ... or by establishing a rival legal norm or institution together with other like-minded states. Exit thus sits at a critical intersection of law and power in international relations.[40]

This is important. For just as quickly as developing countries scrambled to adopt investment treaties, just as quickly could they force through profound changes to the status quo. Although there could be first-mover disadvantages, particularly for very small developing countries,[41] one should not exaggerate this hurdle. Few developing countries would have lost considerable, if any, amounts of foreign capital if they refrained from joining the BIT movement. So as long as they make it painstakingly clear that their exit is not opportunistic and they still protect property rights of foreign investors, it is questionable just how harshly international markets would react. For although investors may increasingly be aware of investment treaty obligations due to the rise of investment arbitration, they have numerous ways other than BITs to protect themselves against political risks.

In fact, rather than continuing to violate their BIT obligations leading to costly investment disputes, withdrawing from the treaties while continuing to adhere to their guiding principles would demonstrate respect rather than contempt for international law. As a result, 'the harm to the withdrawing state's reputation as a law abiding nation may be minimal'.[42] Also, to the extent some investors may react negatively to withdrawals from BITs or some home states may be more inclined to increase political pressure in case of particularly egregious investment disputes, developing countries can always offer individual contracts with the same substantive rights as investment treaties and back them up by investor–state arbitration.

To repeat, this study provides no insights on whether individual developing countries should in fact cancel their agreements. But for those developing countries that joined the BIT movement in a disorganized, chaotic, and uninformed manner and today regret that decision, threats of withdrawal are a potential instrument for voice that should

---

countries would have to terminate the treaties. Yet this would not be an unlawful act. See generally, Helfer 2005.

[40] Helfer 2005, p. 1588.   [41] Montt 2009, p. 103.   [42] Helfer 2005, p. 1621.

not be overlooked. By 2013, 1,300 BITs could be terminated by any party at any time and by 2018 this number will increase to almost 1,600, so the potential for unilateral treaty exit is considerable. For now, however, only a few countries have begun the process. This could be for many reasons. But given the often blind acceptance of default rules when Western BIT models spread in the 1990s, governments should at least consider whether the treaties are kept in place due to an excessive preference for the status quo.

Appendix

Figure 1.3 shows the relationship between domestic investment liberalization and BIT adoption among a broad section of 46 developing countries. This is not a straightforward exercise, as there is hardly any comparable cross-country data on FDI reforms. Identifying exactly the year the shift in policy began is a qualitative assessment, which in some cases is bound to be subject to dispute. A potential indicator could be the year countries adopted a comprehensive liberal foreign investment law, but not all countries have introduced unified foreign investment laws and those that have often began opening up to foreign investment years before. Another indicator could be the year a country offered national treatment to foreign investors, but this again would not adequately reflect when the shifts in investment policy began as national treatment was often introduced in national legislation years after – if introduced at all. The figure is thereby based only on a rough indicator of when the countries began introducing considerable reforms to encourage foreign investment; it makes no assumptions about whether the reforms were comparable. In some cases there were few limitations on foreign ownership; in others foreign investors were not allowed majority participation in joint ventures. In some cases, investors were offered national treatment, free repatriation of capital, and clear-cut protections against expropriation without compensation; in others the FDI regime was very different. The years of liberalization were based on literature on the countries in question and are coded as listed in Table A.1.

204

Appendix 205

Table A.1 *Sources for country FDI liberalization years*

Country	Year of liberalization	Source
Uruguay	1973	Bergstein 1988–1989
Egypt	1974	Salacuse 1975
Chile	1974	Hamilton, Garcia-Boliva, and Otero 2012
Thailand	1977	Nikomborirak 2004.
Sri Lanka	1978	Athukorala 2006
China	1979	Gallagher and Shan 2009
Jamaica	1980	Fishbach 1996
Turkey	1980	Schneider and Bilgen 1992
Ghana	1985	Aryeetey, Harrigan, Nissanke 2000.
Malaysia	1986	Lim and Pang 1991
Indonesia	1986	OECD 2010a
Poland	1986	Gordon 1990
Vietnam	1987	Bath and Nottage 2011
Philippines	1987	Scalise 1995–1996
Russia	1987	Frenkel and Sukhman 1993
Hungary	1988	Marton 1993
Lao	1988	Flipse 1992
Myanmar	1988	McCarthy 2000
Nigeria	1989	Ubezonu 1993
Cambodia	1989	Donovan 1993
Pakistan	1989	Khan 1997
Mexico	1989	Camil 1989
Argentina	1989	Snyder 1994
Venezuela	1989	Di John 2005
Zimbabwe	1991	Brett 2005
Colombia	1991	UNCTAD 2006c
Peru	1991	UNCTAD 2000a
Ecuador	1991	UNCTAD 2001a
Uganda	1991	UNCTAD 2000b
India	1991	Kumar 2005
Syria	1991	Hopfinger and Boeckler 1996
Romania	1991	Costa 1998
Morocco	1992	OECD 2010b
Guatemala	1992	UNCTAD 2011a
Nepal	1992	UNCTAD 2003c
Bulgaria	1992	Levy 1995
Albania	1992	Carlson 1995
Jordan	1992	FIAS 1997
Cuba	1992	Travieso-Diaz and Ferrate 1995–1996
Mozambique	1993	UNCTAD 2012
Tunisia	1993	OECD 2012b
Zambia	1993	UNCTAD 2007b
South Africa	1994	Marais 1998
Domin. Rep.	1995	UNCTAD 2009c
Brazil	1995	OECD 1998
Tanzania	1996	UNCTAD 2002d
Ethiopia	1996	UNCTAD 2011

References

Aaken, Anne van, 2009. 'International investment law between commitment and flexibility: a contract theory analysis', *Journal of International Economic Law* 12, 507–38.

2014. 'Behavioral international law and economics', *Harvard Journal of International Law* 55.

Abbott, Kenneth, 2007. 'Enriching rational choice institutionalism for the study of international law', *University of Illinois Law Review* 5, 5–46.

Abbott, Kenneth, and Duncan Snidal, 2000. 'Hard and soft law in international governance', *International Organization* 54(3): 421–56.

2002 'Filling in the folk theorem: the role of gradualism and legalization in international cooperation to combat corruption', working paper.

Aguilar-Alvarez, Guillermo, and William Park, 2003. 'The new face of investment arbitration: NAFTA chapter 11', *Yale Journal of International Law* 28, 365–401.

Agyemang, Augustus Asante, 1988. 'African states and ICSID arbitration', *Comparative International Law Journal of South Africa* 21(2): 177–89.

1989. 'African courts, the settlement of investment disputes and the enforcement of awards', *Journal of African Law* 33(1): 31–44.

Aisbett, Emma, Larry Karp, and Carol McAusland, 2010. 'Police powers, regulatory takings and the efficient compensation of domestic and foreign investors', *The Economic Record* 86(274): 367–83.

Akinboade, Oludele, Franz Siebrits, and Elizabeth Roussot, 2006. 'Foreign direct investment in South Africa', in S. Ibi Ajayi (ed.), *Foreign Direct Investment in Sub-Saharan Africa: Origins, Targets, Impact and Potential*. Nairobi: African Economic Research Consortium.

Allee, Todd, and Clint Peinhardt, 2010. 'Delegating differences: bilateral investment treaties and bargaining over dispute resolution provisions', *International Studies Quarterly* 54(1): 1–26.

Allison, Graham, 1971. *Essence of Decision: Explaining the Cuban Missile Crisis*. Boston: Little Brown.

Alschner, Wolfgang, 2014. 'Regionalism and overlap in investment treaty law – towards consolidation or contradiction?' *Journal of International Economic Law* 17(4).

Alter, Karen, 1998. 'Who are the "masters of the treaty"?: European governments and the European court of justice', *International Organization* 52(1): 121–47.

References 207

2008. 'Agents or trustees? International courts in their political context', *European Journal of International Relations* 14(1): 33–63.

2014. *The New Terrain of International Law: Courts, Politics, Rights*. Princeton University Press.

Alvarez, Jose, 1992. 'Remarks', *ASIL Proceedings* 86, 550–5.

2005. 'Do states socialize?' *Duke Law Journal* 54(5): 961–74.

2009. 'A bit on custom', *New York University Journal of International Law and Politics* 42, 17-64.

Amerasinghe, Chittharanjan, 1992. 'The Prawn Farm (AAPL) arbitration', *Sri Lanka Journal of International Law* 4, 155.

Aricanli, Tosun, and Dani Rodrik, 1990. *The Political Economy of Turkey: Debt, Adjustment and Sustainability*. Houndmills, Basingstoke, Hampshire: Macmillan.

Ariely, Dan, 2008. *Predictably Irrational: The Hidden Forces That Shape Our Decisions*. New York: HarperCollins.

Arvanitis, Athanasios, 2005. 'Foreign direct investment in South Africa: why has it been so low?' in Michael Nowak and Luca Antonio Ricci (eds.), *Post-Apartheid South Africa. The First Ten Years*. Washington, DC: IMF.

Aryeetey, Ernest, Jane Harrigan, and Machiko Nissanke (eds.), 2000. *Economic Reforms in Ghana: The Miracle and the Mirage*. Oxford: Africa World Press.

Asante, Samuel K., 1988. 'International law and foreign investment: a reappraisal', *The International and Comparative Law Quarterly* 37(3): 558–628.

Asiedu-Akrofi, Derek, 1992. 'ICSID arbitral decision', *American Journal of International Law* 86(2): 371–6.

Athukorala, Prema-chandra, 2006. 'Outward-oriented policy reforms and industrialisation: the Sri Lankan experience', *Journal of South Asian Development* 1(1): 19–49.

Bamert, Justus, Fabrizio Gilardi, and Fabio Wasserfallen, 2014, October. 'Learning and the diffusion of regime contention in the Arab Spring', working paper, University of Zurich.

Bath, Vivienne, and Luke Nottage, 2011. *Foreign Investment and Dispute Resolution Law and Practise in Asia*. London: Routledge.

Bekker, Pieter, and Akiko Ogawa, 2013. 'The impact of bilateral investment treaty (BIT) proliferation on demand for investment insurance: reassessing political risk insurance after the "BIT bang",' *ICSID Review* 28(2): 314–50.

Berger, Axel, 2011. 'The politics of China's investment treaty-making program', in Tomer Broude, Marc Busch, and Amy Porges (eds.), *The Politics of International Economic Law*. Cambridge University Press.

Berger, Axel, Matthias Busse, Peter Nunnenkamp, and Martin Roy, 2011. 'More stringent BITs, less ambiguous effects on FDI? not a bit!' *Economics Letters* 112(3): 270–2.

Beyers, Michael, 1997. 'Taking the law out of international law: a critique of the "iterative perspective"', *Harvard International Law Journal* 38(1): 201–7.

Bidwell, Percy, and William Diebold Jr., 1949. 'The United States and the international trade organization', *International Conciliation* 1, 87–239.

208 References

Bjorklund, Andrea, 2008. 'The emerging civilization of investment arbitration', *Penn State Law Review* 113(4): 1269–300.

2013. 'The role of counterclaims in rebalancing investment law', *Lewis and Clark Law Review* 17(2): 462–80.

Blake, Daniel, 2013. 'Thinking ahead: time horizons and the legalization of international investment agreements', *International Organization* 67(4): 797–827.

Bonnitcha, Jonathan, 2014. *Substantive Protection under Investment Treaties: A Legal and Economic Analysis.* Cambridge University Press.

Bonnitcha, Jonathan, and Emma Aisbett, 2013. 'An economic analysis of the substantive protections provided by investment treaties', in Karl Sauvant (ed.), *Yearbook on International Investment Law & Policy 2011/12.* Oxford University Press.

Boockmann, Bernhard, and Axel Dreher, 2003. 'The contribution of the IMF and the World Bank to economic freedom', *European Journal of Political Economy* 19(3): 633–649.

Braithwaite, John, and Peter Drahos, 2000. *Global Business Regulation.* Cambridge University Press.

Brett, Edward, 2005. 'From corporatism to liberalization in Zimbabwe: economic policy regimes and political crisis, 1980–1997', *International Political Science Review* 26(1): 91–106.

Broches, Aaron, 1995. *Selected Essays: World Bank, ICSID, and Other Subjects of Public and Private International Law.* London: Martinus Nijhoff.

Broude, Tomer, 2013. 'Behavioural international law', *International Law Forum at the Hebrew University of Jerusalem Research Paper,* no. 12–13.

Brower, Charles, 1999. 'Ibrahim Shihata and the resolution of international investment disputes: the masterful missionary', *Studies in Transnational Legal Policy* 31, 79–83.

Brower, Charles, and Jarrod Wong, 2005, May. 'General valuation principles: the case of Santa Elena', in Todd Weiler (ed.), *International Investment Law and Arbitration: Leading Cases from the ICSID, NAFTA, Bilateral Treaties and Customary International Law.* London: Cameron.

Brower, Charles, and Sadie Blanchard, 2014, January. 'From "dealing in virture" to "profiting from injustice": the case against "re-statification" of investment dispute settlement', *Harvard International Law Journal* 55, 45–59.

Brower, Charles, and Stephan Schill, 2009. 'Is arbitration a threat or a boon to the legitimacy of international investment law', *Chicago Journal of International Law* 9(2): 471–98.

Brunetti, Maurizio, 2001. 'The Iran-United States claims tribunal, NAFTA Chapter 11, and the doctrine of indirect expropriation', *Chicago Journal of International Law* 2, 203.

Bubb, Ryan, and Susan Rose-Ackerman, 2007. 'BITs and bargains: strategic aspects of bilateral and multilateral regulation of foreign investment', *International Review of Law and Economics* 27, 291–311.

Burkhardt, Hans-Martin, 1986. 'Investment protection treaties: recent trends and prospects', *Aussenwirtschaft: Schweizerische Zeitschrift für international Wirtschaftsbeziehungen* 41(1): 99–105.

References

Burley, Anne-Marie, and W. Mattli, 1993. 'Europe before the court: a political theory of legal integration', *International Organization* 47(1): 41–76.

Busch, Marc, Eric Reinhardt, Gregory Shaffer, 2009. 'Does legal capacity matter? A survey of WTO members?' *World Trade Review* 8(4): 559–77.

Büthe, Tim, and Helen Milner, 2009. 'Bilateral investment treaties and foreign direct investment', in Karl Sauvant and Lisa Sachs (eds.), *The Effect of Treaties on Foreign Direct Investment: Bilateral Investment Treaties, Double Taxation Treaties, and Investment Flows*. New York: Oxford University Press.

2014. 'Foreign direct investment and institutional diversity in trade agreements: credibility, commitment, and economic flows in the developing world, 1971–2007'. *World Politics* 66(1): 88–122.

Butler, David, 1994. 'South African arbitration legislation – the need for reform', *Comparative International Law Journal of South Africa* 27.

Butler, David, and Eyvind Finsen, 1996. 'Southern Africa', in Eugene Cotran and Austin Amissah (eds.), *Arbitration in Africa*. The Hague: Kluwer Law International.

Callander, Steven, 2008. 'A theory of policy expertise', *Quarterly Journal of Political Science* 3, 123–40.

Cameron, Maxwell, and Brian Tomlin, 2002. *The Making of NAFTA: How the Deal Was Done*. Ithaca: Cornell University Press.

Caplin, Andrew, and Daniel Martin, 2012. 'Defaults and attention: the drop out effect', *National Bureau of Economic Research*, no. w17988.

Carim, Xavier, 2010, September 13. 'Update on EPA negotiations', speaking points to Tralac Seminar, Cape Town, available at http://trade.ec.europa.eu/doclib/docs/2010/september/tradoc_146522.30%20July%202010.2.pdf.

Carlson, Scott, 1995. 'Foreign investment laws and foreign direct investment in developing countries: Albania's experiment', *International Lawyer* 19(3): 577–98.

Central and Eastern European Law Initiative (CEELI), 1993a. *Analysis of Two Draft Proposals on Foreign Investment for Lithuania*. Washington DC: American Bar Association.

1993b. *Country Strategies for the Rule of Law Program for Albania, Bulgaria, Croatia, Czech Republic, Estonia, Hungary, Latvia, Lithuania, Macedonia, Poland, Romania, and Slovakia*. Washington DC: American Bar Association.

1993c. *Report to the United States Agency for International Development on the Activities of the American Bar Association Central and Eastern European Law Initiative (CEELI), July 1993–December 1993*. Washington DC: American Bar Association.

1996. *Analysis of the Draft Law on Foreign Investment Activities in Nizhny Novgorod Oblast*. Washington DC: American Bar Association.

Chaskalson, Arthur, 1994. 'The property clause: section 28 of the Constitution', *South Africa Journal of Human Rights* 10, 131–9.

Christie, Richard, 1993. 'South Africa as a venue for international commercial arbitration', *Arbitration International* 9(2): 153–65.

Christy III, Paul, 1990–1. 'Negotiating investment in the GATT: a call for functionalism', *Michigan Journal of International Law* 12(3): 743–98.

210 References

Cokorinos, Lee, and James Mittelman, 1988. 'Reagan and the *Pax Afrikaana*', in Morris Morely (ed.), *Crisis and Confrontation: Ronald Reagan's Foreign Policy*. Totawa: Rowman and Littlefield.

Colombatto, Enrico, and Jonathan Macey, 1996. 'A public choice model of international economic cooperation and the decline of the nation state', *Cardozo Law Review*, 925–56.

Conlisk, John, 1996. 'Why bounded rationality?' *Journal of Economic Literature* 34(2): 669–700.

Copenhagen Economics, 2012. *EU-China Investment Study*. Copenhagen: Copenhagen Economics.

Dashwood, Hevina, 2000. *Zimbabwe: The Political Economy of Transformation*. Toronto: University of Toronto Press.

Dawson, Erica, Thomas Gilovich, and Dennis Regan, 2002. 'Motivated reasoning and performance on the Wason selection task', *Personality and Social Psychology Bulletin* 28(10): 1379–1987.

Decker, Stephanie, 2012. 'Using archives to understand the difficulties of translating theory into practice: economic advisors in Ghana, 1960–85', presented at the World Bank Conference on Using History to Inform Development Policy: The Role of Archives, 25–26 October.

Delaume, Georges, 1985. 'ICSID and bilateral investment treaties', *News from ICSID*, no. 1, Washington DC: World Bank.

DeLisle, Jacques, 1999. 'Lex Americana? United States legal assistance, American legal models, and legal change in the post-communist world and beyond', *University of Pennsylvania Journal of International Economic Law* 20(2): 179–308.

Denza, Eileen, and Shelagh Brooks, 1987. 'Investment protection treaties: the British experience', *International and Comparative Law Quarterly* 36(4): 908–23.

Department of Minerals and Energy, Republic of South Africa, 1998. *A minerals and mining policy for South Africa*.

Department of Trade and Industry (DTI), Republic of South Africa, 2009, June. *Government position paper on bilateral investment treaty policy framework review*.

    2010, March 29. 'The promotion and reciprocal protection of investments agreement between the governments of the republic of South Africa and the republic of Zimbabwe', Explanatory Memorandum.

    2008, January 30. 'SADC EPA Group – EC Negotiations: Assessing the Emerging Outcome'.

    2008, June 11. 'Trade negotiations update', Parliamentary Portfolio Committee Briefing Session, Cape Town.

Development Committee of the World Bank, 1992. 'Communiqué of the Development Committee', in *Presentations to the 44th Meeting of the Development Committee*, Washington DC: World Bank.

Dezalay, Yves, and Bryan Garth, 1996. *Dealing in Virtue: International Commercial Arbitration and the Construction of a Transnational Legal Order*. Chicago: University of Chicago Press.

Di John, Jonathan, 2005. 'Economic liberalization, political instability, and state capacity in Venezuela', *International Political Science Review* 26(1): 107–24.

Diaz, Fernando, 2009, June 5. 'Ecuador continues exit from ICSID', *Investment Treaty News.*

Dobbin, Frank, Beth Simmons, and Geoffrey Garrett, 2007. 'The global diffusion of public policies: social construction, coercion, competition, or learning?' *Annual Review of Sociology* 33, 449–72.

Dolzer, Rudolf, 2005. 'The impact of international investment treaties on domestic administrative law', *New York University Journal of International Law and Policy* 26, 953–72.

Dolzer, Rudolf, and Margrete Stevens, 1995. *Bilateral Investment Treaties.* Hague: Martinus Neijhof.

Dolzer, Rudolf, and Yun-I Kim, 2013. 'Germany', in Chester Brown (ed.), *Commentaries on Selected Model Investment Treaties.* Oxford University Press.

Donovan, Dolores, 1993. 'Cambodia: building a legal system from scratch', *International Lawyer* 27(2): 445–54.

Douglas, Zachary, 2006. 'Nothing if not critical for investment treaty arbitration: Occidental, Eureko and Methanex', *Arbitration International* 22(1): 27–51.

Eberhardt, Pia, and Cecilia Olivet, 2012. *Profiting from Injustice: How Law Firms, Arbitrators and Financiers Are Fuelling an Investment Arbitration Boom.* Brussels/Amsterdam: Corporate Observatory Europe.

Echandi, Roberto, 2011. 'What do developing countries expect from the international investment regime?' in Jose Alvarez and Karl Sauvant (eds.), *The Evolving International Investment Regime.* New York: Oxford University Press.

Economist Intelligence Unit, 2011, June 11. *Political risk in developing countries focused on expropriation.* Draft survey for MIGA. On file with author.
  2015. *Risk and Return: Foreign Direct Investment and the Rule of Law.* London: Economist Intelligence Unit.

Einhorn, Hillel, 1974. 'Expert judgment: some necessary conditions and an example', *Journal of Applied Psychology* 4(1): 562–71.

Elkins, Zachary, Andrew Guzman, and Beth Simmons (EGS), 2006. 'Competing for capital: the diffusion of bilateral investment treaties, 1960–2000', *International Organization* 60(4): 811–46.
  2007a. 'Replication data for competing for capital: the diffusion of bilateral investment treaties, 1959–2000'.
  2007b. 'Competing for capital: the diffusion of bilateral investment treaties', in Beth Simmons, Frank Dobbin, and Geoffrey Garrett (eds.), *The Global Diffusion of Markets and Democracy.* Cambridge University Press.
  2008. 'Competing for capital: the diffusion of bilateral investment treaties', *University of Illinois Law Review* 1, 265.
  2010a. 'Competing for capital: the diffusion of bilateral investment treaties', in Michael Waibel, Asha Kaushal, Kyo-Hwa Chung, and Claire Balchin (eds.), *The Backlash Against Investment Arbitration.* Alphen Aan den Reijn: Kluwer Law.
  2010b. 'Competing for capital: the diffusion of bilateral investment treaties', in Jeffry Frieden, David Lake, and Lawrence Broz, *International Political Economy*, 5th ed. New York: Norton.

212   References

Elkins, Zachary, Tom Ginsburg, and James Melton, 2014. 'Imagining a world without the universal declaration of human rights', working paper.

Elms, Deborah, 2013. 'New directions for IPE: drawing from behavioral economics', in Rolan Palan (ed.), *Global Political Economy: Contemporary Theories*, 2nd ed., London: Routledge.

Esty, Daniel, 2006. 'Good governance at the supra-national scale: globalizing administrative law', *Yale Law Journal* 115, 1490–1562.

European Commission, 2000. Survey of the attitudes of the European business community to international investment rules, conducted by T. N. Sofres consulting on behalf of the European Commission, DG Trade.

Fatouros, A., 1961. 'An international code to protect private investment: proposals and perspectives', *University of Toronto Law Journal* 14(1): 77–102.

Faya Rodriguez, Alejandro, 2005. 'Mexico signs two new bilateral investment treaties', *North American Free Trade and Investment Report* 15(16): 6–8.

Fecák, Tomáš, 2011. 'Czech experience with bilateral investment treaties: somewhat bitter taste of investment protection', *Czech Yearbook of Public and Private International Law* 2, 233–67.

FIAS, 1994. *Bulgaria: The Climate for Foreign Direct Investments. Diagnosis and Recommendations.* Washington DC: World Bank.

1997a. *Promoting Foreign Direct Investment in Jordan: Policy, Strategy, and Institutions.* Washington DC: World Bank.

1997b. *Republic of Sierra Leone: Formulation of a New Investment Law.* Washington DC: World Bank.

1998. *Former Yugoslav Republic of Macedonia: Improving the Environment for Foreign Direct Investment.* Washington DC: World Bank.

1999a. *Bosnia and Herzegovina: Institutional Framework for Foreign Investment Promotion.* Washington DC: World Bank.

1999b. *Slovak Republic: Legal, Regulatory, and Tax Improvements for Attracting Foreign Direct Investment.* Washington DC: World Bank.

1999c. *Iran: Diagnostic of the Investment Environment.* Washington DC: World Bank.

2001a. *Brazil: Legal, Policy and Administrative Barriers to Investment in Brazil,* vol. 1, Washington DC: World Bank.

2001b. *Albania: Diagnostic Study.* Washington DC: World Bank.

2001c. *Honduras: The Climate for Foreign Direct Investment and How It Can Be Improved.* Washington DC: World Bank.

2001d. *Bosnia and Herzegovina: Commercial Legal Framework and Administrative Barriers to Foreign Investment.* Washington DC: World Bank.

2004. *Grenada: A Diagnostic Review of the Investment Climate.* Washington DC: World Bank.

Finger, Matthias, and Berangere Ruchat, 2000. The transformation of international public organizations: the case of UNCTAD, working paper of IDHEAP 14/2000. Lausanne: Institut de Hautes Etudes en Administration Publique.

Finnemore, Martha, and Kathryn Sikkink, 1998. 'International norm dynamics and political change', *International Organization* 52(4): 887–917.

References

Fishbach, Steven, 1996. '"The quiet revolution": trade and investment liberalization in Chile and Jamaica', *Administrative Law Review* 48(4): 527–43.

Franck, Susan, 2007. 'Empirically evaluating claims about investment treaty arbitration', *North Carolina Law Review* 86(1): 1–87.

Fredriksson, Torbjorn, and Zbigniew Zimny, 2004. 'Foreign direct investment and transnational corporations', in *UNCTAD, Beyond Conventional Wisdom in Development Policy: An Intellectual History of UNCTAD 1964–2004*. New York and Geneva: United Nations.

Frenkel, William, and Michael Sukhman, 1993. 'New foreign investment regimes of Russia and other republics of the former U.S.S.R.: a legislative analysis and historical perspective', *British Columbia International and Comparative Law Review* 16(2): 321–423.

Galbraith, Jean, 2013. 'Treaty options: towards a behavioral understanding of treaty design', *Virginia Journal of International Law* 53, 309.

Galinsky, Adam, and Thomas Mussweiler, 2001. 'First offers as anchors: the role of perspective-taking and negotiator focus', *Journal of Personality and Social Psychology* 81(4): 657–69.

Gallagher, Kevin, and Elen Shrestha, 2011. 'Investment treaty arbitration and developing countries: a re-appraisal', Global Development and Environmental Institute working paper 11-01.

Gallagher, Norah, and Wenhua Shan, 2009. *Chinese Investment Treaties*. Oxford University Press.

Gallins, Glen, 1984. 'Bilateral investment protection treaties', *Journal of Energy and Natural Resources Law* 2, 77.

Gantz, David, 2004. 'The evolution of FTA investment provisions: from NAFTA to the United States-Chile free trade agreement', *American University International Law Review* 19(4), 679–767.

Gardner, James, 1980. *Legal Imperialism: American Lawyers and Foreign Aid in Latin America*. Madison: University of Wisconsin Press.

Gilardi, Fabrizio, 2010. 'Who learns from what in policy diffusion processes?' *American Journal of Political Science* 54(3): 650–66.

2014, March 10. 'Four ways we can improve policy diffusion research', working paper, available at myweb.uiowa.edu/fboehmke/shambaugh2014/papers/Gilardi-4-Theses-Diffusion.pdf.

Gilovich, Thomas, 2000, June. Motivated skepticism and motivated credulity: differential standards of evidence in the evaluation of desired and undesired propositions. Address presented at the 12th Annual Convention of the American Psychological Society, Miami Beach, Florida.

Gilovich, Thomas, and Dale Griffin, 2002. 'Introduction – heuristics and biases: then and now', in Thomas Gilovich, Dale Griffin, and Daniel Kahneman (eds.), *Heuristics and Biases: The Psychology of Intuitive Judgment*. New York: Cambridge University Press.

Ginsburg, Tom, 2005. 'International substitutes for domestic institutions: bilateral investment treaties and governance', *International Review of Law and Economics* 25(1): 107–23.

Goldstein, Judith and Robert Keohane (eds.), 1993. *Ideas and Foreign Policy: Beliefs, Institutions, and Political Change*. Ithaca: Cornell University Press.

214 References

Gordon, David, 1990. 'The Polish foreign investment law of 1990', *The International Lawyer* 24(2): 335–63.

Gottwald, Eric, 2007. 'Levelling the playing field: is it time for a legal assistance center for developing nations in investment treaty arbitration?' *American University International Law Review* 22(2): 237–75.

Graham, Edward, 2000. *Fighting the Wrong Enemy: Antiglobal Activists and Multinational Enterprises*. Washington DC: Institute for International Economics.

Gregory, Neil, Dileep Wagle, and Dale Weigel, 1997. *Foreign Direct Investment*, vol. 5, Washington, DC: International Finance Corporation and Foreign Investment Advisory Services.

Grewlich, Klaus, 1980. *Transnational Enterprises in a New International System*. Alphen aan den Rijn: Sijthoff & Noordhoff.

Gruber, Lloyd, 2000. *Ruling the World: Power Politics and the Rise of Supranational Institutions*. Princeton University Press.

Gudgeon, K., 1986. 'United States bilateral investment treaties: comments on their origin, purposes, and general treatment standards', *International Tax and Business Lawyer* 4(1): 105–31.

Gunawardana, Asoka, 1992. 'The inception and growth of bilateral investment promotion and protection treaties', *ASIL Proceedings* 86, 544–50.

Gurowitz, Amy, 2006. 'The diffusion of international norms: why identity matters', *International Politics* 43(3): 305–41.

Guzman, Andrew, 1998. 'Why LDCs sign treaties that hurt them: explaining the popularity of bilateral investment treaties', *Virginia Journal of International Law* 38, 639–88.

2008. *How International Law Works: A Rational Choice Theory*. New York: Oxford University Press.

Haber, Stephen, Herbert Klein, Noel Maurer, and Kevin Middlebrook, 2008. *Mexico Since 1980*. New York: Cambridge University Press.

Hafner-Burton, Emilie, Brad Leveck, David Victor, and James Fowler, 2012. 'A behavioral approach to international legal cooperation', working paper 13, Laboratory on International Law and Regulation, University of California, San Diego.

Haftel, Yoram, and Alex Thompson, 2014. 'Delayed ratification: the domestic fate of bilateral investment treaties', *International Organization* 67(2): 355–87.

2014. 'When do states renegotiate international agreements? The case of bilateral investment treaties', working paper.

Hale, Thomas. *Between Interests and Law*. Cambridge University Press, forthcoming.

Hamilton, Jonathan, 2012. 'Omar Garcia-Boliva, and Hernando Otero', in *Latin American Investment Protections*. Boston: Martinus Nijhoff.

Hausman, Daniel, and Brynn Welch, 2010. 'Debate: to nudge or not to nudge', *Journal of Political Philosophy* 18(1): 123–36.

Helfer, Laurence, 2005. 'Exiting treaties', *Virginia Law Review* 91(7): 1579–1648.

References 215

Helfer, Laurence, and Anne-Marie Slaughter, 2005. 'Why states create international tribunals: a response to professors Posner and Yoo', *California Law Review* 93, (3): 899–956.

Henkin, Louis, 1979. *How Nations Behave: Law and Foreign Policy*, 2nd ed. New York: Columbia University Press.

Herrera, Yoshiko, 2007. *Imagined Economies: The Sources of Russian Regionalism.* Cambridge University Press.

Hershey, Amos, 1907. 'The Calvo and Drago doctrines', *The American Journal of International Law* 1(1): 26–45.

Hey, Jeanne, and Thomas Klak, 1999. 'From protectionism towards neoliberalism: Ecuador across four administrations (1981–1996)', *Studies in Comparative International Development* 34(3): 66–97.

Hodgson, Matthew, 2014. 'Counting the costs of investment treaty arbitration', *Global Arbitration Review* 9, 2.

Hohenemser, Cristoph, Robert W. Kates, and Paul Slovic, 1983. 'The nature of technological hazard', *Science* 220(4595): 378–84.

Hopfinger, Hans, and Marc Boeckler, 1996. 'Step by step to an open economic system: Syria sets course for liberalization', *British Journal of Middle Eastern Studies* 23(2): 183–202.

Hormeku, Tetteh, 1998. 'NGOs critical of UNCTAD's investment and probusiness approach', *Third World Economics* 187/188, 1.

Hornbeck, Stanley K., 1909. 'The most-favored-nation clause', *The American Journal of International Law* 3(4): 797–827.

Huber, John D., and Nolan McCarty, 2004. 'Bureaucratic capacity, delegation, and political reform', *American Political Science Review* 98(3): 481–94.

ICAS, 2010. *Investing Across Borders, 2010.* Washington DC: World Bank.

ICC, 1977. *Bilateral Treaties for International Investment.* Paris: ICC.

ICSID, 1974. *Annual Report 1973/1974.* Washington DC: World Bank.

    1985. *Annual Report.* Washington DC: World Bank.

    1995. *Annual Report.* Washington DC: World Bank.

IISD, 2004. *An Assessment of the Investment Regime: Thailand Country Report.* Winnipeg: International Institute for Sustainable Development.

    2010. *Report on the Fourth Annual Forum of Developing Country Investment Negotiators.* Winnipeg: International Institute for Sustainable Development.

IMF, 1995. *World Economic Outlook, October 1995.* Washington DC: IMF.

    1998, August 25. 'Bolivia: enhanced structural adjustment facility policy framework paper, 1998–2001'.

    1999, July 29. 'Letter of intent and memorandum of economic and financial policies of the government of Moldova'.

    1999. *World Economic Outlook, October 1999.* Washington DC: IMF.

    2006. *Annual Report for the Executive Board, 2006.* Washington DC: IMF.

    2004, June. 'Uruguay', IMF country report no. 04/172.

    2004, November. 'Uruguay: letter of intent and technical memorandum of understanding', 12.

IMF's Independent Evaluation Office (IEO), 2005. *The IMF's Approach to Capital Account Liberalization.* Washington DC: IMF.

216 References

International Bank for Reconstruction and Development (IBRD), 1947. *Annual Report 1946–1947*. Washington DC: World Bank.
  1969. *The World Bank, IDA and IFC, Policies and Operations*. Washington DC: The World Bank.
International Investment and Development Committee of the American Bar Association's Section of International Law and Practice, 1992. 'Preliminary comments of international investment and development committee on draft Albanian foreign investment law', in CEELI, *Analysis of Albania's Foreign Investment Act*. Washington DC: American Bar Association.
Jandhyala, Srividya, Geoffrey Gertz, and Lauge Poulsen. 2015. 'Legalization and Diplomacy: Does Arbitration De-politicize Investment Disputes?' working paper.
Jandhyala, Srividya and Robert J. Weiner, 2012. 'Institutions sans frontiers: international agreements and foreign investment', *Journal of Business Studies* 45(6): 649–69.
Jandhyala, Srividya, Witold Henisz, and Edward Mansfield, 2011. 'Three waves of BITs: the global diffusion of foreign investment policy', *Journal of Conflict Resolution* 55(6): 1047–73.
Jensen, Nathan, 2005. 'Measuring risk: political risk insurance premiums and domestic political institutions', working paper 512002.
Jervis, Robert, 1976. *Perception and Misperception in International Politics*. Princeton University Press.
Johnson, Eric, John Hershey, Jacqueline Meszaros, and Howard Kunreuther, 1993. 'Framing, probability distortions, and insurance decisions', *Journal of Risk and Uncertainty* 7, 35–51.
Johnson, Lise and Lisa Sachs, 2014. 'International investment agreements, 2011–2012: a review of trends and new approaches', in Andrea Bjorklund (ed.), *Yearbook on International Investment Law and Policy 2012–2013*. New York: Oxford University Press, 219–61.
Johnson, Lise, and Oleksandr Volkov, 2013. 'Investor-state contracts, host-state "commitments" and the myth of stability in international law', *American Review of International Arbitration* 24(361): 361–415.
Jones, Bryan D., 2001. *Politics and the Architecture of Choice: Bounded Rationality and Governance*. Chicago: University of Chicago Press.
Jones, Bryan D., and Frank R. Baumgartner, 2005. *The Politics of Attention*. Chicago: University of Chicago Press.
  'From there to here: punctuated equilibrium to the general punctuation thesis to a theory of government information processing', *Policy Studies Journal* 4(1): 1–20.
Juillard, Patrick, 2001, May 28–29. 'Bilateral investment treaties in the context of international investment law', OECD Roundtable, Dubrovnik, Croatia.
Jupille, Joseph, Walter Mattli, and Duncan Snidal, 2013. *Institutional Choice in Global Commerce: Governance Strategies from the 19th Century to the Present*. Cambridge University Press.
Kahan, Dan, Paul Slovic, Donald Braman, and John Gastil, 2006. 'Fear of democracy: a cultural evaluation of Sunstein on risk', *Harvard Law Review* 119, 1071–109.

Kahneman, Daniel, and Amos Tversky, 1979. 'Prospect theory: an analysis of decision under risk', *Econometrica* 47(2): 263–92.

Kahneman, Daniel, Jack Knetsch, and Richard Thaler, 1991. 'Anomalies: the endowment effect, loss aversion, and status quo bias', *Journal of Economic Perspectives* 5(1): 193–206.

Karsegard, Olof, Pedro Bravo, and Hubert Blom, 2006. *Final In-Depth Evaluation Report, September 2000-July 2005: UNCTAD Work Programme on Capacity Building in Developing Countries on Issues in International Investment Agreements*. New York: United Nations.

Kates, Robert, 1962. 'Hazard and choice perception in flood plain management', research paper no. 78, University of Chicago, Department of Geography.

Katzenstein, Peter, Robert Keohane, and Stephen Krasner, 1998. 'International organization and the study of world politics', *International Organization* 52(4): 645–85.

Kaufmann, Chaim, 1994. 'Out of the lab and into the archives: a method for testing psychological explanations of political decision making', *International Studies Quarterly* 38(4): 557–86.

Kaushal, Asha, 2009. 'Revisiting history: how the past matters for the present backlash against the foreign investment regime', *Harvard Journal of International Law* 50(2): 491–534.

Keller, Carmen, Michael Siegrist, and Heinz Gutscher, 2006. 'The role of affect and availability heuristics in risk communication', *Risk Analysis* 26(3): 631–9.

Kellner, Tomas, 2003, April 28. 'The informer: call it the Ronald Lauder tax', *Forbes*.

Kelman, Mark, 2011. *The Heuristics Debate*. New York: Oxford University Press.

Keohane, Robert, 1984. *After Hegemony: Cooperation and Discord in the World Political Economy*. Princeton University Press.

Kerner, Andrew, and Jane Lawrence, 2014. 'What's the risk? bilateral investment treaties, political risk and fixed capital accumulation', *British Journal of Political Science* 44(1): 107–21.

Khan, Ashfaque, 1997. 'Foreign direct investment in Pakistan: policies and trends', *The Pakistan Development Review* 36(4): 959–85.

Khayat, Dany, 2012. 'Bridging the investment claim gap between sophisticated investors and unprepared host states', in *UNCTAD, Investor-State Disputes: Prevention and Alternatives to Arbitration II. Geneva:* United Nations.

Kim, Jae Hoon, 2011. 'Korea's development of a better investor-state dispute resolution system', in *UNCTAD, Investor-State Disputes: Prevention and Alternatives to Arbitration II. Geneva:* United Nations, 67–70.

Kim, Soo Yeon, and Mark S. Manger, 2013, February 7–9. 'Hubs of governance: path-dependence and higher-order effects of PTA formation', working paper prepared for the Annual Meeting of the Political Economy of International Organizations.

Kinsella, Norman, 1993, November 18. 'Comments on draft project of law on foreign capital investment in the Republic of Lithuania', memorandum to Mr M. Černiauskas, president, Association of Lithuanian Chambers of Commerce and Industry.

218   References

1997, March 25. 'Draft law on stimulation of foreign investment for the Republic of Romania', memorandum to Mr John C. Knechtle, director, Legal Assessments, ABA/CEELI.

Klug, Heinz, 2000. *Constituting Democracy: Law Globalism and South Africa's Political Reconstruction*. Cambridge University Press.

Koh, Harold, 1997. 'Review essay: why do nations obey international law?' *Yale Law Journal* 106, 2599–659.

Kong, Qiangjiang, 2003. 'Bilateral investment treaties: the Chinese approach and practice', *Asian Yearbook of International Law* 8, 105–36.

Koremenos, Barbara, Charles Lipson, and Duncan Snidal, 2001. 'The rational design of international institutions', *International Organization* 55(4): 761–99.

Korobkin, Russell, 1998. 'Inertia and preference in contract negotiation: the psychological power of default rules and form terms', *Vanderbilt Law Review* 51, 1583–1651.

2003. 'Bounded rationality, standard form contracts, and unconscionability', *The University of Chicago Law Review* 70(4): 1203–95.

Krebs, Ronald, and Aaron Rapport, 2012. 'International relations and the psychology of time horizons', *International Studies Quarterly* 56(3): 530–43.

Kumar, Nagesh, 2005. 'India liberalization, foreign direct investment flows, and development: Indian experience in the 1990s', *Economic and Political Weekly* 40(14): 1459–69.

Kunda, Ziva, 1990. 'The case for motivated reasoning', *Psychological Bulletin* 108(3): 480–98.

Laborde, Gustavo, 2010. 'The case for host state claims in investment arbitration', *Journal of International Dispute Settlement* 1(1): 1–26.

Lake, David, 2009. 'Open economy politics: a critical review', *The Review of International Organizations* 4(3): 219–44.

Lamertz, Kai, and Pursey Heugens, 2009. 'Institutional translation through spectatorship: collective consumption and editing of symbolic organizational texts by firms and their audiences', *Organization Studies* 30(11): 1249–79.

Leathley, Christian, 2011 April 13. 'What will the recent entry into force of the UNASUR treaty mean for investment arbitration in Latin America?' *Kluwer Arbitration Blog*.

Lemos, Leany and Daniela Campello, 2013, April 1. 'The non-ratification of bilateral investment treaties in Brazil: a story of conflict in a land of cooperation', working paper.

Leon, Peter, 2009. 'Creeping expropriation of mining investments: an African perspective', *Journal of Energy & Natural Resources Law* 27(4): 597–644.

Levy, David, 1995. 'Bulgarian trade and investment: a realistic assessment', *Case Western Reserve Journal of International Law* 27(2): 203–46.

Levy, Jack, 1992. 'Prospect theory and international relations: theoretical applications and analytical problems', *Political Psychology* 13(2): 283–310.

1994. 'Learning and foreign policy: sweeping a conceptual minefield', *International Organization* 48(2): 279–312.

References

1997. 'Prospect theory, rational choice, and international relations', *International Studies Quarterly* 41(1): 87–112.

Lichtenstein, Sara, Paul Slovic, Baruch Fischhoff, Mark Layman, and Barbara Combs, 1978. 'Judged frequency of lethal events', *Journal of Experimental Psychology: Human Learning and Memory* 4(6): 551.

Lim, Linda, and Eng Pang, 1991. *Foreign Direct Investment and Industrialization in Malaysia, Singapore, Taiwan and Thailand*. Paris: OECD.

Lipson, Charles, 1985. *Standing Guard: Protecting Foreign Capital in the Nineteenth and Twentieth Centuries*. Berkeley: University of California Press.

1991. 'Why are some international agreements informal?' *International Organization* 45(4): 495–538.

Loewenfeld, Andreas, 2003–4. 'Investment agreements and international law', *Columbia Journal of Transnational Law* 42(1): 123–30.

Lundahl, Mats, and Lennart Petersson, 2009. 'Post-apartheid South Africa: an economic success story?' UN-WIDER research paper no. 2009/56.

Lupu, Yonathan, and Paul Poast, 2013, October 21. 'Are bilateral investment treaties really bilateral?' working paper, available at ncgg.princeton.edu/IPES/2013/papers/F900_rm2.pdf.

Manger, Mark, 2008. 'International investment agreements and services markets: locking in market failure?' *World Development* 36(11): 2456–69.

2009. *Investing in Protection: The Politics of Preferential Trade Agreements between North and South*. Cambridge University Press.

Manger, Mark, and Clint Peinhardt, 2013, August. 'Learning and diffusion in international investment agreements', working paper presented at the Annual Meeting of the American Political Science Association, Chicago.

Mangklatanakul, Vilawan, 2012. 'Thailand's first treaty arbitration: gain from pain', in *UNCTAD, Investor-State Disputes: Prevention and Alternatives to Arbitration II*. Geneva: United Nations.

Marais, Hein, 1998. *South Africa: Limits to Change*. London: Zed Press.

March, James, and Johan Olsen 1984. 'The new institutionalism: organizational factor in political life', *American Political Science Review* 78(3): 734–49.

Markusen, James, 2001. 'Commitment to rules on investment: the developing countries' stake', *Review of International Economics* 9(2): 287–302.

Martin, Lisa, and Beth Simmons, 1998. 'Theories and empirical studies of international institutions', *International Organization* 52(4): 729–57.

Marton, Katherin, 1993. 'Foreign direct investment in Hungary', *Transnational Corporations* 2(1): 111–34.

Mason, Edward, and Robert Asher, 1973. *The World Bank Since Bretton Woods*. Washington DC: The Brookings Institution.

Mattli, Walter, and Anne-Marie Slaughter, 1995. 'Law and politics in the European Union: a reply to Garrett', *International Organization* 49(1): 183–90.

Maurer, Noel, 2013. *The Empire Trap: The Rise and Fall of US Intervention to Protect American Property Overseas, 1893–2013*. Princeton University Press.

McCarthy, Stephen, 2000. 'Ten years of chaos in Burma: foreign investment and economic liberalization under the SLORC-SPDC, 1988 to 1998', *Pacific Affairs* 73(2): 233–62.

220 References

McClelland, Gary, William Schultze, and Don Coursey 1993. 'Insurance for low-probability hazards: a bimodal response to unlikely events', *Journal of Risk and Uncertainty* 7, 95–116.

McDermott, Rose, 2004. *Political Psychology in International Relations*. Ann Arbor: University of Michigan Press.

Meaney, Constance, 1995. 'Foreign experts, capitalists, and competing agendas: privatization in Poland, the Czech Republic, and Hungary', *Comparative Political Studies* 28(2): 275–305.

Meseguer, Covadunga, 2005. 'Policy learning, policy diffusion, and the making of a new order', *The ANNALS of the American Academy of Political and Social Science* 598: 67–82.

2006. 'Rational learning and bounded rational learning in the diffusion of policy innovations', *Rationality and Society* 18 (1): 35–66.

2009. *Learning, Policy Making, and Market Reforms*. Cambridge University Press.

Meyer, John, 2000. 'Globalization: sources and effects on national states and societies', *International Sociology* 15(2): 233–48.

Mieg, Harald, 2001. 'Professionalization and professional activities in the Swiss market for environmental services', in Walter Leal Filho (ed.), *Environmental Careers, Environmental Employment and Environmental Training*. Frankfurt: Lang Verlag, 133–60.

Miga Pas, 1991. *Industrialized Countries' Policies Affecting Foreign Direct Investment in Developing Countries*, volume 1, Washington DC: World Bank.

Miles, Kate, 2013. *The Origins of International Investment Law: Empire, Environment, and the Safeguarding of Capital*. Cambridge University Press.

Mintz, Alex, 2007. 'Behavioral IR as a subfield of international relations', *International Studies Review* 9: 157.

Montt, Santiago, 2009. *State Liability in Investment Treaty Arbitration: Global Constitutional and Administrative Law in the BIT Generation*. Portland: Hart Publishing.

Moyer Jr., Homer, Mark Ellis, and Talbot D'Alemberte, 2009. 'The history of CEELI, the ABA's rule of law initiative, and the rule of law movement going forward (panel debate)', *Minnesota Journal of International Law* 18(2): 304–42.

Naudé, Willem, 1998. 'On Ethiopia's economic transition and beyond', *African Development Review* 10(2): 121–42.

Neale, Margaret, and Max Bazerman, 1991. *Cognition and Rationality in Negotiations*. New York: Free Press.

Neumayer, Eric, Peter Nunnenkamp, and Martin Roy, 2014. 'Are stricter investment rules contagious? Host country competition for foreign direct investment through international agreements', Kiel working paper no. 1910.

Neumayer, Eric and Thomas Plümper, 2010. 'Spatial effects in dyadic data', *International Organization* 64(145): 145–66.

Newcompe, Andrew, and Lluis Paradell, 2009. *Law and Practice of Investment Treaties*. New York: Kluwer Law International.

Newfarmer, Richard, 1985. 'Economic policy towards the Caribbean basin', *Journal of Interamerican Studies and World Affairs* 27(1): 63–89.

References 221

Newman, Joseph, William Wolf, and Eliot Hearst, 1980. 'The feature-positive effect in adult human subjects', *Journal of Experimental Psychology: Human Learning and Memory* 6(5): 630–50.

Nikomborirak, Deunden, 2004, March. 'An assessment of the investment regime: Thailand country report', in International Institute for Sustainable Development, *Report of the International Institute for Sustainable Development.*

Nisbett, Richard E., and Lee Ross, 1980. *Human Interference: Strategies and Shortcomings of Social Judgment.* Upper Saddle River, NJ: Prentice Hall.

Nkrumah, Kwame, 1964, March 11. 'Blue print of our goal: launching the seven-year development plan', available at nkrumahinfobank.org/article.php? id=355&c=51.

Ocran, T. Modibo, 1987. 'Bilateral investment protection treaties: a comparative study', *New York Law School Journal of International and Comparative Law* 8(3): 401–30.

Odell, John, 2000. *Negotiating the World Economy.* Ithaca: Cornell University Press.
2002. 'Bounded rationality and the world political economy: the nature of decision making', in David Andrews, C. Randall Henning, and Louis Pauly (eds.), *Governing the World's Money.* Ithaca: Cornell University Press,

OECD, 1985. *Intergovernmental Agreements Relating to Investment in Developing Countries.* Paris: OECD.
1998. *OECD Reviews of Foreign Direct Investment: Brazil 1998.* Paris: OECD.
2010a. *Indonesia—Investment Policy Review.* Paris: OECD.
2010b. *Morocco—Investment Policy Review.* Paris: OECD.
2012a. May 16–July 9. *Investor-State Dispute Settlement, Public Consultation.* Paris: OECD.
2012b. *Tunisia—Investment Policy Review,* Paris: OECD.

Ofusu-Amaah, W. Paatii, 2002. 'Legal and judicial reform in developing countries: reflections on world bank experience', *Law and Business Review of the Americas* 8, 551–82.

Paparinskis, Martins, 2010. 'Limits of depoliticization in contemporary investor-state arbitration', *Select Proceedings of the European Society of International Law* 3.
2013. *The International Minimum Standard and Fair and Equitable Treatment.* Oxford University Press.

Parlett, Kate, 2011. *The Individual in the International Legal System: Continuity and Change in International Law.* Cambridge University Press.

Parliament of the Republic of South Africa, 1994, November 23. 'White paper on reconstruction and development', *Government Gazette.*

Parra, Antonio, 2012. *The History of ICSID.* Oxford University Press.

Paulsson, Jan, 1995. 'Arbitration without privity', *ICSID Review* 10(2): 232–57.
2005. *Denial of Justice in International Law.* Cambridge University Press.
2010. 'The power of states to make meaning promises to foreigners', *Journal of International Dispute Settlement* 1(2): 341–52.

Pauwelyn, Joost, 2014. 'At the edge of chaos? Foreign investment law as a complex adaptive system, how it emerged and how it can be reformed'. *ICSID Review – Foreign Investment Law Journal* 29, 372–418.

222   References

Peinhardt, Clint, and Todd Allee, 2012. 'Failure to deliver: the investment effects of US preferential economic agreements', *The World Economy* 35(6): 757–83.

Pererra, A. Rohan, 2000. 'The role and implications of bilateral investment treaties', *Commonwealth Law Bulletin* 26(1): 607–14.

Pérez-López, Jorge, and Mathias Travieso-Díaz, 2001. 'The contribution of BITs to Cuba's foreign investment program', *Georgetown Law and Policy in International Business Journal* 32, 529–70.

Peters, Paul, 1991. 'Dispute settlement arrangements in investment treaties', in *Netherlands Yearbook of International Law, 1991*. Cambridge University Press.

Peters, Paul, Nico Schrijver and Paul de Waart, 1984. 'Permanent sovereignty, foreign investment and state practice', in Kamal Hossain and Subrata Chowdhury (eds.), *Permanent Sovereignty over Natural Resources in International Law: Principle and Practice*. London: Frances Pinter.

Peterson, Luke, 2003, May 9. 'South Africa's plans for black economic empowerment confronting foreign investor rights', *Investment Law and Policy Weekly News Bulletin*.

  2004. *Bilateral Investment Treaties and Development Policy-Making*. Winnipeg: International Institute for Sustainable Development.

  2004. January, 5. 'Early investment arbitrations against 'improper' use of environmental laws uncovered', *Investment Law and Policy Weekly News Bulletin*.

  2004, October, 13. 'New US ambassador to Korea reiterates obstacles to BIT', *INVEST-SD: Investment Law and Policy Weekly News Bulletin*.

  2005, May, 5. 'French insurance firm alleges Cambodia violated investment treaty', *INVEST-SD: Investment Law and Policy News Bulletin*.

  2005, August, 3. 'India-Singapore FTA inked, investment provisions include important innovations', *INVEST-SD: Investment Law and Policy News Bulletin*.

  2006. *South Africa's Bilateral Investment Treaties: Implications for Development and Human Rights*. Geneva: Friedrich Ebert Stiftung.

  2008, October 22. 'Swiss investor prevailed in 2003 in confidential BIT arbitration over South Africa land dispute', *Investment Arbitration Reporter*.

  2008, December, 11. 'Croatia prevails in confidential arbitration with Canadian investor', *Investment Arbitration Reporter*.

  2009, March, 17. 'South African court rules that mineral rights holders can claim for expropriation following introduction of new minerals rights regime; meanwhile, government about to file its written defense in international arbitration challenging the same legislation', *Investment Arbitration Reporter*.

  2011, April, 14. 'In policy switch, Australia disavows need for investor-state arbitration provisions in trade and investment agreements', *Investment Arbitration Reporter*.

Peterson, Luke and Filip Balcerzak, 2014. 'Amidst concerns about prompt payment of arbitral awards, stays of enforcement are lifted in two ICSID cases', *IA Reporter* 7(9).

References 223

Peterson, Luke, and Damon Vis-Dunbar, 2006, May 15. 'UK and Mexico sign investment treaty, following on heels of UK treaty review', *Investment Treaty News*.

Peterson, Luke, and Ross Garland, 2010. *Bilateral Investment Treaties and Land Reform in Southern Africa*. Montreal: Rights and Democracy.

Pierson, Paul, 2004. *Politics in Time*. Princeton University Press.

Poulsen, Lauge, 2010. 'The significance of south-south BITs for the international investment regime: a quantitative analysis', *Northwestern Journal of International Law and Business* 30(1): 101–30.

2011. Sacrificing sovereignty by chance: investment treaties, developing countries, and bounded rationality, dissertation, London School of Economics and Political Science.

Poulsen, Lauge, and Emma Aisbett, 2013. 'When the claim hits: bilateral investment treaties and bounded rational learning', *World Politics* 65(2): 273–313.

Poulsen, Lauge, Martins Paparinskis, and Michael Waibel, 2015. 'Investment law before arbitration', working paper.

Price, Daniel, 2009, May 14. 'Keep international protections', *The Washington Times*.

Raghavan, Chakravarthi, 1997. 'Bilateral investment treaties play only a minor role in attracting FDI', *Third World Economics* 162, 1–15.

Raiffa, Howard, 1982. *The Art and Science of Negotiation*. Cambridge, MA: Harvard University Press.

Ramamurti, Ravi, 2003. 'Can governments make credible commitments? Insights from infrastructure projects in developing regions', *Journal of International Management* 9, 253ff.

Ramirez, Francisco, John Meyer, Christin Wotipka, and Gili Drori, 2002. 'Expansion and impact of the world human rights regime: longitudinal and cross-national analyses over the twentieth century', National Science Foundation grant proposal.

Ranjan, Prabhash, 2014. 'India and bilateral investment treaties – a changing landscape', *ICSID Review* 29(2): 419–50.

Ranjan, Prabhash, and Deepak Raju, 2014. 'Bilateral investment treaties and Indian judiciary', *George Washington International Law Review* 46(4).

Rao, Sreenivasa, 2000. 'Bilateral investment protection agreements: a legal framework for the protection of foreign investments', *Commonwealth Law Bulletin* 26(1): 623–30.

Reiter, Dan, 1996. *Crucible of Beliefs: Learning, Alliances, and World Wars*. Ithaca: Cornell University Press.

Reyna, Valerie, and Farrell Lloyd, 2006. 'Physician decision-making and cardiac risk: effects of knowledge, risk perception, risk tolerance, and fuzzy processing', *Journal of Experimental Psychology: Applied* 12(3): 179–95.

Reyna, Valerie, Farrell Lloyd, and Charles Brainerd, 2003. 'Memory, development, and rationality: an integrative theory of judgment and decision making', *Emerging Perspectives on Judgment and Decision Research*, 201–45.

Roberts, Anthea, 2010. 'Power and persuasion in investment treaty interpretation: the dual role of states', *American Journal of International Law* 104(2): 179–225.

224 References

2014. 'State-to-state investment treaty arbitration: a hybrid theory of interdependent rights and shared interpretive authority', *Harvard International Law Journal* 55(1): 1–70.

Robin, Patricia, 1983–84. 'The BIT won't bite: the American bilateral investment treaty program', *American University Law Review* 33, 931–58.

Robinson, Patrick, 1993. 'Treaty negotiation, drafting, ratification and accession of CARICOM states', *West Indian Law Journal* 18(1).

Rodrik, Danni, 2006. 'Understanding South Africa's economic puzzles', NBER working paper 12565.

Rose-Ackerman, Susan, 2009. 'The global BITs regime and the domestic environment for investment', in Karl Sauvant and Lisa Sachs (eds.), *The Effect of Treaties on Foreign Direct Investment*. New York: Oxford University Press.

Rosert, Diana, 2014. *The Stakes Are High: A Review of the Financial Costs of Investment Treaty Arbitration*. Winnipeg: International Institute for Sustainable Development.

Ross, Alison, 2010a. 'From ICCA to the icecaps: an interview with Francisco Orrego Vicuña', *Global Arbitration Review* 5(4).

2010b. 'South Africa – is it time?' *Global Arbitration Review* 5(4).

Rothstein, Robert, 1979. *Global Bargaining: UNCTAD and the Quest for a New International Economic Order*. Princeton University Press.

Rovine, Arthur, 1987. 'Report on bilateral investment treaties', *The International Lawyer* 21, 274–7.

Rowe, Gene, and George Wright, 2001. 'Differences in expert and lay judgments of risk: myth or reality?", *Risk Analysis* 21(2): 341–56.

Ryan, Brendan, 2005, September 15. 'Offshore investors may sue SA government', available at www.miningmx.com.

Ryans, John, and James Baker, 1976. 'The International Centre for the Settlement of Investment Disputes (ICSID)', *Journal of World Trade Law* 10, 65–79.

Sagafi-Nejad, T., 2008. *The UN and Transnational Corporations: From Code of Conduct to Global Compact*. Bloomington: Indiana University Press.

Salacuse, Jeswald, 1975. 'Egypt's new law on foreign investment: the framework for economic openness', *The International Lawyer* 9, 647–60.

2010 'The emerging global regime for investment', *Harvard International Law Journal* 51, 427–73.

2013. *The Three Laws of Foreign Investment*. New York: Oxford University Press.

Salacuse, Jeswald, and Nicholas Sullivan, 2005. 'Do BITS really work? An evaluation of bilateral investment treaties and their grand bargain', *Harvard International Law Journal* 46, 67–75.

Sands, Philippe, 2006. *Lawless World*. London: Penguin Books.

Sauvant, Karl, 2009. 'Driving and countervailing forces: a rebalancing of national FDI policies', in Karl Sauvant (ed.), *Yearbook on International Investment Law and Policy 2008/2009*. New York: Oxford University Press.

Sauvé, Pierre, 2006. 'Multilateral rules on investment: is forward movement possible?' *Journal of International Economic Law* 9(2): 325–55.

References 225

Schelling, Thomas, 1960. *The Strategy of Conflict.* Cambridge, MA: Harvard University Press.

Schneider, Eric, and Alev Bilgen, 1992. 'Foreign investment laws in the republic of Turkey: a model for reform', *Transnational Lawyer* 5(1): 99–130.

Schneiderman, David, 2008. *Constitutionalizing Economic Globalization: Investment Rules and Democracy's Promise.* Cambridge University Press.

2009. 'Promoting equality, black economic empowerment, and the future of investment rules', *South African Journal on Human Rights* 25(2): 246.

2010. 'Judicial politics and international investment arbitration: seeking an explanation for conflicting outcomes', *Northwestern Journal of International Law and Business* 30(3): 383–416.

2013. *Resisting Economic Globalization: Critical Theory and International Investment Law.* London: Palgrave.

Schreuer, Christoph, 2005. 'A decade of increasing awareness of investment arbitration and increasing activity: an assessment', available at www.oecd.org/dataoecd/5/54/36055388.pdf.

Schrijver, Nico, 2008. *Sovereignty over Natural Resources: Balancing Rights and Duties.* Cambridge University Press.

Schwarzenberger, Georg, 1969. *Foreign Investments and International Law.* London: Stevens.

Schwebel, Stephen, 2008. 'The overwhelming merits of bilateral investment treaties', *Suffolk Transnational Law Review* 32, 263.

Senses, Fikret, 1991. 'Turkey's stabilization and structural adjustment program in retrospect and prospect', *The Developing Economies* 29(3): 210–34.

Sergeant, Barry, 2010, August 19. 'South Africa: an inflection point?' *Mineweb*, available at www.mineweb.com/mineweb/content/en/mineweb-political-economy?oid=110032&sn=Detail.

Shabu, Martin, 2011 April 7. 'Czechs face uphill battle to cancel US investment treaty', *Czech Position*.

Shafir, Eldar, 1992. 'Prospect theory and political analysis: a psychological perspective', *Political Psychology* 13(2): 311–22.

Shawcross, Hartley, 1995. *Life Sentence: The Memoirs of Hartley Shawcross.* London: Constable.

Shelley, Marjorie, 1994. 'Gain/loss asymmetry in risky intertemporal choice', *Organizational Behavior and Human Decision Processes* 59(1): 124–59.

Shihata, Ibrahim, 1987. 'Factors influencing the flow of foreign investment and the relevance of a multilateral guarantee scheme', *The International Lawyer* 21(3): 671–94.

1988. *MIGA and Foreign Investment.* The Hague: Martinus Nijhoff.

1991. 'Promotion of foreign direct investment – a general account, with particular reference to the role of the world bank group', *ICSID Review* 6(2): 484–509.

1992. *Legal Treatment of Foreign Investment: The World Bank Guidelines.* Washington DC: World Bank.

1993, February. 'Judicial reform in developing countries and the role of the World Bank', paper presented at the Seminar on Justice in Latin America and the Caribbean in the 1990s, Inter-American Development Bank, San José, Costa Rica.

226 References

Shishi, L., 1988. 'Bilateral investment promotion and protection agreements: practice of the People's Republic of China', *International Law and Development*, 163.

Siegel, Deborah, 2013. 'Capital account restrictions, trade agreements, and the IMF', in Kevin Gallagher and Leonardo Stanley (eds.), *Capital Account Regulations and the Trading System: A Compatibility Review*. Boston University Press.

Sikkink, Kathryn, 1993. 'Human rights, principled issue-networks, and sovereignty in Latin America', *International Organization* 47(3): 411–41.

Simon, Herbert, 1957. *Models of Man*. New York: Wiley.

1959. 'Theories of decision making in economics and behavioral science', *American Economic Review* 49(3): 253–83.

1982. *Models of Bounded Rationality*. Cambridge: MIT Press.

1985. 'Human nature and politics: the dialogue of psychology with political science', *American Political Science Review* 79(2): 293–304.

1997. *An Empirically Based Microeconomics*. Cambridge University Press.

Slovic, Paul, 1987. 'Perception of risk', *Science* 236(4799): 280–5.

Smith, James, 2000. 'The politics of dispute settlement design: explaining legalism in regional trade pacts', *International Organization* 54(1): 137–80.

Snyder, Edward, 1994. 'The Menem Revolution in Argentina: progress toward a hemispheric free trade area', *Texas International Law Journal* 29(1): 95–122.

Society to Advance the Protection of Foreign Investment, 1957. International Convention for the Mutual Protection of Private Property Rights in Foreign Countries. Cologne, Germany.

Sornarajah, Muthucumaraswamy, 1994. *The International Law on Foreign Investment*. Cambridge University Press.

South African Law Commission, 1998. *Arbitration: an international arbitration act for South Africa*, report.

St John, Taylor, 2014. 'The power of modest multilateralism: the International Centre for Settlement of Investment Disputes (ICSID), 1964–1980', dissertation, University of Oxford.

Ste-Marie, Diane, 1999. 'Expert-novice differences in gymnastic judging: an information-processing perspective', *Applied Cognitive Psychology* 13(3): 269–81.

Stein, Jana von, 2013. 'The engines of compliance', in Jeffrey Dunoff and Mark Pollack (eds.), *Interdisciplinary Perspectives on International Law and International Relations: The State of the Art*. Cambridge University Press.

Stewart, Terence, 1993. *The GATT Uruguay Round: A Negotiation History (1986–1994), Volume Four: The End Game (Part I)*. The Hague: Kluwer Law International.

Stigler, George, and Gary Becker, 1977. 'De Gustibus Non Est Disputandum', *American Economic Review* 67(2): 76–90.

Stockwell, Sarah, 2000. *The Business of Decolonization: British Business Strategies in the Gold Coast*. Oxford University Press.

Strang, David, and John Meyer, 2009. 'Institutional conditions for diffusion', in Georg Krücken and Gili Drori (eds.), *World Society: The Writings of John W. Meyer*. Oxford University Press.

References   227

Sunstein, Cass, (ed.), 2000. *Behavioural Law and Economics*. Cambridge University Press.
  2013. 'Deciding by default', *University of Pennsylvania Law Review* 162(1): 1–58.
Szasz, Paul, 1971. 'The investment disputes convention and Latin America', *Virginia Journal of International Law* 11, 256–65.
Taber, Charles, and Milton Lodge, 2006. 'Motivated skepticism in the evaluation of political beliefs', *American Journal of Political Science* 50(3): 755–69.
Taylor, Ian, and Karen Smith, 2007. *United Nations Conference on Trade and Development (UNCTAD)*. New York: Routledge.
Thaler, Richard H., and Cass Sunstein, 2008. *Nudge: Improving Decisions about Health, Wealth, and Happiness*. New Haven: Yale University Press.
Tienhaara, Kyla, 2009. *The Expropriation of Environmental Governance: Protecting Foreign Investors at the Expense of Public Policy*. Cambridge University Press.
Tignor, Robert, 1998. *Capitalism and Nationalism at the End of Empire: State and Business in Decolonizing Egypt, Nigeria, and Kenya, 1945–1963*. Princeton University Press.
Trade Law Centre for Southern Africa, 2004. *Investment Project: South African Case Study* 10.
Travieso-Diaz, Matias, and Alejandro Ferrate, 1996. 'Recommended features of a foreign investment code for Cuba's free market transition', *North Carolina Journal of International Law and Commercial Regulation* 21(3): 511–60.
Tversky, Amos, and Daniel Kahneman, 1971. 'Belief in the law of small numbers', *Psychological Bulletin* 76(2): 105–10.
  1973. 'Availability: a heuristic for judging frequency and probability' *Cognitive Psychology* 4(2): 207–32.
Ubezonu, Chudi, 1993. 'Some recent amendments to laws affecting foreign investment in Nigeria', *ICSID Review* 8(1): 123–31.
United States Policy Toward International Investment, 1981, July 30, September 20, and October 28. Hearings before the subcommittee on international economic policy of the Committee on Foreign Relations, US Senate.
UNCTAD, 1992. *World Investment Report 1992*. Geneva: United Nations.
  1995. *World Investment Report 1995*. Geneva: United Nations.
  1996a. *World Investment Report 1996*. Geneva: United Nations.
  1996b. *International Investment Instruments: A Compendium*, vol. III. Geneva: United Nations.
  1996c, April 27. *Midrand Declaration and Partnership for Growth and Development*, adopted at the ninth session, Midrand.
  1996d, August 1. 'Current international arrangements governing foreign direct investment', TD/B/(43)/5.
  1997a, June 2. 'Expert meeting on existing agreements on investment and their development dimensions: chairman's summary', TD/B/COM.2/EM.1/5.
  1997b, October 3. 'Draft report of the commission on investment, technology and related financial issues on its second session', TD/B/COM.2/L.4/Add.1.
  1997c. *World Investment Report 1997*. Geneva: United Nations.
  1998a, September 17. 'Draft report of the commission on investment, technology and related financial issues on its third session', TD/B/COM.2/L.7.

228 References

1998b. *Bilateral Investment Treaties in the Mid-1990s*. Geneva: United Nations.

1998c. *World Investment Report 1998*. Geneva: United Nations.

1999a. *World Investment Report 1999*. Geneva: United Nations.

1999b. *Trends in International Investment Agreements: An Overview*. Geneva: United Nations.

1999c, January 14. 'Seven G-15 countries negotiated eight bilateral investment treaties hosted by UNCTAD', press release.

1999d, January 7. 'UNCTAD hosts bilateral investment treaty negotiations by group of fifteen countries', press release.

1999e, January 14. 'Bilateral investment treaties among the G-15: bilateral negotiations, final report, closing statement by Ambassador Hill', UNCTAD/ITE/Misc.7/Rev.L,

2000a. *Investment Policy Review: Peru*. Geneva: United Nations.

2000b. *Investment Policy Review: Uganda*. Geneva: United Nations.

2000c. *World Investment Report 2000*. Geneva: United Nations.

2000d. *International Investment Instruments: A Compendium*, vol. 5. Geneva: United Nations.

2000e. Twenty-two bilateral investment treaties signed at Sapporo (Japan), TAD/INF/PR/048 29/06/00.

2001a. *Investment Policy Review: Ecuador*. Geneva: United Nations.

2001b. *World Investment Report 2001*. Geneva: United Nations.

2001c. *Environment, UNCTAD Series on Issues in International Investment Agreements*. Geneva: United Nations.

2002a. *Investment and Innovation Policy Review: Ethiopia*. Geneva: United Nations.

2002b. *Progress report: Work Undertaken within UNCTAD's Work Programme on International Investment Agreements between the 10th Conference of UNCTAD, Bangkok, February 2000 and July 2000*. Geneva: United Nations.

2002c, June, 12 to 14. 'Report of the expert meeting on experiences with bilateral and regional approaches to multilateral cooperation in the area of long-term cross-border investment, particularly foreign direct investment'.

2002d. *Investment Policy Review: Tanzania*. Geneva: United Nations.

2003a. *Investment Policy Review: Ghana*. Geneva: United Nations.

2003b. *Investment Policy Review: Lesotho*. Geneva: United Nations.

2003c. *Investment Policy Review: Nepal*. Geneva: United Nations.

2003d. *World Investment Report 2003*. Geneva: United Nations.

2003e. *Course on Dispute Settlement: International Centre for Settlement of Investment Disputes*. Geneva: United Nations.

2004. *World Investment Report 2004*. Geneva: United Nations.

2005a. *World Investment Report 2005*. Geneva: United Nations.

2005b. *Investment Policy Review: Kenya*. Geneva: United Nations.

2005c. *South-South Cooperation in International Investment Agreements*. Geneva: UNCTAD.

2005d. *Investment Policy Review: Brazil*. Geneva: United Nations.

2006a. *World Investment Report 2006*. Geneva: United Nations.

2006b. *Investment Policy Review: Botswana*. Geneva: United Nations.

2006c. *Investment Policy Review: Colombia*. Geneva: United Nations.

References 229

2006d. *Investment Policy Review: Nigeria*. Geneva: United Nations.

2006e. *Investment Policy Review: Rwanda*. Geneva: United Nations.

2006f. 'The entry into force of bilateral investment treaties (BITs)', *IIA Monitor* 3.

2007a. *Investment Policy Review: Dominican Republic*. Geneva: United Nations.

2007b. *Investment Policy Review: Zambia*. Geneva: United Nations.

2007c. *Worldwide Survey of Foreign Affiliates*, Occasional Note. Geneva: United Nations.

2007d. *Investor-State Dispute Settlement and Impact on Investment Rulemaking*. Geneva: United Nations.

2007e. *International Investment Rule-Making: Stocktaking, Challenges and the Way Forward*. Geneva: United Nations.

2009a. *The Role of International Investment Agreements in Attracting Foreign Direct Investment to Developing Countries*. Geneva: United Nations.

2009b. 'The impact on foreign direct investment of BITs', in Karl Sauvant and Lisa Sachs (eds.), *The Effect of Treaties on Foreign Direct Investment: Bilateral Investment Treaties, Double Taxation Treaties, and Investment Flows*. New York: Oxford University Press.

2009c. *Investment Policy Review: Dominican Republic*. Geneva: United Nations.

2009d. 'Recent developments in international investment agreements (2008–June 2009)', *IIA Monitor* 3.

2010a. *Investment Policy Review: Sierra Leone*. Geneva: United Nations.

2010b. *Investment Policy Review: Guatemala*. Geneva: United Nations.

2010c. *Investor-State Disputes: Prevention and Alternatives to Arbitration*. Geneva: United Nations.

2011a. *Investment Policy Review: Guatemala*. Geneva: United Nations.

2011b. *Investment Policy Review: Ethiopia*. Geneva: United Nations.

2011c. 'Interpretation of IIAs: what states can do', *IIA Issues* 3.

2012. *Investment Policy Review: Mozambique*. Geneva: United Nations.

2013a. *World Investment Report*. Geneva: United Nations.

2013b. *International Investment Policy Making in Transition: Challenges and Opportunities of Treaty Renewal*. Geneva: United Nations.

2013c. *Reform of Investor-State Dispute Settlement: In Search of a Roadmap*. Geneva: UNCTAD.

2014a, April. 'Recent developments in investor-state dispute settlement (ISDS)'.

2014b. *Investor-State Dispute Settlement, UNCTAD Series on Issues in International Investment Agreements II*. Geneva: UNCTAD.

UNCTC, 1983. 'Report on ninth session', *Official Records of the Economic and Social Council*, supplement no. 7a, E/C.10/1983/15.

1984a. 'Bilateral, regional and international arrangements on matters relating to transnational corporations', *Official Records of the Economic and Social Council*, E.C.10/1984/8.

1984b. 'Report on the tenth session', *Official Records of the Economic and Social Council*, supplement no. 8, E/C.10/1984/20.

1985. 'Report on the eleventh session', *Official Records of the Economic and Social Council*, supplement no. 8, E/C.10/1985/19.

230   References

1986. 'Bilateral arrangements and agreements related to transnational corporations', *Official Records of the Economic and Social Council*, E/C.10/1986/7.

1987. 'Report on the thirteenth session', *Official Records of the Economic and Social Council*, supplement no. 9, E/C.10/1987/16.

1988a. *Bilateral Investment Treaties*. New York: United Nations.

1988b, March 10. *Joint Ventures as a Form of International Economic Co-operation, Background Documents of the High-Level Seminar Organized by the United Nations Centre on Transnational Corporations in Co-operation with the State Foreign Economic Commission, and the State Committee on Science and Technology of the Union of Soviet Socialist Republic, Moscow*. New York: United Nations.

1991a. 'Other international, regional and bilateral arrangements and agreements related to transnational corporations', *Official Records of the Economic and Social Council*, E/C.10/1991/9.

1991b.'Report on seventeenth session', *Official Records of the Economic and Social Council*, supplement no. 10, E/C.10/1991/17.

1992a. 'Report on eighteenth session', *Official Records of the Economic and Social Council*, supplement no. 6, E/1992/26.

1992b. *The Determinants of Foreign Direct Investment: A Survey of the Evidence*. New York: United Nations.

1993a. 'Report on nineteenth session', *Official Records of the Economic and Social Council*, supplement no. 10, E/1993/30.

1993b. 'International framework for transnational corporations', *Official Records of the Economic and Social Council*, E/C.10/1993/8.

UNCTC and ICC, 1992. *Bilateral Investment Treaties, 1959–1991*. New York: United Nations.

United States Department of State, 2009, September 30. Advisory committee on international economic policy submits report on U.S. model bilateral investment treaty, available at www.state.gov/r/pa/prs/ps/2009/sept/130097.htm.

United States Intergovernmental Policy Advisory Committee (IGPAC), 2004, March 12. Advisory Committee Report to the President, the Congress and the United States Trade Representative on the US-Australia Free Trade Agreement'.

USAID, 1990, July. 'Private sector investment climate assessment of Balochistan', available at http://pdf.usaid.gov/pdf_docs/PNABU894.pdf.

Van Harten, Gus, 2007. *Investment Treaty Arbitration and Public Law*. Oxford University Press.

2010. 'Five justifications for investment treaties: a critical discussion', *Trade, Law and Development* 2(1): 19–58.

2013. *Sovereign Choices and Sovereign Constraints: Judicial Restraint in Investment Treaty Arbitration*. Oxford University Press.

Vandevelde, Kenneth, 1988a. 'The bilateral investment program of the United States', *Cornell International Law Journal* 21(2): 201–76.

1988b. 'Treaty interpretation from a negotiator's perspective', *Vanderbilt Journal of Transnational Law* 21, 281.

References

1992a. 'The BIT program: a fifteen-year appraisal', *American Society of International Law Proceedings* 86, 532–9.

1992b. *United States Investment Treaties*. Deventer: Kluwer.

1993. 'U.S. bilateral investment treaties: the second wave', *Michigan Journal of International Law* 14(4): 621–704.

1998a. 'Sustainable liberalism and the international investment regime', *Michigan Journal of International Law* 19(2): 373–400.

1998b. 'The political economy of a bilateral investment treaty', *American Journal of International Law* 92(4): 621–41.

1998c. 'Investment liberalization and economic development: the role of bilateral investment treaties', *Columbia Journal of Transnational Law* 36(2): 501–28.

2006. 'Investment arbitration and sustainable development: good intentions—or effective results?' *International Environment Agreements* 6, 459–66.

2007. 'The present state of research carried out by the English-speaking section of the Centre for Studies and Research', in Philippe Kahn and Thomas Wälde (eds.), *New Aspects of International Investment Law*. Hague: Martinus Neijhoff.

2009. *U.S. International Investment Agreements*. Oxford University Press.

Vasciannie, Stephen, 1992. 'Bilateral investment treaties and civil strife: the AAPL/Sri Lanka arbitration', *Netherlands International Law Review* 29, 332.

Vernon, Raymond, 1971. *Sovereignty at Bay: The Multinational Spread of U.S. Enterprises*. London: Longman.

Vertzberger, Yaacov, 1998. *Risk-Taking and Decision Making: Foreign Military Intervention Decisions*. Stanford University Press.

Veselá, Gita, 2009. 'Bilateral investment treaty overview – Czech Republic', available at www.investmentclaims.com.

Vickers, Brandan, 2002, February. 'Foreign direct investment (FDI) regime of South Africa', *Institute for Global Dialogue*.

Vicuña, Francisco, 2002. 'Regulatory expropriations in international law: Carlos Calvo, honorary NAFTA citizen', *New York University Environmental Law Journal* 11(1): 19–34.

Vis-Dunbar, Damon, 2006, August 23. 'French investor criticizes governments' handling of Cambodian dispute', *Investment Treaty News*.

Voss, Jurgen, 1981. 'The protection and promotion of European private investment in developing countries – an approach towards a concept for a European policy on foreign investment. A German contribution', *Common Market Law Review* 18(3): 363–95.

Waibel, Michael, and Yanhui Wu, 2014. 'Are arbitrators political?' Working paper on file with author.

Wakslak, Cheryl, and Yaacov Trope, 2009. 'The effect of construal level on subjective probability estimates', *Psychological Science* 20(1): 52–8.

Wälde, Thomas, 2000. 'Treaties and regulatory risk in infrastructure investment', *Journal of World Trade* 34(2): 1–61.

Walker, Herman, 1956. 'Treaties for the encouragement and protection of foreign investment: present United States practice', *The American Journal of Comparative Law* 5(2): 229–47.

232 References

Wall, Tim, 1996. 'New investment rules cause concern', *Africa Recovery* 10, 3.
Walter, Andrew, 2001. 'NGOs, business, and international investment: the multilateral agreement on investment, Seattle, and beyond', *Global Governance* 7(1): 51–73.
Walter, Stefanie, and Thomas Willett, 2012. 'Delaying the inevitable: a political economy approach to currency defenses and depreciation', *Review of International Political Economy* 19(1): 114–39.
Wedel, Janine, 1998. *Collision and Collusion: The Strange Case of Western Aid to Eastern Europe.* New York: Palgrave Macmillan.
Weiler, Todd, 2002. 'NAFTA investment arbitration and the growth of international economic law', *Canadian Business Law Journal* 36(3): 405–35.
Weinstein, Neil, 1989. 'Effects of personal experience on self-protective behavior', *Psychological Bulletin* 3105(1): 31–50.
Wellhausen, Rachel, 2015. 'Investor–state disputes: when can governments break contracts?' *Journal of Conflict Resolution* 59(2): 239–61.
Wellhausen, Rachel and Leslie Johns, 2014. 'Modern day merchant guilds supply chains and informal property rights enforcement', working paper.
Wells, Louis, 2010. 'The emerging global regime for investment: a response', *Harvard International Law Journal* [online] 52, 42–57.
Wells, Louis, and Rafiq Ahmed, 2006. *Making Foreign Investment Safe: Property Rights and National Sovereignty.* Oxford University Press.
West, Gerald, 1999. 'Political risk investment insurance: a renaissance', *Journal of Project Finance* 5(2): 27–36.
Weyland, Kurt, 2006. *Bounded Rationality and Policy Diffusion: Social Sector Reform in Latin America.* Princeton University Press.
  2008. 'Toward a new theory of institutional change', *World Politics* 60(2): 281–314.
  2009. 'The diffusion of revolution: "1848" in Europe and Latin America', *International Organization* 62(3): 391–423.
  2010. 'The diffusion of regime contention in European democratization, 1830–1940', *Comparative Political Studies* 43(8–9): 1148–76.
White, Nicholas, 2000. 'The business and the politics of decolonization: the British experience in the twentieth century', *Economic History Review* 53(3): 544–64.
Wilcox, Clair, 1949. *A Charter for World Trade.* New York: Macmillan.
Wilkie, Christopher, 2001. 'FDI, development and investment rules: a critique of the UNCTAD series on issues in international investment agreements', *Transnational Corporations* 10(2): 135–60.
Williamson, John, 1990. 'What Washington means with policy reform', in John Williamson (ed.), *Latin American Adjustment: How Much has Happened?* Washington DC: Institute for International Economics.
Williamson, Oliver, 1986. *Economic Organization: Firms, Markets, and Policy Control.* Brighton: Wheatsheaf.
Woodhouse, Erik, 2006. 'The obsolescing bargain redux? Foreign investment in the electric power sector in developing countries', *New York University Journal of International Law and Politics* 38, 121–219.

References

233

World Bank, 1992, July 13. *Development credit agreement between republic of Zambia and International Development Association.*

1993, September 30. *Development credit agreement between republic of Zambia and International Development Association.*

1997. Technical *annex to the memorandum and recommendation on a proposed loan* to FF 56.7 million to the Gabonese Republic for Privatization and Regulatory Capacity Building Technical Assistance Project. Washington DC: World Bank.

World Bank OEU, 2004. *An Evaluation of World Bank Investment Climate Activities.* Washington DC: World Bank.

Wright, George, Fergus Bolger, and Gene Rowe 2002. 'An empirical test of the relative validity of expert and lay judgments of risk', *Risk Analysis* 22(6): 1107–22.

WTO WGTI, 1999. Communication from India – stocktaking of India bilateral agreements for the promotion and protection of investments, WT/WGTI/W/71.

2000a. Communication from India, WT/WGTI/W/86.

2000b. Report on the meeting of 11 October 2000, WT/WGTI/M/12.

2001. Report on the Meeting of 7 and 8 March 2001, WT/WGTI/M/14.

2002. Report on the Meeting held on 16–18 September 2002, WT/WGTI/M/19.

Yackee, Jason, 2008a. 'Conceptual difficulties in the empirical study of bilateral investment treaties', *Brooklyn Journal of International Law* 33(2): 405–62.

2008b. 'Do we really need BITs? Toward a return to contract in international investment law', *Asian Journal of WTO and Health Law* 3(1): 121–46.

2009a. 'Pacta Sunt Servanda and state promises to foreign investors before bilateral investment treaties: myth and reality', *Fordham International Law Journal* 32(5): 1550–1613.

2009b. 'Do BITs really work? Revisiting the empirical link between investment treaties and foreign direct investment', in Karl Sauvant and Lisa Sachs (eds.), *The Effect of Treaties on Foreign Direct Investment: Bilateral Investment Treaties, Double Taxation Treaties, and Investment Flows.* New York: Oxford University Press.

2010. 'Do bilateral investment treaties promote foreign direct investment – some hints from alternative evidence', *Virginia Journal of International Law* 51(2): 397–441.

2014a. 'Do investment promotion agencies promote bilateral investment treaties?' *Yearbook of International Investment Law & Policy 2013-2014.* New York: Oxford University Press.

2014b. 'Do states bargain over investor–state dispute settlement? Or, toward greater collaboration in the study of bilateral investment treaties', *Santa Clara Journal of International Law* 12(1): 277–301.

Yamin, Alicia, and Pilar Garcia, 1999. 'The absence of the rule of law in Mexico: diagnosis and implications for a Mexican transition to democracy', *Loyola International and Comparative Law Journal* 21(3): 467–520.

Yannaca-Small, Katia, 2008. 'Fair and equitable treatment standard: recent developments', in August Reinisch (ed.) *Standards of Investment Protection.* Oxford University Press.

Zaidé, Nassib, 1991. 'Some recent decisions in ICSID cases', *ICSID Review* 6, 514–5.

Archives

West Germany

PA, AA Politisches Archiv des Auswärtiges Amt (Political Archive, Federal Foreign Office)

Netherlands

NA, AOK, AZ, KMP Nationaal Archief, Ministeries voor Algemeene Oorlogvoering van het Koninkrijk (AOK) en Algemene Zaken (AZ): kabinet van de Minister-President (KMP) (National Archive, General War Department of the Kingdom and General Affairs: Cabinet of the Prime Minister)

NA, BZ Nationaal Archief, Buitenlandse Zagen (National Archive, Ministry of Foreign Affairs)

NA, MF Nationaal Archief, Ministerie van Financiën, Directie Bewindvoering (National Archive, Ministry of Finance)

United Kingdom

FCO National Archive, Foreign and Commonwealth Office

FO National Archive, Foreign Office

Denmark

UM Udenrigsministeriet (Foreign Ministry)

Agreements, arbitration awards, and constitutions

All BITs quoted are from UNCTAD's online website at: investmentpolicyhub. unctad.org/IIA. When not available, the treaties were compiled directly from governments. BITs are simply referred to by the two treaty parties followed by the date of signature. Some Model BITs were obtained from governments.

Investment arbitration awards and decisions are available at Andrew Newcombe's Investment Treaty Arbitration website at: italaw.com.

Constitutions are quoted from the Constitute Project: www.constitu teproject.org.

Index

Abs, Herman, 50–2, 196
Abs-Shawcross Draft Convention, 50–3, 55
Aguilar-Alvarez, Guillermo, 118
aid. *See* foreign aid
Aisbett, Emma, 145
Albania, 79
  CEELI, 84–6
Algeria, 63
Ali Khan, Makhdoom, xiii
American Bar Association (ABA), 51, 86
  CEELI. *See* Central and Eastern
    European Law Initiative (CEELI)
anchoring. *See* status-quo bias
arbitration. *See* investment arbitration
arbitrators
  as policy advisors, 83–7, 96–8, 113, 118,
    186, 201
  individuals
    Aguilar-Alvarez, Guillermo, 118
    Böckstiegel, Karl-Heinz, 186
    Brower, Charles, 81
    Park, William, 89
    Paulsson, Jan, 20, 96, 98, 186
    Schreuer, Christoph, 20, 96
    Vicuña, Francisco, 20, 97, 123
  motives of, 3, 20, 136
  relevance of book for, 192–4
  v. judges, 199
Argentina, 52, 83, 123
  BIT adoption strategy of, 53, 116, 117,
    120, 121, 159–60
  BIT claims against, 4, 44, 141, 154,
    157
  Calvo Doctrine, 57
  early BIT adoption strategy of, 63
  policy makers, 97
Armenia and CEELI, 84
Asian Agricultural Products (AAPL) v. Sri
  Lanka, 138–9
Austria and UNCTAD, 95
Azerbaijan, 116
  CEELI, 84

Bahrain
  and Jan Paulsson, 98
Ballén, Sixto, 120
Bangladesh, 59, 116
Barbados, 61
Belarus
  CEELI, 84
  UNCTAD, 95
Belgium, 59
  UNCTAD, 95
Benin and UNCTAD, 95
Böckstiegel, Karl-Heinz, 186
Bolivia, 4
  BIT claims against, 161
Bosnia and Herzegovina, 79
Botswana and UNCTAD, 92, 95
bounded rationality
  biases. *See* motivated reasoning, salience
    bias, status-quo bias
  cognitive constraints, 16–17, 26, 194
    developing countries v. developed
      countries, 18, 27–9, 194
    role of expertise and experience,
      18–19, 27–9, *See* also expertise and
      experience
  competition, 31–5, 110–34, 183
  constructivism, 25
  fast and frugal problem solving, 26
  intended rationality, 17, 26, 182
  learning, 30–1, 35–45, 135–60, 170–3,
    182–4, 188–90
  organizational v. experimental studies, 21
  path dependency, 27, 43, 196–203
  prospect theory, 21, 43
  relevance for IPE theory, 9–22
  satisficing. *See* satisficing
Brazil, 79, 199
  BIT adoption strategy of, 53
  Calvo Doctrine, 57
  early BIT adoption strategy of, 61
  Petrobas, 7
  UNCTAD, 95

237

238 Index

Broches, Aron, 56, 58, 60, 73, 127, 136
Brower, Charles, 81
Bulgaria, 86, 102
  BIT adoption strategy of, 116
  CEELI, 84
  FIAS, 79
  negotiators, 98
Burkina Faso and UNCTAD, 95
Burundi and UNCTAD, 95
Bush, George H.W., 82–3, 104

Calvo doctrine, 48, 83
  Chile, 122
  Latin American support for, 53, 57, 89,
    118, 121, 147
  UN General Assembly support for, 66,
    118
Cambodia, 80, 144
  UNCTAD, 95
Cameroon and UNCTAD, 95
Canada, 18, 115, 121, 123
  BIT negotiations with South Africa,
    176–7, 185
  complaining about lacking expertise, 155
  NAFTA, 118–19, 140, 176
  NAFTA claims against, 37
  policy makers, 97
  UNCTAD, 95
Caribbean Basin Initiative, 82
Carter, Jimmy, 81
Central and Eastern European Law
    Initiative (CEELI), 83–7
  Kenneth Vandevelde's role in. *See*
    Vandevelde, Kenneth
Chad and UNCTAD, 95
Chile, 52–3, 57, 119–20
  arbitration lawyers as policy advisors to,
    97
  BIT adoption strategy of, 61, 122–4, 150
  policy makers, 97
China, 79, 183, 200
  BIT adoption strategy of, 158–9
  impact of BITs on investment flows to, 8
  UNCTAD, 95
coercion, 30, 34
  cannot explain BIT-movement, 9–13
  Caribbean Basin Initiative, 82
  EC aid policy, 59
  Germany, 64
  Netherlands, 64
  United Kingdom, 64
Cold War, 10, 13, 56, 59, 82
Colombia, 54, 120
  negotiators, 97
  UNCTAD, 92, 95

colonialism, 44, 46, 158
  investment protection under, 48–9, 69,
    124
  investment treaties as continuation of, 51,
    55
Comoros and UNCTAD, 95
competition, 31–5, 110–34, 183, 187
Congo, 60
contracts, 7, 48, 58
  Argentina, 140
  as substitutes for investment treaties, xv,
    7, 202
  Ecuador, 3, 122
  Ghana, 100
  incomplete. *See* incomplete contracts
  negotiation experiments, 35, 40, 66
  Pakistan, xiii
Costa Rica, 82
  BIT adoption strategy of, 156–8
  policy makers, 97
cost-benefit analysis, 17, 27, 33, 47, 99,
    120, 178, 191
courts, 44, 85, 158
  Calvo Doctrine, 48, 60
  decisions subject to investment
    arbitration, 153
  enforcement of arbitration awards, xiv
  European Court of Human Rights, 198
  European Court of Justice, 19
  exhaustion of local remedies, xiv, 63, 65,
    198
  International Court of Justice, 19, 35
  regional investment courts, 149, 199
  World Investment Court, 200
  WTO, 19
credible commitments, 5–9, 111–12
Croatia, 105, 116
  CEELI, 84
  UNCTAD, 95
Cuba, 102
  BIT with South Africa, 180, 185
  revolutionary, 50
Czech Republic, 183
  American advisors, 103
  BIT adoption strategy of, 102–6, 112,
    117, 141
  BIT claims against, 3, 141
  CEELI, 84

default rules, 19, 26, 35, 43, 193
  early investment treaties as, 46, 69, 108,
    116
  experiments, 35
  expertise and experience, 45
  re-anchoring from, 43

Index

resulting in incoherent policies, 120, 124, 152
satisficing. *See* satisficing
World Bank Guidelines as, 76
Denmark, 44, 69, 105, 130, 159
UNCTAD, 95
de-politicization, 31, 53, 56, 58, 199–200
Costa Rica, 44, 156
United States, 44, 156
developing countries
classification of, 16
experience. *See* experience
expertise. *See* expertise
subject to bounded rationality.
See bounded rationality
diplomatic protection, 31, 48–9, 56, 58, 85
de-politicization. *See* de-politicization
Egypt, 59
Germany, 50
gunboat diplomacy, 48
Iran, 59
Libya, 59
United Kingdom, 59
United States, 56
Dominican Republic, 53, 80, 82, 150

economic diplomacy
BITs as new instrument of, 53
book rooted in rationalist, 25
bounded rationality and study of, xvi, 192, 21–2
Odell, John, 192
role of experience for, 29
role of expertise for, 28
Ecuador, 83
BIT adoption strategy of, 120–2, 148–9, 198
BIT claims against, 3, 148–9, 161
Calvo Doctrine, 57
cancelling BITs, 4, 149
early BIT adoption strategy of, 61
policy makers, 97
UNCTAD, 91
Egypt, 59
early BIT adoption strategy of, 61, 65–6
expertise, 66
liberalisation, 115–17
Suez crisis, 59
UNCTAD, 93, 95
El Salvador, 82
Elkins, Guzman, and Simmons (EGS), 31, 110–15
emulation, 26, 30
cannot explain BIT movement, 13–16
Energy Charter Treaty (ECT), 11

Estonia and CEELI, 84
Ethiopia
BIT adoption strategy of, 131–2, 154
UNCTAD, 95
Ethyl Corporation v. Canada, 140, 142
European Economic Community (EEC), 50–1
experience, 29, 156–60, 194–6
Argentina, 44, 159
bureaucratic turnover, 44, 157, 159, 195
Costa Rica, 44, 157
developing countries, 18, 44, 160, 182
Lebanon, 44, 159
Lithuania, 195
Pakistan, 196
role for salience bias, 18, 41–2, 155
role for status-quo bias, 19, 44–6
South Africa, 184
Turkey, 44, 159
expertise, 28–9, 194–6
Africa, 153
Argentina, 44, 159
China, 44, 159
Costa Rica, 44, 157
developed countries complaining about lack of, 156, 176
developing countries, 44, 89, 160, 182
Egypt, 66
India, 151
Jamaica, 67
Korea, 45
Latin America, 148
Lebanon, 40, 159
Lithuania, 85, 195
Mali, 181
Pakistan, xiii, 196
role for salience bias, 18, 44, 135, 157
role for status-quo bias, 19, 44–6
South Africa, 170, 184–5
Thailand, 151
Turkey, 44, 159
expropriation
1938 Mexican, 49, 118, 136, 147
China, 44, 158
Czech Republic, 103
Czechoslovakia, 103
decline of direct, 1–2
diplomatic protection, 48, 55–6
FCN-treaties, 135
Foresti v. South Africa, 167
Germany, 52, 58
Ghana, 100
Hull standard. *See* Hull standard of compensation
in domestic laws, 10

240   Index

expropriation (cont.)
  indirect, 136, 140, 163
  lacking salience of, 44
  Libya, 59
  Nigeria, 132
  political risk management, 6
  post-colonial rise of, 55
  Romania, 63
  salience of, 65
  Shawcross comments on Middle East, 51
  South Africa, 169–70, 176, 183
  United Kingdom, 58, 60–1
  World Bank, 55
  Zaire, 63
  Zambia, 79
  Zimbabwe, 107

fair and equitable treatment, xiv, 2, 38,
    42–3, 136, 167
  in domestic laws, 10, 18
  lacking salience of, 18, 44
  South Africa, 183
  UNCTC reports, 136
  World Bank Guidelines, 77
Fecák, Tomáš, 103, 105
Fiji, 61
financial crises, 10, 71, 100, 124, 130, 140
Finland and UNCTAD, 95
foreign aid, 10, 71, 100
  American policy, 56
  Caribbean Basin Initiative, 82
  Dutch policy, 64
  German policy, 64
  political risk insurance, 6
  South Africa, 174
  United Kingdom policy, 59
foreign investment, 6, 8, 10
  impact of investment treaties on, 5–9,
    113
  1991 MIGA survey, 8, 113
  Chile expectations, 122
  Czech Republic expectations, 103
  Ecuador expectations, 122
  Ethiopia expectations, 132
  Ghana expectations, 101
  India expectations, 131
  Jamaica expectations, 94
  Mexico expectations, 119
  Nigeria expectations, 133
  Pakistan expectations, 129
  South Africa expectations, 174, 183,
    189
  Thailand expectations, 126
  Turkey expectations, 125
  UNCTAD position, 91–8, 106

  United Kingdom position, 68
  United States position, 87
  Zimbabwe expectations, 107
  regulation of, 11, 91
Foreign Investment Advisory Services
    (FIAS), 77–81, 92, 100–1, 107
Foreign, Commerce, and Navigation
    (FCN) treaties, 49, 51–2, 58, 69, 81,
    135
France, 59, 133
  early BIT adoption strategy of, 72
  support for a multilateral investment
    treaty, 74, 76
  threat of claim by French investors, 144
  UNCTAD, 95
full protection and security, 135

Gabon, 79
General Agreement on Tariffs and Trade
    (GATT), 12, 50, 82
Germany
  aid policy, 156
  BIT claims by German investors, 150–1
  BIT with Costa Rica, 44, 157
  BIT with India, 130
  BIT with Pakistan, xv, 1, 53, 195
  BIT with Turkey, 124
  complaining about lacking expertise, 155
  de-politicization, 53, 200
  early BIT adoption strategy of, 50–5, 58,
    61, 68, 72, 111
  investors and BITs, 8
  Metallgesellschaft, 68
  negotiators, 74, 98
  political risk insurance, 9, 52, 68, 74,
    126
  support for a multilateral investment
    treaty, 55, 57, 74, 76
  UNCTAD, 95
Ghana, 183
  BIT adoption strategy of, 99–102, 153
  UNCTAD, 91, 95, 101
Golsong, Heribert, 73
Gorbachev, Mikhail, 10
Greece, 105
  skepticism towards 1962 OECD
    Convention, 55
Grenada, 79, 82
Guinea and UNCTAD, 95
Guinea-Bissau and UNCTAD, 95
gunboat diplomacy. *See* diplomatic
    protection

Honduras, 79, 82
Hoppe, Hans-Herman, 85

Index

Hull standard of compensation, 49, 60, 83, 118–19, 135
Hull, Cordell, 49
Hungary, 87, 103, 123, 130
  CEELI, 84

Imperialism. *See* colonialism
incomplete contracts, 20, 37, 39
India, 59
  BIT adoption strategy of, 53, 130–1, 151–3
  Calvo Doctrine, 57
  early BIT adoption strategy of, 60, 61
  intellectual property rights, 131
  reconsidering BITs, 4
  UN General Assembly, 66
  UNCTAD, 93, 95, 101
  WTO v. BITs, 12
Indonesia
  early BIT adoption strategy of, 58, 61, 65–6
  reconsidering BITs, 4
  UN General Assembly, 66
  UNCTAD, 93, 95, 101
  WTO v. BITs, 12
inertia. *See* status-quo bias
information
  about risks of BITs, 135–41
  imperfect, 30, 37, 39, 42, 161, 181
  imperfect processing of. *See* bounded rationality
institutional choice
  de-coupling, 14
  fully v. bounded rational. *See* bounded rationality
intellectual property rights, 176
  India, 131
  Pakistan, 12
  South Africa, 186
International Centre for the Settlement of Investment Disputes (ICSID)
  as promoter of investment treaties, 58, 72–4, 137
  availability of negotiation records, 22
  Calvo doctrine, 57
  CEELI promotion of, 85
  Chile's justification for joining, 122
  China, 44, 158
  claims against Argentina, 4
  contracts referring to, 7
  counterclaims, 197
  de-politicization, 44, 56, 156, *See* also de-politicization
  early Jamaican support, 65

early skepticism about impact on investment flows, 57, 114, 127
enforcement, 5
establishment of, 55–9
ignorance of, xiii–xiv, 44, 159
Indian and Sri Lankan opposition, 57, 130
lack of cases in early years, 57
lacking definition of investment, 139
Latin American alternative, 149, 198
Latin American opposition to, 4, 57, 149
model clauses, 58, 69, 72–4, 76, 136–7
South Africa, 187
staff members, 74, 97, 186
transparency rules, 139, 143, 167
United Kingdom model clauses, 60
International Court of Justice (ICJ), 19, 35
International Labor Organisation (ILO)
  investor guidelines, 89
International Monetary Fund (IMF), 49
  enforcement of arbitral awards, 4
  not strong supporter of BITs, 72
  structural adjustment. *See* structural adjustment
International Trade Organization (ITO), 49–51
investment arbitration
  Calvo doctrine. *See* Calvo doctrine
  de-politicization. *See* de-politicization
  enforceable, xiv, 20, 137–8
  exhaustion of local remedies, xiv, 63, 65, 198
  ICSID. *See* International Centre for the Settlement of Investment Disputes (ICSID)
  information about, 37, 135–41
  lacking salience of, 40, 66, 70
  legitimacy of, 2–4
  rise of, 2, 37, 138–41
  treaty v. contract, xv
  unanticipated consequences of, xiii–xv, 2–4, 9–18, 37, 141–60, 188–9, 193–4, 197
  unimportant during early BIT negotiations, 65
  v. interstate dispute settlement, 199–200
investment laws
  Albania, 86
  American advisors, 83–7
  Cambodia, 80
  correspondence with investment treaties, 10, 86
  Cuba, 180
  Dominican Republic, 80
  Gabon, 79

242 Index

investment laws (cont.)
  Ghana, 101
  Honduras, 79
  United Nations, 88
  World Bank, 57
  World Bank Guidelines on the
    Treatment of Foreign Investment,
    76–81
  Zambia, 79
  Zimbabwe, 106
investment treaties
  as credible commitments, 5–9
  as incomplete contracts. *See* incomplete
    contracts
  cancelling, 4, 201–3
  correspondence with investment laws,
    10, 86
  default rules. *See* default rules
  impact on investment flows. *See* foreign
    investment
  lacking investor obligations, 18, 52, 198
  normative considerations, 21
  re-negotiating, 106, 149, 185, 189, 195,
    200–1
  vague and open-ended, xiii, 1–3, 18–20,
    36–7, 44, 193
Iran, 59, 79, 183
  early BIT adoption strategy of, 62
  UNCTAD, 95
Iraq, 13, 59, 63
Italy
  Foresti v. South Africa, 165–6
  UNCTAD, 95
Ivory Coast, 60, 64

Jamaica, 94
  BIT adoption strategy of, 117
  early BIT adoption strategy of, 63, 65, 67–8
  expertise, 67
  UNCTAD, 93
Japan, 115, 152
  UNCTAD, 95
Jordan, 57, 117
  FIAS, 79

Kazakhstan, 139
  CEELI, 84
Kenya, 60, 62
  BIT adoption strategy of, 53, 154
  UNCTAD, 91, 95
Khan, Ayub, 53
Klaus, Vaclav, 102, 104
Korea, 152
  BIT adoption strategy of, 62
  BIT with South Africa, 175

  early BIT adoption strategy of, 65–6
  expertise, 45, 175
  UNCTAD, 95
Korobkin, Russell, 40, 66
Kunda, Ziva, 26
Kuwait, 13, 66
Kyrgyzstan, 116
  CEELI, 84
  UNCTAD, 95

Laos, 127
  UNCTAD, 95
Latvia, 117
  CEELI, 84
  UNCTAD, 95
Lauder, Ronald, 141
learning, 30–1, 35–45, 135–60
  South Africa, 170–3, 182–4, 188–90
Lebanon
  BIT adoption strategy of, 159
  early BIT adoption strategy of, 63
  UNCTAD, 95
Lesotho and UNCTAD, 91, 95
Liberia, 53
Libya, 53
  BIT adoption strategy of, 63, 154–5
  expropriation, 59
  UNCTAD, 95
Lithuania, 84–5, 139
  CEELI, 84
  Kenneth Vandevelde advising, 85–7, 195
logic of appropriateness. *See* emulation

Macedonia and CEELI, 84
Madagascar and UNCTAD, 95
Major, John, 168, 174
Malawi, 62
  UNCTAD, 95
Malaysia, 152, 197
  BIT with South Africa, 177–8
  early BIT adoption strategy of, 53, 62,
    65, 67
  UNCTAD, 93
  WTO v. BITs, 12
Mali, 181
  UNCTAD, 95
Malta and UNCTAD, 95
Mandela, Nelson, 162, 174
Mauritania and UNCTAD, 95
Mauritius, 183
  arbitration lawyers as policy advisors to,
    97
  UNCTAD, 95
McNamara, Robert, 72
Metallgesellschaft, 68

Index

243

Mexico, 123
  1938 expropriations by, 49, 136
  arbitration lawyers as policy advisors, 97
  BIT adoption strategy of, 53, 118–20
  BIT claims against, 140, 146–8
  Calvo doctrine, 65
  NAFTA, 97, 118–20
  negotiators, 98
Moldova, 117
  CEELI, 84
  UNCTAD, 95
Mongolia, 117
Montt, Santiago, 36
Morocco, 53
  arbitration lawyers as policy advisors, 97
most favoured nation (MFN) clauses, 41, 49, 107, 115, 136
  South Africa, 183
  Turkey, 125
motivated reasoning, 17–18, 26–7, 34, 70, 109, 134, 197
  Chile, 123
  Ecuador, 122
  Ethiopia, 132
  Ghana, 101
  India, 131
  Mexico, 119
  Nigeria, 133
  Pakistan, 129
  Thailand, 127
  Turkey, 126
Mozambique, 106, 116, 182
  UNCTAD, 95
Mugabe, Robert, 106–7
Multilateral Agreement on Investment (MAI), 6, 44, 91, 133, 140, 157, 178
Multilateral Investment Guarantee Agency (MIGA), 74–8
  early survey on investment impact of BITs, 8, 113
  Ghana, 101
Muñoz, Guillermo Leon Valencia, 54
Myanmar and UNCTAD, 95

national treatment clauses, 115, 167
  China, 82
  Czechoslovakia, 104
  Egypt, 66
  Malaysia, 177
  Mexico, 118
  Philippines, 53
  pre-establishment, 117
  salience of, 44, 65, 70
  Singapore, 63

South Africa, 162, 168–9, 177
  Turkey, 125
nationalisation. *See* expropriation
Nepal and UNCTAD, 91
Netherlands
  aid policy, 64
  BIT adoption strategy of, 201
  BIT claims by Dutch investors, 140–1, 153
  BIT with Czechoslovakia, 105
  BIT with South Africa, 175
  complaining about lacking expertise, 155
  early BIT adoption strategy of, 64, 68, 72
  political risk insurance, 68
  Shell, 8, 51, 68
  UNCTAD, 95
  Unilever, 68
New International Economic Order (NIEO), 36, 60, 66, 88, 118
Nicaragua, 120
Nigeria
  BIT adoption strategy of, 132–4, 154
  UNCTAD, 92
Nixon, Richard, 51
Nkrumah, Kwame, 99, 221
North American Free Trade Agreement (NAFTA), 11, 37, 39
  arbitration lawyers as policy advisors on, 97
  arbitrators defence of, 201
  Chile, 122, 150
  claims, 140, 152, 176, 197, 200
  Mexico, 118–20, 140
Norway, 105

Odell, John, 192
Organization for Economic Co-operation and Development (OECD)
  as promoter of investment treaties, 137
  expropriation policy, 59
  inspiration for BITs, 60, 94, 169, 176–8
  investor guidelines, 89
  multilateral investment treaty, 6, 52, 55–6, 91, 178
Overseas Private Investment Corporation (OPIC), 52, 107
Ozal, Turkut, 124

Pakistan, 59
  arbitration lawyers as policy advisors to, 97
  BIT adoption strategy of, xiv–xv, 53, 127–30
  BIT claims against, xiii, 2–3

244   Index

Pakistan (cont.)
  BIT negotiations with United States, 12,
    87
  BIT with Germany, 1, 53, 195
  early BIT adoption strategy of, 62
  UNCTAD, 95
Papua New Guinea, 62
  Ok Tedi, 68
Park, William, 89
path dependency. *See* status-quo bias
Paulsson, Jan, 20, 96, 98, 118, 186
Peru, 52, 127
  UNCTAD, 95
Petrobas, 7
Philippines, 51, 57
  BIT adoption strategy of, 53
  BIT claims against, 3
  early BIT adoption strategy of, 62
  UNCTAD, 95, 101
Poland
  BIT adoption strategy of, 117
  BIT claims against, 139
  CEELI, 84
political risk insurance, 56, 73–5
  as substitute for investment treaties, 7
  France, 68
  Germany, 9, 52, 68
  Netherlands, 68
  relevance of investment treaties for, 7, 68
    Chilean expectations, 122
    ICSID position, 73
    South African expectations, 173
    UNCTAD position, 94
  United Kingdom, 59, 68
  United States. *See* Overseas Private
    Investment Corporation (OPIC)
  World Bank. *See* Multilateral Investment
    Guarantee Agency (MIGA)
Portugal
  skepticism towards 1962 OECD
    Convention, 55
pre-establishment clauses, 115–16
  Czech Republic, 104
  Ecuador, 120
  Mexico, 118–20
  salience of, 19
  South Africa, 176
  Turkey, 125–6
preferential trade agreements (PTAs), 119,
    142, 151, 186
  more salient than BITs, 146
  politicization of, 14
prospect theory, 21, 43
public choice theory and BIT adoption, 27,
    33, 41, 168, 181–2

Reagan, Ronald, 11, 81–2
Romania, 102
  BIT adoption strategy of, 117
  CEELI, 84, 86
  early BIT adoption strategy of, 62, 65
Rothbard, Murray, 85
Russia, 183
  BIT adoption strategy of, 117
  BIT claims against, 3, 139
  CEELI, 84
Rwanda
  arbitration lawyers as policy advisors to,
    97
  UNCTAD, 91

salience bias, 26, 31, 34, 40–2, 70, 134
  BIT adoption patterns as indication of,
    142–6
  Chile, 150
  Czech Republic, 105–6
  early BIT negotiations, 65–6, 70
  Ecuador, 149
  Ethiopia, 153
  Ghana, 102
  India, 151–3
  Kenya, 154
  Libya, 154–5
  Mexico, 146–8
  Nigeria, 154
  role of expertise and experience, 18,
    41–2, 44–5, 135, 171, 156–60
  role of mass media, 201
salience enhancement, 71
  CEELI, 83–8
  UNCTAD, 91–9, 106, 108
  World Bank, 76–81
  South Africa, 167–79, 185, 188–90
  Thailand, 150–1
  Zimbabwe, 109
Salinas, Carlos, 118
satisficing, 19, 27, 31, 35, 99, 109–10,
    115–16, 134
  Argentina, 121
  Chile, 124
  Czech Republic, 104
  Ecuador, 121
  Ethiopia, 132
  India, 131
  Mexico, 118–20
  Nigeria, 133
  Pakistan, 127–30
  South Africa, 174–8, 181, 183
  Thailand, 126–7
  Turkey, 125
  Zimbabwe, 108

Index

245

saturation, 143–5
Schreuer, Christoph, 20, 96
Senegal, 117
   UNCTAD, 95
Serbia, 102
Shawcross, Hartley, 51–2
Shell (Royal Dutch), 8, 51, 68
Shihata, Ibrahim, 74–81, 90
Sierra Leone, 63
   FIAS, 79
   UNCTAD, 94
signalling
   competition, 16, 32, 73, 91, 94, 177, 187
   emulation, 13–15
   UNCTAD, 96
Simon, Herbert, 27, 182
Singapore, 68, 152
   early BIT adoption strategy of, 63, 65–6,
     68
   UN General Assembly, 66
Slovakia and CEELI, 84
Société Générale de Surveillance (SGS) v.
   Pakistan, xiii, 3
soft law
   as alternative to multilateral investment
     treaty, 76
   BITs mistaken for, 18, 188
Somalia, 70
South Africa
   arbitration lawyers as policy advisors to,
     97, 186
   as deviant case, 161
   BIT adoption strategy of, 162–91
   BIT claims against, 163–8, 188–9
   BIT with the United Kingdom, 168–74,
     190
   cancelling BITs, 4, 189
   early BIT program, 174–85
   UNCTAD, 95
sovereignty costs, 5–6, 55, 83, 114
   expectations in rationalist models, 31, 36,
     111, 160
   expertise and awareness of, 44
   multilateral treaty, 179
   other international legal regimes, 19
Soviet Union, 10, 59, 90
   assistance, 131, 180
Spain, 154
   aid policy, 156
Sri Lanka, 59
   AAPL v., 138–9
   BIT adoption strategy of, 10, 116–17
   early BIT adoption strategy of, 63
   early scepticism towards ICSID, 57
   UNCTAD, 93

status-quo bias, 19, 26–7, 134, 160, 196,
   200
   Chile, 124
   Czech Republic, 104
   default rules. *See* default rules
   Ecuador, 149
   Ethiopia, 132
   India, 131, 152
   Mexico, 118–20, 147
   Pakistan, 130
   role of expertise and experience, 45
   South Africa, 174–8
   Thailand, 127, 151
   treaty design, 35, 42–4, 114–16
   Turkey, 125
   Zimbabwe, 108
structural adjustment, 80–1
   Ethiopia, 131
   Ghana, 100
   Mexico, 118
   Nigeria, 132
   Turkey, 124
   Zambia and Gabon, 79–80
Sudan, 63
   UNCTAD, 95
Summers, Lawrence, 77
Sunstein, Cass, 45
survival clauses, 201
Sweden
   early BIT adoption strategy of, 72
   investors and BITs, 8
   UNCTAD, 95
Switzerland, 79, 123
   BIT claims by Swiss investors, xv
   BIT with Pakistan, xv
   early BIT adoption strategy of, 54
   UNCTAD, 95

Tanzania, 59, 63
   UNCTAD, 95
Thailand
   anchoring to UK BIT, 127
   arbitration lawyers as policy advisors to,
     97
   BIT adoption strategy of, 126–7,
     150–1
   BIT claims against, 150–1
   early BIT adoption strategy of, 63, 65
   early scepticism towards ICSID, 57
   FCN treaty with US, 58
   UN General Assembly, 66
Togo
   FCN treaty with US, 58
   UNCTAD, 95
transaction costs, 30, 33

246   Index

transfer clauses, 156
  Chile, 123
  Costa Rica, 44, 157
  Egypt, 61
  FCN treaties, 135
  Germany, 52
  Ghana, 100
  IMF obligations, 72
  Pakistan, xiv
  Romania, 62
  salience of, 44, 65, 173
  South Africa, 162, 173
  Zambia, 79
  Zimbabwe, 108
Trujillo, Rafael, 53
Tubman, William, 53
Tunisia
  BIT adoption strategy of, 116
  Dutch BIT linked to aid, 64
  early BIT adoption strategy of, 63
Turkey
  BIT adoption strategy of, 44, 124–6, 159
  non-compliance with German BIT, 111
  skepticism towards 1962 OECD
    Convention, 55

Uganda, 59
UNCTAD, 95
Ukraine
  BIT adoption strategy of, 117
  CEELI, 84
  policy makers, 97
umbrella clauses, 3
uncertainty, 36, 38
Unilever, 68
United Kingdom, 58, 130
  BIT with Ghana, 100
  BIT with South Africa, 168–74
  BIT with Thailand as default, 128
  early BIT program, 59–69, 72
  Hartley Shawcross, 51
  investors and BITs, 8, 174
  negotiators, 97
United Nations Centre on Transnational
    Corporations (UNCTC), 88–91
  Code of Conduct, 76
  informing developing countries, 136–8
  South Africa, 171, 173
United Nations Conference on Trade and
    Development (UNCTAD)
  as Global OECD, 91
  negotiating and signing sessions, 92–6
  promotion of BITs, 91–9, 106–9, 114,
    133, 143
  role during MAI, 91

  South Africa, 171, 173
  staff members, 97, 99
  teaming up with arbitration community,
    96–8
  US power, 90–1
United States
  1938 Mexican expropriations, 49
  Abs-Shawcross Draft Convention, 52
  aid policy, 156
  availability of negotiation records, 22
  BIT adoption strategy of, 81–3, 86–7
  BIT claims by US investors, 141
  BIT model, 14–15, 18, 81, 84, 114–17,
    186, 197
  BIT negotiations with India, 131
  BIT negotiations with South Africa, 186
  BIT with Czech Republic, 104, 106
  BIT with Ecuador, 120
  BIT with Egypt, 115
  BIT with Panama, 144
  BIT with Turkey, 124
  Caribbean Basin Initiative, 82
  CEELI, 83–7
  diplomatic protection, 44, 49, 56, 59, 156
  early BIT negotiations with China, 82
  FCN treaties, 49, 58, 69, 81
  GATT, 82
  ICSID, 56
  investors and BITs, 8
  ITO, 49–50
  MAI, 201
  NAFTA, 118
  NAFTA claims against, 37
  negotiators, 98
  OPIC, 52
  PTA negotiations with South Africa,
    185
  refusing to sign BIT with Pakistan, 12, 130
  salience of BITs with, 14
  subrogation agreements, 52, 61, 64, 69
  take-off in BIT program, 11
  UNCTAD, 90–1
  UNCTC, 90
  Wall Street Brigade in Czech Republic,
    102–3
  Zimbabwe refusing to sign BIT with, 107
Uzbekistan and CEELI, 84

Vandevelde, Kenneth
  advising Lithuania, 85–7, 195
Venezuela
  BIT claims against, 139, 161
  cancelling BITs, 4
Vicuña, Francisco, 20, 97, 123
Vietnam, 127

Index

Washington Consensus, 10, 17, 71, 89, 145
Wedel, Janine, 83
West Indies Associated States, 61
Weyland, Kurt, 29, 173
Williamson, John, 10, 30
World Bank
  FIAS. *See* Foreign Investment Advisory
    Services (FIAS)
  Guidelines on the Treatment of Foreign
    Investment, 76–81, 90, 104
  ICSID. *See* International Centre for the
    Settlement of Investment Disputes
    (ICSID)
  influence on developing countries' BIT
    adoption strategies, 99–102
  MIGA. *See* Multilateral Investment
    Guarantee Agency (MIGA)
  promotion of BITs, 71–81
  structural adjustment. *See* structural
    adjustment
World Trade Organization (WTO)

Doha-Round, 152
inter-state dispute settlement, 111
multilateral investment treaty, 179
South Africa, 178–80
unanticipated consequences of, 19
v. BITs, 12, 146

Yemen, 63
  UNCTAD, 95
Yugoslavia, 63, 79, 107

Zaire, 63
  BIT claims against, 139
Zambia, 79–80
  UNCTAD, 92, 95
Zedillo, Ernesto, 119
Zimbabwe
  BIT adoption strategy of, 106–9,
    141
  FIAS, 107
  UNCTAD, 93, 106–9

For EU product safety concerns, contact us at Calle de José Abascal, 56–1°, 28003 Madrid, Spain or eugpsr@cambridge.org.

www.ingramcontent.com/pod-product-compliance
Ingram Content Group UK Ltd.
Pitfield, Milton Keynes, MK11 3LW, UK
UKHW020454090825
461507UK00007B/225